THE SMART GUIDE TO

Understanding Your Cat

BY CAROLYN JANIK

SECOND EDITION

The Smart Guide To Understandering Your Cat

Published by

Smart Guide Publications, Inc.
2517 Deer Chase Drive
Norman, OK 73071
www.smartguidepublications.com

For information, address: Smart Guide Publications, Inc. 2517 Deer Creek Drive, Norman, OK 73071

SMART GUIDE and Design are registered trademarks licensed to Smart Guide Publications, Inc.

International Standard Book Number: 978-1-937636-66-1

Library of Congress Catalog Card Number:
11 12 13 14 15   10 9 8 7 6 5 4 3 2 1

Printed in the United States of America

Cover design: Lorna Llewellyn
Copy Editor: Ruth Strother
Back cover design: Joel Friedlander, Eric Gelb, Deon Seifert
Back cover copy: Eric Gelb, Deon Seifert
Illustrations: Carolyn Janik
Production: Zoë Lonergan
Indexer: Cory Emberson
V.P./Business Manager: Cathy Barker

ACKNOWLEDGMENTS

Many thanks to Dalia Remys who read and commented upon the text and told me stories of the stray and rescue cats that she and her husband Edmund had come to love. For particular insights into the rewards and challenges of living with a Siamese Cat, I owe warm hugs to Linda Reimer and Heidi and Jim Crane. Marv Atkins was kind enough to let me use one of his photos as reference for a drawing.

The veterinarians at Animal Medical Hospital in St Petersburg were available for special questions and they cared for my own Becky when she was left in a rusty cage at a dumpster downtown. (Since coming to our house Miss Becky Sharp always finds the most comfortable places to sleep!) Thanks to my housekeeper, Marie Howell, for being able to spot accumulated cat hair in the most unusual places. Thanks to my friends at Ace Hardware in St Pete for talking with me about Cotter Pin, an aging cat with the spirit of a two year old. And I gratefully acknowledge all the time the members of The Academy of Senior Professionals at Eckerd College spent listening to and adding to my stories, and especially Ellen Hersh and Bob Shepherd (co-chairs of the ASPEC Poetry Group) who encouraged me to spend an entire meeting reading and discussing poems about cats.

Thanks also to the people who contributed photographs and suggestions:

Max Adams, Merle Allshouse, Marv Atkins, Mary Fullerton, Dot Goldsmith, Clark Lambert, Gene Norris, Linda Reimer, Mary Robison, and Nicole Witmer. And on-going

Thanks to my agent, Jeanne Fredericks, who introduced me to The Smart Guide series.

Thanks to photographer Dianne Blyler who photographed my cat Becky.

And most of all, love and gratitude to my husband, Joe, who tried to stay out of the office while I was writing and who made himself innumerable sandwiches for lunch, not to mention going out to fetch the take-out dinners when I had forgotten what time it was.

Carolyn Janik

St Petersburg, FL

The cats in this book are referred to as he and she in alternating chapters unless their sexes are apparent from the content.

To the ailurophiles in my family:

Laura, Chris, Caitlin, and Tommy

Bill, Meredith, Sarah, Michael, and Kristin

and

In Memoriam

Alan P. Zimmerman
who loved cats, and children, and life

TABLE OF CONTENTS

INTRODUCTION

Some of the greatest minds and hearts in human history have saved space for the love of cats. Think about people as diverse as Theodore Roosevelt, Dr. Samuel Johnson, John Keats, Charles Dickens, Mark Twain, Leonardo Da Vinci, Emily Dickinson, Oscar Wilde, Jules Verne, Albert Schweitzer, Charles Baudelaire, J.R.R. Tolkien, Pablo Neruda, Emily Brontë, Edouard Manet, T.S. Eliot, and Cardinal Richelieu, to name just a scattering. Among the rest of us, cats now claim a place in the homes of more Americans than any other pet. What is the magnetism of this small animal?

 If you have ever lived with a cat, you'll have your own answers to those questions. But you'll also have lots of questions and puzzlements about our complex, cunning, cute, cuddly, comical, curious, sometimes contentious, often contented, and always companionable housemates. The sometimes mysterious and seemingly unpredictable elements of the cat's personality are definitely a part of its allure. This book is written to help you to recognize and differentiate the traits and behaviors that are endemic in the species—in other words, part of cat-ness—and the activities and behaviors that are unique to your particular cat. And to appreciate, care for, and love your cat, just the way he or she is.

 I am one of the many cat lovers in the world. But I am neither a veterinarian, nor a breeder, nor an expert on cats. The material in this book comes from my experiences with the cats who have lived in my home and from research among the many, many books and articles written on the subject of cats. This second edition, however, incorporates the knowledge and experience of a noted cat-specialist veterinarian, Dr. Donna Shannon. She reviewed the entire book and brought medical information up to date.

The Smart Guide to Understanding Your Cat (2nd edition) contains information about the anatomy and physiology of the cat, information essential to understanding how to share your home with another species. It also examines the role of the cat as a human companion and the contributions that cats have made to our culture and civilization. (Don't laugh! There have been many, and you'll be fascinated by the scope and variety of cat activities in the sidebars to the text.)

If you are new to having a cat in your life, I hope this book will provide you with the necessary guidelines for good care and good cat communication. If you have known many cats in your life, I hope the book will give you pleasure in the reading, and bring clarity to any areas of uncertainty or confusion in your relationships with your feline friends. The Smart Guide to Understanding Your Cat was written not only to provide information, but also to enhance intangible feelings of admiration, awe, aesthetic appreciation, and just plain love for our cats.

Carolyn Janik

FORWARD

All through history, cats (domestic cats, who looked and acted very much as we know them today) seem to have shown up everywhere in the world where humans have gathered and lived in communities. Why? What is the mutual attraction? Do cats understand us, more than we know? Do we humans have a subconscious need for what cats can give us? What does it mean to love a cat?

Also from time to time throughout history, cats have inspired hatred, fear, awe, and puzzlement among some human communities. And even today, certain people (ailurophobes) are irrationally terrified of even the smallest cat. Again we must ask why? Is it cats' uncanny insight and sensibility, their self-preservation instincts, the bodily perfection that gives them abilities we humans cannot match?

Everyone who has ever loved or hated a cat has at least one cat-story to tell. Most of us have many. Let me begin by sharing a few of my own; they will almost surely be similar to some of your own.

Ever since I was a little girl, cats have attracted and enticed me with their beauty, intelligence, and mystery. My first feline contacts were the cats at my Granddaddy's farm. Yes, they were barn cats in charge of keeping the barns free from vermin and no, they were never allowed into the farmhouse. Nevertheless, they were loved, each had a name, and each had his/her share of baby-talk conversation with my grandfather virtually every day.

Of course, kittens were always being born. My sister and I would catch and tame them with stroking and cuddling. Again and again we tried to get my parents to let us take a favorite or two home with us. But ironically, my mother was terrified of cats. So I lived in a house without a cat. Until, that is, I turned 16.

At that time my "big brother" was an MP in the Army, stationed in Savannah, GA. By chance he came upon a stray kitten and could not resist bringing it home to us. My "little sister" and I collaborated on how to persuade our mother to change her NO CATS! rule. (The kitten was ours, we had to keep her!) I tried logical persuasion, but my sister cried a lot, and a lot, and a lot more. Finally, our mother gave in. We had a cat! We named her Cricket because she jumped sideways and played such silly kitten games.

Cricket grew into a beautiful "torbie" – that's a tortise shell cat with with some tabby stripes mixed in. When I left for college at 17, I took her with me. As a high school junior, I was in an early-entry program and therefore required to live in a dorm for the summer and to pass all the college classes I had been assigned before I could be officially admitted as a freshman. (Needless to mention: pets were NOT allowed in the dorm.) My roommate allowed Cricket out into the hallway and I got thrown out of the dorm. Cricket did just fine; she ended up back at home with my sister. I found a room off campus, finished the summer program, and got accepted anyway.

In the fall, I was in the dorm again. And I had another cat, this one all my own. She was a beautiful silvery gray and chirped melodies to me, so I named her Krrra, as close as I could come to the sounds that delighted me so much. Krrra was about a year old when I got her.

But my life as an ailurophile seemed to be touched by the Wicked Witch of the West. Yes, my new roommate was desperately afraid of cats (an ailurophobe of the first order). Because we didn't really hit it off in any other way either, she moved out. That left me and Krrra with a room to ourselves. Gloriously, that room was up on the 6th floor. She and I had a view and nobody ever saw her sitting in the window. Whenever I left the dorm for an overnight, I took her with me. Returning, I would sneak her up the back staircase with Krrra held close to my body.

Sometimes I wonder how many college kids are more traumatized by leaving their beloved pets than they are by leaving their hometowns. And I wonder just how many uncounted pets are living in dormitory rooms. The author of this book, Carolyn Janik, remembers the "found" kitten of her junior year. She and her fellow conspirators called the tabby Geranium because she looked so right sitting in the sunshine of the east-facing window. Food being smuggled in napkins from the dinner table was referred to as "watering the Geranium." Of course, animals were strictly forbidden back in the 1960s and there were "housemothers" who did periodic inspections. On one such inspection, Carolyn had Beethoven's Ode to Joy playing at max volume while Geranium complained about being locked in the closet! Today a few colleges actually have pet-friendly dorms; our local Eckerd College is one of them.

During the winter quarter of my freshman year, I was lucky enough to go on a college-sponsored program to Colombia, South America, where I got to live with a local family. Of course I didn't want to leave Krrra, but my boyfriend promised he would take care of her. Taking care of her included keeping her inside the house since I hadn't had her spayed yet. Predictably, his mom let her out. I came home to a beautiful but very pregnant cat! She had 3 gorgeous kittens, and I was well on my way to becoming a "crazy cat lady."

As I had always leaned toward a career in the medical field, my love for animals made the choice to become a veterinarian both satisfying and virtually inevitable. By the time I entered vet school, I had acquired 7 cats and a dog, and a 3-legged gray fox named Merlin the Magic Fox. As penniless students, it was not easy for me and my new husband to find an affordable place to keep them all. But there was no question that they were going with us. We moved 3 times before finding the right place. And we picked up more cats along the way!

I considered myself very lucky to be able to study veterinary medicine and to spend my life caring for animals. I discovered a veterinarian in Chicago who had opened one of the very first all feline practices, and I was hooked. I vowed that someday; someday I would have an all-feline practice as well. And I did this even though I loved dogs and horses and wild (exotic) animals too.

Being a veterinarian is a little bit like being a pediatrician. Your patients can't always tell you what hurts. And in some ways, it's even more complicated because there are so many different kinds of patients. As a new graduate who owed student loans, had no spare money, and little practical experience, I didn't feel that I had the luxury of starting an all- cat practice. So I went to work for a vet in Vermont where I got plenty of real and varied experience. I saw and treated all kinds of animals: cows, pigs, goats, horses, cats, dogs, and whatever else was around. I was getting just what I wanted at the time, living in a rural area and proving to myself that I could work on large animals just as well as "the guys". Satisfied of that challenge after a year, I went to a small animal practice in New Hampshire. My boss was an excellent doctor, recognized my competence, and encouraged me to open my own practice.

Because I now had a horse as well as my small animal family, I chose to stay rural and opened my first practice in Vermont. I was willing to work with every kind of animal, but even in a small town in a rural area, people began to find out that I truly loved cats and had an intuitive and well-developed understanding of their problems and their needs. Cat owners came from miles around with much-loved cats that needed help.

I saw about 60% cats and 40% dogs (an unusual ratio for a small animal practice). This was great, but circumstances changed in my life, and I decided it was time to make the big move and open my feline only practice. I sold the practice in Vermont and moved to Florida, to the "big city" of Ft. Myers, where there were as many people in the county I lived in as there were in the whole state of Vermont. Naturally I figured there would be lots of cats. But I didn't expect the negative obstacles.

My own parents didn't think I could make it as a cats-only specialist. Other vets in the area were disparaging about the idea. (I can't help but think that some of them were just plain jealous.) The business-loan reps at the banks thought I was nuts. And maybe I was, a little. Or maybe a lot nuts about cats. In any case, I was different. At that time there were very few cats-only practices in America.

This book, The Smart Guide to Understanding Your Cat, is a little like my choosing a cats-only specialty. It's a little bit daring and it's written with a lot of caring. The book focuses upon understanding the domestic feline, not just from the human perspective of taking care of, tolerating, training, or adapting to a cat in your home, but also from the feline perspective of learning to live as a part of a human family. To understand a cat, a human must understand how a cat's body is different from all other animals, and how a cat interacts with other cats and with people, and what a cat needs, and what a cat gives, and how a cat expresses its feelings. With this understanding comes love, both from human to cat and from cat to human. Such love is truly a unique relationship, unique between each cat and each human. The better you understand your cat, the better you will appreciate the many facets of its intelligence, its sensitivity, its caring, its honesty, and its loyalty.

Donna Shannon, DVM

St Petersburg, FL

PART ONE

Cat Think Simplified

CHAPTER 1

What Do Cats Want?

In This Chapter

➤ A brief feline history
➤ What cats need
➤ What cats want
➤ What cats give

Early in the twentieth century, the great psychologist and philosopher Sigmund Freud (1856–1939) wrote, "I have not yet been able to answer… the great question that has never been answered: What does a woman want?" He said those words as a man who loved and lived with a wife and daughter.

Many men and women who love and live with cats have looked upon our sometimes puzzling, sometimes exasperating, and always interesting household companions and, like Freud, asked, "What does a cat want?"

Observing cats is a lot like looking through a kaleidoscope: so many different images, always changing, always beautiful. In this chapter, we'll begin the challenging and rewarding experience of trying to understand your cat.

Someone Said

"Perhaps God made cats so that man might have the pleasure of fondling the tiger…"

—Robertson Davies (1913-1995) Canadian novelist and literary critic

The Feline Species

Animals you might recognize as belonging to the feline species evolved over a million years ago, at about the same time that humans first appeared on Earth. The earliest cats were, of course, wild and didn't live with or near any human communities. They began their existence as hunters in Africa. From there they migrated, pretty much as humans did.

Did they follow the spread of human villages? Who knows? Maybe in the night they picked up scraps from human campfires or caught the vermin attracted by the scraps. Maybe they just found us fascinating.

In 2007, *The New York Times* reported on a study that connected the lineage of the cats we now keep as pets to about five African wildcats (*Felis silvestris*) who chose to become domesticated. (I write *chose* because we all know that it's extremely difficult to force cats to do anything they don't want to do, and it's unlikely that this was any different a million years or so ago.)

CATch Words

Felis silvestris is the biological species name for wild cats.

Felis catus is the biological subspecies name for the domestic cat. It is sometimes identified with its species name as well: *felis silvestris catus*.

Both wild and domestic cats are in the class Mammalia and the order Carnivora.

It quite naturally follows that two of our most famous cats are named Felix and Sylvester! Felix was created in the silent film era. He went on to become a popular comic strip character and a commercial promoter of many kinds of goods.

Sylvester made his first appearance in the film *Life with Feathers* on March 24, 1945. *Looney Tunes* and *Merrie Melodies* made him famous as he sparred with his archrival Tweety Bird. Certainly you remember "I tawt I taw a puddy tat."

Unlike dogs, human interference in the breeding of cats has not changed the species very much. The body and brain of virtually every cat born today would allow it to survive on its own, without human help. Compare that to, let's say, a Pekingese or an English bulldog or in fact most any other dog breed. Few of our dogs could revert to the wild and become highly organized group hunters like their wolf ancestors.

Around the world, cats similar to those we keep as pets are now surviving in the wild. Cats are so adaptable to their environments that they can be found in cities, the open plains, the great deserts, and the deepest forests. They can survive in almost any climate where people survive, except, of course, in the very coldest.

And size doesn't seem to be a factor in that survival. In fact, there is today a species of wild cat that is smaller than the average adolescent house cat. It's *Felis nigripes,* an African black-footed cat that reaches a top weight of only 5 or 5.5 pounds. These cats are loner-hunters, but when they want company (as in a mate), they let it be known with an extraordinarily strong roar. If you want to see one, you'll do best in the Great Karoo of Namibia, the Kalahari, Botswana, and South Africa.

Did You Notice the Cat?

Cats and angels keep company in La Recoleta Cemetery outside Buenos Aires, Argentina, where Eva "Evita" Perón is buried. In these magnificent monuments also rest the remains of presidents, scientists, poets, military generals, and many of Argentina's wealthiest citizens. Hundreds of cats have chosen to live there. At night they gather at the cemetery gates, and the people of Rio bring them food.

"Around the world, feral cats make their homes, uninvited, with the wealthiest and wisest. This cat is comfortable after slipping inside the gate of a family crypt at La Recoleta Cemetery near Buenos Aires."

CATch Words

Feral cats are those who live outside the comforts of a human home. Dictionary definitions of *feral* include relating to or suggestive of a wild beast; not domesticated; having escaped from domestication and become wild. But the cats we call *feral* are almost always associated with human habitation. Sometimes food is left out for them by several different families, sometimes they forage in human rubbish, sometimes they live entirely on the prey they capture. But always they are wary of human interaction.

There are an estimated 60 million feral cats in the United States alone.

Cats who have never slept inside a house can be seen hunting in virtually every city in the world. These solitary hunters also gather as members of cat communities in cemeteries, parks, civic building complexes, and on the steps of some of our most prestigious historical buildings. They have been photographed, studied, and featured in best-selling books. Often particularly prominent groups appear on tourist brochures. These cats who live on their own but quite near to human habitation are called feral cats.

Cats in Early Human History

Experts estimate that the first cat-human domestic partnerships occurred about 8000 BCE. It happened somewhere in what we now call the Near East. Our earliest certain evidence of cats in the household, however, was found in a 9,500-year-old burial site, where the remains of a kitten were laid alongside a human.

Myth, Magic and Medicine

Thousands of years BCE, cats were considered divine in ancient Egypt. In the fifth dynasty (about 5,000 years ago), the goddess Bastet was depicted with the head of a lioness and symbolized light and warmth. But the divine image changed over hundreds of years and later she became a sensuous female with the head of a cat. Feline Bastet was associated with the moon and night. The Egyptians believed that she controlled fertility, cured illness, and protected the dead. She was also the protector of women and all persons who cared for cats.

Some millennia later, cats were an important part of human civilization in ancient Egypt. In the minds of the Pharaohs and the people they ruled, cats were deities, not to be maligned. The penalties for harming a cat were severe: some cat-cruel people were ostracized, some even put to death. But those were the very few.

Egyptian cats were well loved and appreciated as well as worshipped. They provided a significant service by keeping grain sheds free of vermin, but they also lived in the home and often shared the beds of the human inhabitants.

Feline Essentials

The essentials for survival of the feline species are the same as those of humans and other animals: food, water, shelter, sleep, and reproduction. As with humans, individual cats assign different degrees of importance and particular preferences to each of these needs. Could they talk, feral cats would probably discuss their needs somewhat differently than domesticated cats.

Food

Technically cats are carnivores, but in reality they can and will eat much more like omnivorous humans. Feral cats catch mice and birds, but they also forage in garbage dumps, hang around outside the local fast-food chains, and sustain themselves with cat food kibble put out by kindly people.

Domestic cats are the beneficiaries of the approximately $15 billion pet food industry in the United States. (The current world pet food industry is close to US$50 billion.) But our cats also eat brie and Camembert from their owners' hands, Kentucky Fried Chicken, the finest French pâté, grilled tuna, some vegetables, milk (or preferably cream), and sometimes even flowers. If you leave the Thanksgiving turkey on your table unattended, you might just find your carnivorous cat chewing on the skin or even the stuffing!

Myth, Magic and Medicine

Poinsettias are traditional Christmas decorations in many homes. Beware of them if a cat lives with you. They are poisonous to cats, although cats have been known to chew on the leaves. Better you should decorate with evergreens.

Water

Unlike humans, dogs, and most of our other domestic animals, the cat has a urinary tract that can accommodate minimal water intake. The reason goes back to its being descended from the African Wildcat (*Felis silvestris*), who dwelled primarily in deserts and other dry environments.

Your cat won't tell you that she is thirsty because she rarely feels thirsty. Cats tend to ignore mild levels of dehydration. This biological compensation is evidenced by their tendency to produce very concentrated urine. (You've surely noticed this condition if you've ever tried to clean up an area where a cat has urinated.)

On the other hand, when a cat wants water, she will find water. Perhaps you've seen a cat licking the dew from the early morning grass. Among cats who live entirely indoors, most are adept at figuring out exactly which faucet has even the slightest leak and how to get into the shower or tub still wet from human use.

Did You Notice the Cat?

Some experts think cats like high places because they get a better view of the world.

Shelter

Near the beginning of this chapter, I wrote that cats can survive in just about any climate habitable to humans. Although true, I must add that cats, like humans, seek and need shelter. Outdoor cats can become the prey of larger animals, and indoor cats the object of chase by the family dog. Every cat knows instinctively to seek out a place or places of shelter. This need for shelter functions on two levels: shelter from the elements and shelter from predators.

Fame and Fortune

Dewey Readmore Books is the full name of a cat who recently became famous among both adults and children everywhere. Most of us know him from the book titled *Dewey: The Small-Town Library Cat Who Touched the World* by Vicki Myron (Grand Central Publishing, 2008). After many weeks on the *New York Times* best-seller list, more books were written including translations, children's books, audio books, and now rumors of a movie.

Why such fame? On a cold night in January of 1988, a two-month-old kitten was dropped into the book depository of the Public Library in Spencer, Iowa. That dark bin turned out to lead to exactly the shelter the shivering kitten needed. Dewey grew into a gregarious long-haired orange tabby and became the library mascot until his death nineteen years later on November 29, 2006.

For cats in the wild, shelter usually means a cave or cavelike thicket or rock formation. In developed areas, a cavelike structure is usually of human construction. (Think of broken drainpipes, discarded appliances, storage sheds.)

Domestic cats get shelter complete with heat and air-conditioning, sofas, beds, and sometimes even the bathroom sink as a perfectly fitting place to curl up rent-free. But their choice of favorite places in your house is rooted in their instincts for survival in the wild. An open paper bag or recently unpacked box, the far corner of a closet or under a bed or couch, or even a high shelf on a bookcase is the domestic cat's version of a cavelike hiding place.

CATch Words

Our English term *cat nap* is certainly a contribution to the language drawn from our observation of cat behavior. Cats can fall asleep for very brief periods of time at virtually any time of the day and in just about any place. A person who nods off in a chair or lays atop the bed for a short rest is said to be taking a cat nap.

Sleep

With the possible exception of sharks, we all need sleep, some of us more than others. Cats too. In fact, our cats are among the best sleepers in the animal world. All the energy demanded by the intensity and precision of their hunting is conserved and created through an uncanny propensity for sleep. After all, when nothing is going on in the house and boredom threatens, why not sleep?

The daily duration of cat-sleep varies, of course, but the range is usually twelve to sixteen hours. Some cats, particularly indoor cats, can sleep as much as twenty hours in a twenty-four-hour period. Older cats generally sleep more than younger cats.

Like humans, cats dream. Researchers have recorded that while they are sleeping, cats experience short periods of rapid eye movement and muscle twitches. What's happening in their brains? What are they dreaming about—a chase, a love affair? After they awaken, stretch, and stop by for a head rub, they'll never tell.

Reproduction

To survive, all species need a means of procreation. So we mammals have sex, or, more accurately, we copulate. Unlike humans, however, cats are not particularly interested in sex except when they are given the biochemical cue from nature.

Female cats are seasonally polyestrous. This scientific term means that they have many periods when they are sexually receptive over the course of a mating season. The mating season is usually from early spring to late fall. During that time, the mature female will be in heat (receptive to mating) for between four and seven days at about two-week intervals until she becomes pregnant.

A female cat in estrous sprays urine, scent-marking prominent objects to let all the male cats in the area know that she is ready. Very often the male cats fight over female cats in estrous. The strongest, loudest, most aggressive, or perhaps just the most persistent, male wins. He gets to copulate. But that does not necessarily mean that he will be the father of her kittens.

After copulation, the female cleans herself, rests for a half hour or so, and then lets it be known that she is willing to consider another mating with the same or another male. Among cats, sexual pairings can occur fifteen or more times per day during the entire four to seven days of estrous. Several different male cats can father kittens born in the same litter.

What Cats Want

Even though there's a movement afoot in the twenty-first century to simplify life, few of us are willing to accept without objection (or perhaps depression) a life with only the bare necessities. Would you give up all chances for a good bottle of wine shared among friends, owning your home, fine clothes and jewelry, a night at the opera, an occasional soak at the spa, or a game of golf?

Some simplicity advocates would say all of those are luxuries, not needed for the survival of our species or even our civilization. But most of us want more, more, more. Life is not just about survival. Humans are the most complex of creatures, with desires far exceeding needs. Freud was right to be puzzled by the question of what women want. But he should have looked inward a bit, too; what men want is just as tangled an enigma.

Cats too have wants as well as basic needs. In fact, wanting is one of their charms. Each cat is a little different and chooses and expresses her preferences a little differently. Understanding the instinctive wants of the species *felis catus*, however, may help you understand your particular cat. Let's talk about territory, socializing, cleanliness, and play.

Territory

Cats are territorial. They scent-mark the area they consider theirs but may on occasion (especially when answering the mating urge) range far beyond their declared place. The territorial range of indoor-outdoor cats has been the subject of serious study, and the research came up with the conclusion that the size of a cat's territory is pretty much up to the individual cat. David Barratt's published work shows a range from a little over 1 acre to 69 acres. Most of the time, however, cats stay pretty close to home.

Feral cats often live in groups gathered in specific outdoor areas such a monument or fountain steps or even the outskirts of a dump or a cargo loading area. These cats recognize and accept each other. Members of the group often groom each other and sleep comfortably side by side. With the exception of kittens, newcomers are not usually welcomed.

Indoor cats in a multi-cat household may stake out certain places in the house as their own, or they may willingly share virtually everything with other members of their cat family. Bringing in a new cat, however, often causes some problems. Resident cats may chase or hiss at the newcomer. Sometimes owners have to keep the new cat separate for days or even weeks. Usually peace prevails eventually. But sometimes two particular cats may tolerate each other yet never become friends.

Socializing

In their own unique way, cats are social animals. Unlike wolves and wild dogs, however, cats hunt solo. And they do not form organized packs or communities such as those in which an alpha dog and alpha bitch run the show. In groups, cats respect the space of each fellow cat and they are unlikely to interfere with each other. Some cats, usually the largest and smartest, do achieve dominance, however.

Indoor cats make more sounds than feral cats. Research has identified about twenty different variations of meow. And you thought cats couldn't talk! The variations are based upon intentional changes in intonation, tone, volume, and pitch. If you listen carefully, you'll soon catch the meaning of each meow. And, of course, there's no need to explain the meaning of purring! This vocal communication is a way for your cat to socialize with you.

Someone Said

"Cats seem to go on the principle that it never does any harm to ask for what you want."

— Joseph Wood Krutch (1893–1970) American author, critic, and naturalist

Cats simply like humans, and they crave human company. If you were to leave your cat home alone for a week or so, you'd realize just how much she missed you. Oh, cats can get the food and water they need and they can be warm and comfortable while you're away, but they can't be close to you. And being close is very important to a cat who has come to love her human companion. When you return from your time away, you may have a constant shadow for a few days at least. This human-cat bonding is the same all over the world.

Cleanliness

The old Hebrew proverb *Cleanliness is next to godliness* can be traced back to at least the second century. Cats take these words to heart. They love to sleep on clean laundry and they need no housebreaking: once shown where an adequate litter box is being kept or where to find a door to the outdoors, cats will not soil indoor areas with their waste. They even cover up whatever they have deposited, either with cat litter or with soil.

Unlike many animals (including dogs and some people), cats keep themselves clean. Everyone has seen them grooming their fur and "washing" their faces with their paws. Cats remove old, dead hair by grooming.

Cleanliness and good grooming seem to be programmed into cat DNA. The trait has claimed human admiration for millennia and it is definitely a contributing factor to the popularity of cats as house pets around the world.

Besides keeping a cat clean, grooming is important to a cat's well-being. The cat's coat is its primary protection from extremes of weather. True fur is

Did You Notice the Cat?

Cat hair grows at the same rate as human hair, but its ultimate potential length is nowhere near as long. In pedigreed cats, hair length and texture is intentionally determined by the genetics of selective breeding.

Did You Notice the Cat?

Many humans enjoy wearing or using fur. Unfortunately, in some parts of the world cat fur is commonly used for coats, gloves, hats, shoe linings, stuffed toys, and blankets. (It takes about twenty-four cats to make a fur coat.) The practice of using cat fur in manufacturing and trade has been outlawed in the United States and by Australia and the European Union. But, sadly, it's likely that some cat-fur products get by international trade inspections.

made up of two kinds of hair: the outer primary guard hairs and the softer hairs close to the skin sometimes called awn or down. Selective breeding has changed the character of many cat coats; some coats are now more efficient than others. But all coats respond to the climate, becoming thicker with cold and thinner with warmth.

Cats who live only indoors shed more or less regularly all through the year as new hair pushes out the old in the constant regulated temperature. And, yes, strands and puffs of hair found in corners or woven into the upholstery are one of the joys of living with a cat!

Play

Cats love to play. They play with each other, with humans, sometimes by themselves, and sometimes with other animals. Most authorities say we shouldn't attribute human characteristics to animals, but I'm just about certain that cats are curious, have a sense of humor, and like to master puzzling situations.

Someone Said

Mark Twain wrote about a kitten from his cat Tammany:

"One of them likes to be crammed into a corner-pocket of the billiard table—which he fits as snugly as does a finger in a glove and then he watches the game (and obstructs it) by the hour, and spoils many a shot by putting out his paw and changing the direction of a passing ball."

—Mark Twain (Samuel Clemens) (1835–1910) American humorist, novelist, and philosopher

They can also play tricks. For example, Clara Schumann, one of my cats, lived in our house with two miniature dachshunds. Being very low to the ground, the dogs always had a little trouble getting up the steps to our deck in the back yard. Clara would hide on a ledge beside the steps waiting. Just as the dogs were making the jump upward, she would pounce out, legs spread in best Halloween fashion. The dogs would have a fright reaction and sometimes fall backwards off the stairs. Clara would laugh.

Most cat owners keep cat toys in the house. But specialized commercial products are rarely necessary to keep a cat amused. Yarn, balls, shoelaces, shadows, toilet paper, flowing curtains at the window, even the computer keyboard will do nicely. And nothing but the sense of a game is needed to play hide-and-seek with one's owner.

Cats play together, sometimes chasing, sometimes swatting, sometimes twirling after their own tails. Kittens have been known to go into frenzies of crazy pointless running; pointless, but oh such fun.

Someone Said

"As anyone who has ever been around a cat for any length of time well knows, cats have enormous patience with the limitations of the human kind."

—Cleveland Amory (1917–1998) Animal rights advocate, founder of the Fund for Animals

What Cats Give

Near the end of her best-selling humor book *All I Need to Know I Learned From My Cat* (Workman Publishing, 1990), Suzy Becker dedicates a full page to "be loved." Every cat I have ever known knew just how to do that. Cats allow themselves to be loved, and humans need to love.

Earlier in the same book is the advice, "love unconditionally." Cats do that too. And it works. Every human craves unconditional love, but most of us rarely get it—except from our cats (and dogs).

One of the most beautiful stories of unconditional love between a man and a cat (and the effects it had on both of them) has been told by Cleveland Amory in the three books he wrote about his cat Polar Bear: *The Cat Who Came for Christmas*, *The Cat and the Curmudgeon*, and *The Best Cat Ever*.

CHAPTER 2

Silent Signals and Wordless Messages

> ## In This Chapter
>
> ➤ How ears talk as well as listen
>
> ➤ The tails tell
>
> ➤ What else body language has to say
>
> ➤ Cat compassion for needful humans

"How do I love thee? Let me count the ways."

So begins Elizabeth Barrett Browning's famous poem about loving. Love is the emotion writers love to write about. It's the feeling we all love to feel. It's the word we love to hear spoken in a soft voice, perhaps with a kiss. And don't you wish, sometimes, that it might just be that one special word your cat could say to you?

It is! It is! Well, not quite with words, but cats "talk" of love and other emotions every day, in many different ways. In this chapter, we'll explore how cats communicate the feelings that we humans tag with words.

Let Me Tell You How I Feel About You

If we humans take the time to respond with some sensitivity, cats can teach us to understand everything they want us to know. And they can do it in just a few days. In fact, everywhere in the world, cat language is exactly the same. In this universal language, a Maine Coon can tell a Turkish Van exactly what he thinks of her. An Abyssinian, a Scottish Fold, and an American Shorthair can all be friends. And all of them can tell a man from China that they love him.

Modern research has finally acknowledged that all living creatures, in fact even the cells that make up living creatures, can communicate with each other. In all species except humans, the messages are conveyed without words. It's no surprise, therefore, that dogs, horses, mice, rats, and even birds and pet fish quickly pick up enough cat language to get the major messages. With our larger brains and sometimes with an intuitive sensitivity that is almost equal to that of the cat species, humans can often understand or interpret even the most subtle cat messages.

Someone Said

"A cat has absolute emotional honesty; human beings, for one reason or another, may hide their feelings, but a cat does not."

—Ernest Hemingway (1899-1961) American novelist and cat-aholic

The Purrrrrrrrrr

Even with all the research and applied science of the twenty-first century, we're still not sure exactly how the cat purr works. But we know why. The purr is to the cat what the smile is to us humans. It is a characteristic of the species, a sign of contentment, and a means of social communication. The cat in your lap purring as you stroke his head is a happy cat.

Cats don't purr, however, no matter how sensuously pleased and at ease they are, without human company; not while warming on the hearth, not while stretched out on your down comforter, not while curled up on a sunny windowsill. Purring is a part of cat language; it is meant to communicate contentment. The sound is made with the cat's mouth closed, but it can vary quite a lot in volume. The moderate purr may be more felt than heard; the extremely happy purr can sometimes be heard across a room.

Myth, Magic and Medicine

Cats purr at the rate of 25 to 150 vibrations per second. Some research indicates that a vibration frequency of about 26 per second benefits bone and tissue growth and/or repair. If so, purring might well help contented cats to live longer. But what about their humans? Does the purring cat in your grandmother's lap help her live a little longer or maybe smooth a few wrinkles in her face? Or does it just make her days a little happier? (Being happy, of course, can smooth some wrinkles and soothe some aches.)

Rubbing Round and Round

If you've been with cats, even briefly, you've experienced the possession rub of a cat twisting his body around and around your legs. This action can be translated as, "I like you, you're mine, and I'd like to keep you near me." The cat is intentionally leaving his scent on you.

Cats have scent glands located in the face, behind the ears, in the tail area, and in the feet. The scent that each cat produces and rubs off is unique to that cat. Cats can recognize each other by scent, even in the dark. The sense of smell in humans, however, is not developed well enough to pick up scent markings, much less differentiate one from another. So our cats leave their marks on us and we don't even know it!

Scent glands are an important part of cat communication. The cat's substitute for our word *love* is intimate and sensuous touching that uses the scent glands to mark the loved one. Your cat will put his face next to yours or perhaps in the crook of your neck and rub up and down, back and forth, sometimes purring at the same time. He is announcing to all the known world that you are his, his property, as it were. But the statement is made affectionately, not aggressively. When your cat's face touches your face, it is an expression of sincere love demonstrated by close and gentle physical contact.

CATch Words

A gland is an organ in an animal's body that synthesizes a substance for release. A scent gland releases a substance with an odor identifiable to its possessor.

Back to the rubbing round your legs. A particularly assertive cat will carry that activity a step further, particularly if he wants to be noticed. This type of cat will stand on his hind legs, stretching to his full length to plant his two front feet as high on his person's leg as possible. (No scratching or clawing, just friendly pressure.) Cats who do this definitely want to let the person know that he or she belongs to them. Scent glands in the feet leave their imprint.

Did You Notice the Cat?

Were there cats in the Garden of Eden? World-class artists Peter Paul Rubens and Jan Brueghel thought so. The two great artists were friends and often worked on the same canvases together. In the painting titled *The Original Sin*, Rubens painted the two human figures and the horse; Brueghel painted the landscape and all the other beautiful animals. And he included a cat that makes a very positive statement indeed. But if you glance quickly at the whole painting, you may miss the cat. Pause a second and look carefully at Eve's legs and at the enlarged detail. There he is, rubbing her ankles, declaring possession and loyalty.

The entire painting:

The enlarged detail:

When a cat rubs his face against another cat (or sometimes a dog or other befriended animal), it is also a sign of affection, but in a slightly different way. When the rubbing is cat to cat or cat to animal friend, it's a sign of submission as well as the desire to please.

Cats use other tactile ways to communicate.For instance, touching noses is a friendly greeting between cats, and a lowered head is another sign of submission.

Bonking and Kissing

What do cats have in common with football players?

"Huh?" you say. "Probably not much!"

You might be surprised. Think of the last football game you watched. To express affection or approval for a good play, you most likely saw football players bump their chests against one another, or bang their helmets into a teammate's shoulder, or just dole out a good pat on the back.

Without the benefits of roaring crowds, cats developed and perfected that activity long before football was invented. To express affection and approval, cats do something called head bonking, or bunting. A happy and approving cat will deliberately bump a person or another cat with his head.

Cats also "kiss," Cats also "kiss," which is an activity not found in football. Cats licking each other (the cat equivalent of a kiss) is not only an act of grooming but also of trust and bonding. Cats lick humans for the same reasons.

Gift Giving

Humans give presents, presents like roses on Valentine's Day or perhaps monogrammed golf balls on a birthday. These gifts are meant as a tangible expression of affection. Cats give presents too, and for the same reason. Of great value in the eyes of your cat is a dead frog on your pillow, or the carcass of a little gray field mouse on your doorstep.

Someone Said

"What greater gift than the love of a cat?"

—Charles Dickens (1812-1870) English novelist

Don't forget to thank your generous gift giver! No harsh words, shouting, or whacking with a rolled-up newspaper will ever change this behavior.

Fame and Fortune

Charles Dickens owned a cat named William until, that is, "he" had kittens. The name was quickly changed to Williamina. After a short time, Williamina insisted on moving her kittens into the writer's study, and (you guessed it!) Charles decided to keep one. For all his life, Williamina's son was called The Master's Cat, a title he never knew since he was deaf.

Someone Said

"A cat determined not to be found can fold itself up like a pocket handkerchief if it wants to."

—Dr. Louis J. Camuti, (1893-1981) New York City cat veterinarian and author of *All My Patients Are Under The Bed*

I Don't Like You, Yet

Not all cats are trusting and outgoing, especially when meeting a new human for the first time. Some will simply run into a favorite hiding place when someone enters the room. It's usually a place you couldn't possibly get to, like under the king-size bed. It may take catnip, playthings, or treats to get such a cat to come out. Dewey, the famous library cat that you met in chapter 1, sometimes "hid" on the top shelf of the library stacks.

Other cats won't run away but will keep a safe distance while sizing up the new person's behavior and scent. (Many people believe cats can differentiate emotions like fear and aggression in people or other animals by the scent a body is emitting at any given moment.)

The somewhat timid or fearful cat may circle the new person and avoid making eye contact. If you find yourself in this position, don't stare. Staring tends to intimidate both cats and humans. Instead, use the slow blink. Close your eyes very slowly and then open them very slowly, all without losing eye contact. Experts have written that this action eases tension, intimidation, and anxiety in the cat.

CATch Words

Scaredy-cat is a favorite children's taunt, a challenge, and a put-down of the frightened person. The term came into our language in 1948 and is still being used to voice the speaker's judgment that another person is being unduly cautious.

Body Language

Behavior is one way cats communicate to us and other animals. Another way they communicate is through body language, a different form of feline "talk" for you to pay attention to when interacting with your cat companion. It seems that every part of a cat and his every action says something about what the cat is thinking. The key to good communication with your cat, therefore, is careful observation as well as a well-honed knowledge of what the silent signals mean.

Talking Ears

Perhaps you know a few people who can wiggle their ears. For most of us, however, the external ear is simply ornamental, if something so shaped and so located can be called an ornament. Not so for cats.

Aesthetically, most cats' external ears are quite beautiful, clean of line and perfectly placed. They are also a working system. With their tremendous flexibility, the ears of a cat can indicate its mental focus and its prevailing emotion. Each ear can move independently of the other or both ears can move together. Ears can turn a half circle and perk up for peak hearing. They can also move to the horizontal or go flat as an indication of various aggressive emotions or motivations.

Sometimes humans think that a calm or aloof cat, even one who may be looking right at them, is simply not listening. But the clue to a cat's attention level is not in the eyes, it's in the ears. A cat who is responding to your voice will adjust the angle of his ears. When ears are pointed in the direction of your head, you can be assured that he is listening attentively. But you understand, of course, that he still might choose to respond by doing absolutely nothing.

A secure cat carries his ears erect, forward, and slightly to the side. An anxious or fearful cat carries his ears in a horizontal position, out from the sides of his head. When feeling aggressive or defensive, a cat pins his ears back against his head. The hunting cat carries his ears erect and pointing forward.

Fame and Fortune

If you love cats (or dogs) and have children, you've probably seen the Warner Brothers Family Entertainment movie *Cats & Dogs: The Revenge of Kitty Galore*. But, did you notice the changing ear positions?

In your opinion, were they accurate? Will you ever be able to watch another film about cats without noticing their ears?

What the Tail Tells

A cat's highly developed nervous system extends right to the tip of his tail. So it's not surprising that cat tails tell tales. Think about the welcome-home greeting, for example. No cat will ever jump up and down, make gleeful noises, and run circles around his returning beloved. Dogs hold that copyright. Instead, once the cat's person is inside the door, Mr. Tom or Ms. Kitty appears out of nowhere quite naturally. He or she will move at a refined yet quick pace, head up, eyes bright, and tail erect. Carrying the tail high over the body is always a sign of cat happiness, and also, just maybe, some self-satisfaction.

A tail held low delivers very different messages. Moderately low and loose from the body, is a "situation normal" position. No powerful emotions are stirring; it's just an ordinary moment. If a cat is whipping a low-held tail back and forth, however, he is feeling nervous, perhaps threatened, possibly even angry. A cat also holds his tail low when he is hunting, but the tail is absolutely motionless—except, perhaps, for a tiny twitch on the very last vertebra.

A cat who is feeling challenged or frightened and is ready to fight puffs out his tail—in fact, all of his body hair bristles. As it is with a porcupine ready to release its quills, the message is "don't mess with me!" Even more indicative of a fighting mood, however, is when a cat puffs out the fur over his hackles. In contrast, a defeated and fearful cat carries his tail down between its legs, and the hair is not puffed up.

CATch Words

Hackles are erectile hairs along the neck, shoulders, and back of a cat or dog and some other animals. They rise straight up when the animal is angry, being challenged, or frightened. In American and English idiom, a person who is responding negatively to insult or challenge might be told, "Don't get your hackles up!"

With all those nerve endings running to the very end of his body, the tail of a cat is very sensitive. Often the cat protects his tail by wrapping it around his feet when sitting, or around his body when lying down. If you see a tail hanging down over the edge of a bookshelf or countertop or just fully extended from a cat lying on a bed or the floor, you'll know that the sleeping cat is completely relaxed. But be warned (and warn your children): it's never a good idea to grab a cat by his tail.

Evidence in the Eyes

When a cat is calm, interested, and feeling friendly, his eyes are comfortably open (not strained to the max) and the pupils are in normal response to the available light. But when a cat is frightened, his eyes strain wider and the pupils dilate. Combine this eye change with fur-raised hackles and a tail with hairs like cactus spikes, and the frightened cat can be a frightening sight.

Someone Said

"If you hold a cat by the tail you learn things you cannot learn any other way."

— Samuel Clemens (pen name Mark Twain) (1835-1910) American author and humorist

On the other hand, when a cat is feeling aggressive and wants to frighten a challenger, his eyes narrow and then focus with seemingly laser precision. As the old saying goes, "If looks could kill."

The cat power stare is intimidating but interesting. It's a weapon cats never have to learn how to use. The power of staring is bred into some dog breeds like the Border Collie, who uses it to intimidate and herd sheep. Other dogs and even some people have no knowledge of how to use unrelenting eye focus. All cats know all about it. The power stare is inherent in cat nature, which is also exactly why a cat does not like to be stared at.

The hunting or stalking eyes of a cat are slightly different from his ready-to-fight eyes. Rather than narrowing the eyes for focus as in the aggressive stare, the hunting cat keeps his eyes wide open. The center of the visual field never wavers from the object of the hunt.

Whisker Signals

A cat's whiskers are not just long-bristle facial hair. They actually help the cat move through the dark. They work almost like a mini-sonar system. Because whiskers respond to touch, vibrations, and, some researchers say, sound waves and air pressure, a cat can become aware of things he cannot see.

There are twenty-four whiskers distributed in rows on either side of a cat's nose; additional whiskers grow on each cheek, over the eyes, on the chin, and on the back of each foreleg. Whiskers are twice as thick as ordinary cat hairs, and their roots are embedded three times deeper into the surface of the cat's skin. These roots meet a concentration of nerve endings at the end of the follicle. This abundance of nerve endings contributes to the sensitivity of whiskers.

CATch Words

Cat's whisker once had a different meaning, now all but forgotten. In the old crystal wireless sets and radio receivers, *cat's whisker* was the name of the fine-pointed wire that made contact with the crystal.

The top two rows of whiskers on either side of a cat's nose are moveable, and how they are positioned is another indication of what's going on in a cat's mind. A cat walking with his whiskers pointed only slightly forward and somewhat down is probably attentive but essentially calm. When his whiskers point forward and up, however, he is either excited or anxious. He could be excited to see you or he could be anxious that you haven't fed him yet. When pointed even more forward, up, and bristled, the whiskers indicate defensive or aggressive feelings. And watch out if you see a cat with whiskers bent backward. That cat is ready to bite, and it has gotten its whiskers out of the way.

Did You Notice the Cat?

What does W-H-I-S-K-A-S spell? There's no such word in the English language. But add this picture and virtually all of us will say whiskers. We see the cat, we know the cat has whiskers, and we subconsciously translate a brand name into a cat characteristic.

Hiss Means Watch Out!

Most animals give warning signals to frighten an adversary or to indicate a readiness to attack. Dogs growl, for example, horses scrape the ground with their hooves, birds fluff up their feathers, open their beaks, and make the loudest noises they can. Cats hiss.

To hiss, a cat opens his mouth partway, pulls back his upper lip, and strongly releases his breath. (When moisture accompanies a hiss, it's called spitting.) It is not a good idea to take a cat's hissing lightly, especially if the cat is unknown to you. Although a rather small animal, an angry or scared cat can do a lot of damage to human skin. Drawing blood is not unusual.

Arching the Back

The arching of a cat's back can send many different signals. The particular situation that the cat is in and the manner in which the arching is done, however, will give you pretty accurate clues as to the meaning of this behavior.

➤ A cat arching his back slowly is usually greeting someone affectionately, especially if he is also rubbing against the person's legs.

➤ A cat arching his back sensuously while being petted is probably luxuriating in the pleasure of the moment.

➤ A cat arching his back after a nap is probably just stretching.

➤ A cat arching his back while standing on stiff legs with bristling hair (think Halloween silhouette) is either frightened or trying to frighten.

Fame and Fortune

Given their potential to look both mysterious and menacing, cats have always been favored creatures in the world of witches and wizards. In the Harry Potter books by J. K. Rowling, Hermione's cat is called Crookshanks. She is now famous the world over.

Tapping and Swiping

Cats are attracted to movement. And they like to participate in movement whenever they can. Think about your Goldie sitting on the desk and batting at your pen as you try to write checks. Think about Blackie batting at the bob on the unused fishing tackle standing in the corner. There is no aggression in their repeated taps. These cats just want to play.

But change the situation, extend the claws, and add some power. Then playful tapping can turn into a nasty swipe. A swipe is a cat's way of giving an aggressive warning. It says very clearly, "You're annoying me!" And, yes, sometimes swipes break the skin and leave bloody trails.

Cat Compassion

There are many situations in human life where words fail us and our feelings simply cannot be expressed. This is especially true in times of illness and stress. But cats seem to have a special sensitivity to situations of human need. Do they have psychic powers or perhaps a sixth sense?

In our most stressful times, cats communicate with us without words. Their closeness, their warmth, their silken fur, and, of course, their purr gives us comfort in even the most hopeless circumstances. Is there more tangible evidence anywhere of unconditional love?

Believe it or not, cats are getting real jobs, and in the most unexpected places, because of their potential for caring and companionship. Because cats can pretty much take care of their own basic needs and yet choose to be our companions, they are being "employed" across the country in nursing homes, psychiatric hospitals, assisted living facilities—even in some prisons and facilities for the mentally challenged.

Therapy cats have long been brought into these places, so often far removed from "normal" society, by relatives and visitors to brighten the days of the residents. But some nursing homes and assisted living facilities are now allowing patients to keep their own pet cats in their rooms. Some particularly creative facilities are actually housing resident cats who stroll at will among the patients' rooms.

Besides providing purring companionship, some cats also seem to have a sixth sense that enables them to predict epileptic seizures or other medical events in humans. In 2006, BBC News honored Tee Cee, a cat who knew when her owner was about to have a seizure and would always run to warn his wife. More recently, Dr. David Dosa, a geriatrician in Rhode Island, published an article in the *New England Journal of Medicine* about Oscar, a cat who could predict when a patient was about to die and would remain with that person until the passing.

Fame and Fortune

In 2010, Dr. David Dosa expanded a medical journal article that he wrote into a best-selling book, *Making Rounds with Oscar: The Extraordinary Gift of an Ordinary Cat* (Hyperion, 2010). Oscar's love and sensitivity became known to the world and has paved the way for other cats to be accepted into long-term care facilities. Slowly, cats are being allowed to give the gift of warmth and compassion to the very old and mentally challenged that few humans have the time or patience to provide.

In ages past, mythical cats have also been associated with fertility, the harvest, predicting luck (bad and good), the casting of evil spells, and the curing of disease. For example, as late as 1883, common folklore regarding a sty on an eye advised that if you brush the sty seven times with the tail of a black cat, the sty would be gone by the following morning. In 1942, a believer wrote, "I suffered from styes as a child and one day, when I was out with my mother, a gipsy [sic] woman approached us and, in a somewhat hesitant manner, said that if my eyelids were stroked with a cat's tail the styes would disappear. . .The experiment was tried with the result—strange as it may seem—that the styes vanished and have not recurred." (From *A Dictionary of Superstitions*, Oxford University Press, pp 65–6.)

Even today, many people believe that cats can predict the coming of rain in a village, gales at sea, thunder and lightning storms, and even earthquakes. In fact, many people think that cats have many powers we haven't yet recognized. Perhaps some of the secrets lay hidden in the brain of the cat. Do read the next chapter.

CHAPTER 3

Those Little Gray Cells at Work

In This Chapter

➤ The size and structure of the cat's brain

➤ How well does a cat see?

➤ Taste and smell: a close relationship

➤ Hearing far more than the human ear

"I think, therefore I am."

Of course you've heard that declaration of seventeenth-century philosopher René Descartes. But did you know that he attributed the art of thinking only to the human brain? He believed that all other animals acted from instinct. Almost three hundred years passed before Charles Darwin declared that higher animals like apes, cats, and dogs not only think but also make decisions based upon available evidence.

Anyone who has ever loved or lived with a cat can verify the power of a cat's mind. In fact, we all admit (although sometimes silently, secretly, or sheepishly—shhhhh) that perhaps we've been outsmarted by our cats more than a few times in our lives. In this chapter, we'll consider the brain of the cat, how it works, and how it compares to the human brain.

The Brain of the Cat

What do brains do? This most complex organ in the animal body processes information sent from other parts of the body and sends signals back. It is also the source of meaningful life. In humans, meaningful life includes our senses, our movements, our emotions, and our decisions. In cats, too. The feline brain is remarkably similar to the human brain. Like humans, cats rely upon a mixture of instinct, learned behavior, and intelligence.

Did You Notice the Cat?

Everyone knows that Siamese cats are smart. But can you imagine that one particular cat might be smart enough to coauthor an article in the field of low temperature physics and have it published in the prestigious journal *Physical Review Letters* in 1975? It happened. Officially, at least.

The physicist who actually did the research and wrote the article was Jack H. Hetherington of Michigan State University, yet he named F. D. C. Willard as his coauthor. F stands for *Felis*, D for *Domestica*, and C for Chester (the cat's name). Willard was Chester's sire's name, another Siamese cat from Aspen, Colorado.

Why joint authorship? Hetherington wanted to use the pronoun *we* in making his research posits. The publisher said he couldn't use *we* unless there was more than one author. It was easier (in the precomputer, pre-word processing age) to create a coauthor than to go back into the manuscript and change every *we* to an *I*.

Months later with the authors' copies of the published article in hand, the vanity of outsmarting the boss took over. Chester's paw was dipped in ink and pressed to each of a dozen or so copies distributed to friends. In 1978, that well-researched article was considered for presentation at the 15th International Conference on Low Temperature *Physics* in Grenoble, France. It was disqualified when someone leaked the real identity of F. D. C. Willard.

CATch Words

A neuron is a grayish granular cell with specialized processes that make it the fundamental functioning unit of all nerve tissues. In the brain, each neuron contains everything it needs to do its job.

A synapse is the point at which a nerve-generated impulse in the brain passes from one neuron to another. In other words, it's the wireless jump of information that forms the communication network of the brain. Brain synapse speed is astounding even in this age of wireless instant everything.

Size and Intelligence

The average adult human brain weighs about 3.25 pounds. The average adult cat brain weighs about 1 ounce. So how could a cat possibly outsmart a human, or any other large animal for that matter? Well, it's not the size of the brain, or even the number of cells in the brain, that counts. It's the density and specialization of the neurons and synapses and how they interconnect.

Compared to the cat, the hippopotamus has a very big brain, which stands to reason because its brain has to be large enough to manage its huge body. Yet that hippopotamus brain doesn't work very fast or make very many decisions. Why? Because there are not a lot of specialized cells in the thinking areas of hippopotamus brain tissue and relatively few connections between the brain cells. Rats and mice with much smaller brains think and act more quickly and sometimes more creatively because their synapse connections are more complex and more developed than that of the hippopotamus. Cats have a proportionately larger brain to body size ratio than do rats and mice, and most other animals, and they use every bit of it to the betterment of their lives.

The Arrangement of the Working Parts

The working structure of the cat brain is remarkably similar to the structure of the human brain. The two largest areas are the cerebellum of the hindbrain and the cerebral cortex of the forebrain. These two parts are in the same positioning in the cat and the human brain. And as in our brain, certain sites or areas control specific functions such as speech (vocalization for the cat), vision, hearing, touch, and smell.

The cerebellum at the rear of the brain (above the back of the neck) is responsible for the control of muscles (including heartbeat) and for balance. In most mammals, this area is highly convoluted, allowing more space for more cells. The cerebellum, however, is proportionally larger in the cat than it is in most other species. If ever there's a question about your cat's ability to balance, that extra cerebellum size is a factor to remember. Say to yourself *she can do it!* as you watch her walk confidently along the narrow top edge of a fence, even in the dark.

CATch Words

Catwalk is a term familiar to everyone who works in or loves the theater. It's a narrow bridgelike structure above the visible stage area by which stagehands can manipulate scenery, lighting, and microphones, or suspend and swing Peter Pan about. Humans usually need safety equipment to work on a theater catwalk, but of course any well-balanced cat could do it with ease.

In the world of high fashion, *catwalk* has a somewhat different meaning. It is the narrow elevated runway used by models to display a designer's newest creations and take them far into the midst of an audience. One can't help but wonder if the structure got its name because it was elevated and narrow enough to require exceptional balance or because beautiful women are quite naturally associated with cats.

In American urban areas, *catwalk* is also a term for an enclosed or open pedestrian bridge over a street, expressway, railroad, or body of water.

The spinal cord enters a cat's brain beneath the cerebellum and makes its connections through the brain stem. It is the carrier for information from the body to the brain. Sensations from the extremities (extreme hot or cold, for example) travel the spinal column to the brain with amazing speed. The brain then sends action messages back to the body just as fast, also through the spinal cord. This ultra-high-speed, two-way system is why your cat pulls back her paw and you pull back your finger if you touch the hot surface of a stove.

Located in the forebrain, the cerebrum, or cerebral cortex, is the site of consciousness. It's also the thinking part of the brain. In other words, personality and intelligence derive from the frontal lobes. These delicate jellylike thinking tissues are protected by the forehead skull. In humans, the frontal lobes are highly convoluted, and the more convoluted the more the potential for thinking. The cat's cerebrum is located in the same position under the skull as the human's and is also highly convoluted.

Observation power is greater in cats than in any other domestic animal. So is memory. Tests that were done at the University of Michigan and the Department of Animal Behavior at the American Museum of Natural History charted a cat's recall potential as bordering on sixteen hours. (Dogs ranked at five minutes!) The consensus opinion was also that the memory capacity of cats was greater than that of monkeys or chimpanzees.

Cat Vision

Lustrous and expressive, the eyes of cats can mesmerize their adoring "owners." We see in them a range of emotions that almost mirrors all that we can feel: love, anger, joy, curiosity, pain, embarrassment, hunger, and even the urge to kill, to name just a sample. Through their eyes, cats send and get messages, not only to and from their trusted humans but also to and from their brains.

Like most animals that hunt at night, the cat's eyes are set forward in the skull and are large in proportion to the size of the head. To accommodate hunting, the cat's field of vision is about 285 degrees, considerably greater than ours at 180 degrees. This wide range of peripheral vision helps cats detect motion on either side of their head. Peripheral vision, however, is the vision of each eye separately and does not include depth perception.

Just as in humans, what's caught in the corner of a cat's eye is a blurred sense of something moving. Binocular vision is much more accurate and is reserved for the central vision area (about 130 degrees). In that range, the brain takes the images from the retinas of both eyes and synthesizes them to create depth perception. Accurate depth perception is as essential for cats when they're hunting as it is for humans when they're driving!

Myth, Magic and Medicine

Wherever English is spoken, *brain* and *rain* are a perfect rhyme. It's no wonder the British came up with the prophecy "Cat on its brain, it's going to rain."

"How could a cat be on its brain?' you ask.

Without any effort at all. You'll see her sleeping curled up in such a way that the part of her head between the ears (where the cerebrum is protected by the top of the skull) rests on the ground or the floor.

Someone Said

In the eyes of the cat

Is the color of the sea,

On a sunny day, in winter.

—Yorie (1884–1941) Japanese poet

Fine-Tuned Pupils

Your cat can see in almost total darkness. She needs only one-sixth the amount of light that we humans need. The cat's exceptional sensitivity to light is aided by a layer of reflective cells behind the retina of each eye called the *tapetum lucidum*. This membrane bounces light back through the retina to allow motion-detecting cells greater ability to gather images. It is this same layer of reflective cells that causes the cat's eyes to reflect back as two round globes in the headlights of a car.

With extraordinary light-gathering power comes a high sensitivity to light. A cat is protected from intense blinding dazzle by incredibly responsive pupils. Unlike the round human pupil, which expands and shrinks rather slowly in response to changes in light, the cat pupil narrows to the slimmest vertical slit rather quickly. When the light gets low, however, the cat's eye can dilate the pupil to 90 percent of the iris.

With cats (but not with humans), pupil changes can be a clue as to what's going on inside the cat's brain. If a cat is feeling angry, his pupils tend to narrow. If he's feeling frightened, excited, or aggressive, the pupils tend to open wider. These changes work together with the eye alterations discussed in chapter 2, Evidence in the Eyes.

CATch Words

The word *tapetum* in *tapetum lucidum* comes from a Greek word meaning carpet. Knowing that, you'll understand that the *tapetum lucidum* is made up of membranes behind the retina (like a carpet) that reflect *lucidum* (from the Latin for light). Pretty good wordplay, no?

Moggy (sometimes shortened to just mog) is the British word for a cat without a pedigree, or, more casually, for any cat. It came into the language about 1911 and is probably derived from the woman's name Maggie, a familiar version of Margaret.

Chatoyancy is a word used primarily in regard to gemstones. It is derived from French for "eye of the cat" (*oeil de chat*). *Merrium-Webster's 11th Collegiate Dictionary* defines chatoyant as "having a changeable luster or color with an undulating narrow band of white light."

Rods for Motion, Cones for Color

As with humans, the cat's retina has two kinds of receptor cells: rods and cones. The more rods there are, the higher the visual definition and sensitivity to motion. Compared to human vision, cats have six times the number of rod cells for each cone cell. No wonder they love to hunt!

Cone cells detect color. In this function, the human eye is greatly superior to the cat's eye. The human retina has several varieties of specialized cone cells to help us differentiate not only all the wavelengths of the light spectrum but mixtures of every variety as well. Cats are not so well endowed. Until the 1960s, most people, and even most scientists, believed that cats were color-blind. It's now proven that cats can differentiate blue, green, and yellow, but not red. Therefore, the color of the world they see is less intense and less varied than ours.

Whether for the feral cat or for the homebody moggy just out for a night on the town, that color perception deficiency doesn't seem to matter much. As the old proverb goes, "All cats are gray in the dark." And most cats don't seem to care whether a daytime mouse is reddish brown or gray.

Fame and Fortune

Cats' eyes are so alluring, so mysterious, and so beautiful that we humans have named a gem category after them. If you're curious about what kind of gem category, stop by and talk with an upscale jeweler about chatoyancy.

Many stones are said to have cat's-eye properties, but the most famous and valuable is the chrysoberyl cat's-eye. It is a hard stone commonly found in Brazil and Sri Lanka, with some deposits in India, China, and Zimbabwe.

Far Sight is Better

By human standards, cats are a bit farsighted. Their perception at a distance is actually better than ours in many ways, but when anything is less than 8 inches from their eyes, its image becomes blurred in the cat's mind.

If you've seen a cat play with a captured mouse, you're probably finding that last sentence a little hard to believe. But remember, a cat uses all his senses together. When a cat is playing with a prey or toy that is close to his body, his whiskers contribute to the accuracy of his vision. They are so very sensitive to every motion and change of position that they act as cat radar.

Extra Protection

Have you ever seen a cat blink? They don't—not ever, honestly!

We humans blink to protect our eyes and to lubricate them. Instead of needing to blink, cats have a so-called third eyelid (actually named the nictitating membrane) that is a thin, pliable tissue that unfolds over the eye. This membrane is located at the inner corner of each eye. It moves across the eye horizontally to protect and to moisten it. Because it is transparent, the cat can see through it.

In a healthy cat, we usually don't notice this membrane. When we do, especially when it is chronically visible partially across a cat's eye, it is usually an indicator that the cat is not feeling well. He might even need a visit to the vet.

The Two Chemical Senses: Smell and Taste

There's an area in the cat brain called the olfactory lobe that responds particularly to odor. It is located in the forebrain nearest the nose and, not so surprisingly, near the mouth. Why not so surprising? Because a cat has a special scent tool in his mouth called the Jacobson's organ. More about that in just a bit.

We all know about taste buds on the tongue, but taste is also in the mind. As every pet food manufacturer has discovered, there's a pretty well-defined area of the cat's brain devoted to what he really likes to eat. And odor plays a pretty big role in that venue.

Myth, Magic and Medicine

Cats are very sensitive to odors from nitrogen compounds. Unfortunately for some outdoor cats, nitrogen chemicals are abundant in rotting animal flesh and other food products. A cat may be attracted to a carcass teeming with bacteria, and he may eat enough to make him seriously ill. Fortunately, well-fed house cats are picky about food and often disregard such temptations completely, or leave them after just a few nibbles.

What the Nose Knows

There's a bakery off I-95 near Bridgeport, Connecticut, that awakens primitive desires every morning among truck drivers and Wall Street commuters alike. The bakers bake bread there and the aroma permeates everything, even closed car windows. What happens to humans in response to the scent of baking bread is a lot like what happens to cats when the electric can opener whirrs and the scent of salmon wafts into the air: mmmmmmm, mmmmmm, good!

Cats, however, have a more sensitive sense of smell than do humans. In both species, olfactory cells in the nose carry scent messages to the brain. But humans have only 5 to 20 million of these specialized cells; cats have 60 to 80 million. Dogs beat us both out. Depending upon the breed, the canine nose has between 100 million and 300 million olfactory cells. In fact, smell is the chief hunting and tracking sense in many dog breeds, whereas cats rely more on sound and sight in their stalking of prey.

Odor for cats is a signpost of marked territory and sometimes an invitation to an intensely romantic rendezvous. Cats can mark any vertical object with urine. Females in season emit pheromones as a come-hither invitation for male cats. A healthy Mr. Tom can catch a whiff of these pheromones from a distance farther than a Super Bowl stadium measured end to end.

Tasting Tricks and Trials

Cats can transmit both taste and smell to the brain at the same time. The enabler is the Jacobson's organ located in the roof of the mouth. Airborne scent molecules are trapped on a cat's sandpaper-like tongue. The cat then flicks his tongue back and presses it to the opening of the specialized organ. Odor information is relayed to the brain's hypothalamus, which determines the cat's response. This is not really a thinking response, however. It is an instinctual response, and there's not much a cat can do (or wants to do) to control it.

The process of using the Jacobson's organ is called the flehmen reaction. You may have seen

CATch Words

The hypothalamus is a region of the front part of the brain that controls body temperature, thirst, and hunger. It is also involved in controlling sleep and emotional responses.

a male cat draw back his lips and not realized that you were watching the flehmen reaction. Maybe you thought Caesar was trying to smile or, perhaps, snarl. You saw him stretch his neck, open his mouth (but not too wide), and curl his lips back. He may even have begun to salivate. Male cats use the flehmen to test the air more accurately, particularly when they think there may be a ready, willing, and able female cat nearby.

In addition to odor sensitivity, cats have excellent taste differentiation. They may even prefer the taste of water from one source over another. But taste, although sensitive, seems to vary greatly among individuals: one cat's delight may be another's disdain.

Despite their discriminating sense of flavor, cats cannot taste sweetness. They may, indeed, eat sweets, but it is a behavior learned from their human companions. In a cat's life, those big Valentine's Day heart-shaped boxes are best for sleeping in after they have become "magically" emptied of their confections.

Fame and Fortune

Samuel Johnson was an ailurophile. In the eighteenth century, he wrote the first dictionary of the English language with the help of his cat, Hodge, of course. To reward Hodge's diligence, patience, perseverance, and companionship, "Dictionary" Johnson would walk to the marketplace himself to buy oysters or other favorite treats for his "very fine cat."

Years later, the British government was so impressed with the lexicography accomplished by Dr. Johnson and Hodge that it erected a statue to commemorate the dictionary for ages to come. It still stands in Gough Square near the house where Johnson and Hodge lived. If you go to visit, notice that Hodge is sitting on Johnson's dictionary next to an oyster!

CATch Words

An ailurophile is a person who fancies or loves cats. An ailurophobe is a person who hates or fears cats. Both words derive from the Greek *ailourus*, meaning cat. But neither word was included in Dr. Johnson's English dictionary. Actually, these words did not come into common usage until the early twentieth century.

What Cats Hear

Sounds enter a cat's ears and are sent to and processed by the brain. But cats can hear much more than humans. Hearing, in fact, is a highly developed sense that has added to the feline species' survival ability.

For deep sounds (thunder, the kettle drum, the purr), cats and humans have a lower range of about 20 cycles per second. In the higher range of sound (peeping baby birds, piccolos, some cell phone alerts), human hearing stops at about 20,000 cycles per second; cat hearing continues up to about 60,000 cycles per second.

Have you ever seen your cat perk up and look around when you're sitting quietly reading and the room is totally quiet? In actuality, you only think the room is totally quiet. Your cat can hear the squeak of a mouse that is pitched beyond your range of hearing. Mice, by the way, can hear sounds up to 95,000 cycles per second.

Besides hearing a wider range of sounds, cats also hear better than humans. The human auditory nerve has about 30,000 fibers, whereas the cat's has about 40,000. If your cat were to choose to listen, you could give cat commands in a whisper—which means, of course, that your cat always hears you when you say, "I love you."

Myth, Magic and Medicine

Handed down over centuries, in many versions and in many lands, there's a fable that tells of a community of mice who were being terrorized by a cat, a cat who was a particularly silent hunter. The mice called a meeting. The meeting brought forth a decision: to hang a bell around the cat's neck. A brilliant idea! All the mice were busy celebrating their collective genius when an old gray mouse in the corner spoke up: *Who will bell the cat?*

Today, the phrase *"to bell the cat"* describes an attempt to do something dangerous, especially for the benefit of a group.

In the real world, putting a bell around a cat's neck is not a good idea. While the bell may protect birds or other small prey, it will interfere with the cat's hearing. In the worst case, the sound could be disorienting to the cat; in the least, it will be annoying.

How Do You Feel, Dear Friend?

We think of ourselves as rational beings, but humans are not in total rational control of our emotions or our reactions to certain stimuli. Neither are cats. In both species, hormonal systems and control areas of the brain often influence our behaviors long before we can think anything through.

If you don't think that's true, just ask a young premenstrual woman or somewhat older perimenopausal woman or a man of any age at a topless beach or a tomcat who catches a scent of invitation from a female cat or a mother cat with her kittens. The limbic system, particularly the pituitary gland (sometimes called the controller gland), in both the human and the cat brains monitor hormone production and activity in the body. Most commonly, hormones influence motivation, function, and emotion.

CATch Words

Hormones are substances produced by a body to circulate within its system. Different hormones work on specific body cells or regions and have predictable outcomes, although their effects can manifest rather differently from one individual to another.

Stimulating Substances

Adrenalin is a hormone released by the adrenal glands. It is generally thought to produce the fight-or-flight response. In cats and humans, this hormone activates and intensifies anxiety, fear, rage, and aggression.

In addition to producing adrenalin, the adrenal glands produce cortisol, a steroid. As in humans, cortisol modifies a cat's metabolism in times of mental stress, such as territorial disputes within the house. So if you are wondering why your cat is gaining or losing weight, stop a moment and consider how he may be feeling about life in general. This, of course, applies to humans too.

Chronic stress can lead to constantly high levels of cortisol in your cat's system. In both humans and cats, this condition is known to affect the body's immune response and it can increase susceptibility to some diseases.

In a similar way, testosterone, a hormone that affects male sexuality, controls much of the behavior of male cats. When stimulated by it, the tomcat can become driven and aggressive. The quantity of testosterone in any given cat's genetic makeup can also influence the build of his body. For females, the sexually linked hormone is estrogen. Small amounts of testosterone, however, do show up in some female cats and some women too.

The Happy Hormone

You may not think your cat is being very funny when he learns that swiping at the toilet paper roll can produce an endless stream of white stuff that he can pull anywhere in the house. But he is just playing and play is very important to cats. Humans too.

Play almost always produces pleasure, and pleasurable activity releases the hormone dopamine in the brain. Dopamine is a neurotransmitter. Simply put, dopamine is a happiness producer. It joins food, sleep, warmth, sex, security, and love.

Someone Said

A meow massages the heart.

—Stuart McMillan, twentieth-century New Zealand journalist and author

Cat Intelligence

How smart are cats, really? Well, if we could think like cats, we might be able to devise some testing procedures that would answer that question. But behavioral scientists haven't been too successful in using human evaluation methods so far. About the best we can do is watch.

One measure of intelligence is certainly an animal's ability to adapt to his environment and use the elements he finds there for his own survival and comfort. Cats do that very well. So well, in fact, that cats have become the most popular household pet in many nations around the world, including the United States.

Although they can't be trained, especially to obey, as easily as dogs can be trained, cats do learn. You've probably heard about Pavlovian experiments with dogs that led to the observation that when dogs associated bell ringing with food, the dogs eventually salivated at the sound of the bell, even when there was no food available. Likewise, doesn't your cat often come running at the sound of the can opener, even when it's not dinner time?

Unlike dogs, cats do not obey or comply with our wishes with the hope of getting praised. They simply don't need the gold stars and prestige. When they get a favorite food reward, however, training can be amazingly simple.

Science has determined that cats can distinguish and remember complex shapes, and they can even differentiate among geometrical shapes such as a triangle, a circle, and a square. That kind of learning, however, is really rather academic. You don't have to be a scientist to know that cats also learn quickly by trial and error and that their attained knowledge is lasting. Before trial and error, a cat's earliest experience with learning is by imitating their mothers.

Someone Said

I have studied many philosophers and many cats. The wisdom of cats is infinitely superior.

—Hippolyte Taine (1828-1893) French critic and historian

Cats also learn the characteristics and parameters of their homes and the surrounding area. When a family moves, some cats struggle to return to their original residences. Others just philosophically accept life as it is and settle in for the duration. They choose a home and make it theirs.

Did You Notice the Cat?

Look at those sun-warmed stone steps in the garden. Can't you just imagine a cat or two stretched out in perfect harmony with the environment?

During World War II and afterward, Chartwell was the home of British Prime Minister Winston Churchill. He was an ailurophile of the first order. His cats even accompanied him to most cabinet meetings. Favorites among them were orange or ginger tabbies with white chests and feet.

After Churchill died in 1965, Chartwell was willed to the National Trust with the provision that the estate always include an orange cat with white chest and feet to be named Jock. The legal mandate stipulated that every Jock was to live "in comfortable residence" on the property.

In November 2010, the newest orange cat at Chartwell became Jock V. This beautiful kitten was found in a cat shelter, but it took him no time at all to adapt to being lord of the manor. If you visit Chartwell, you might see him mousing or (more likely) sleeping in the garden. Indoors, you might find him curled up in a sink. (Jock V seems to love water.)

PART TWO

Why Do They Do That?

CHAPTER 4

Body Design by Purr-fection

In This Chapter

➤ When a skeleton is not scary

➤ On little cat feet

➤ What the mouth does

➤ About skin and fur

In this chapter you'll learn not only what makes a cat beautiful to look at but also beautiful to watch. In the masterpiece that is the cat, everything works in synergy and harmony. The cat is perfectly designed. While breeds of dogs can look vastly different from each other, the silhouette of a cat in a window is the same everywhere!

Body and Skeleton

Today most adult pet cats weigh in somewhere between 10 and 15 pounds, with a few heavyweights (the Maine Coon and the Ragdoll, for example) topping 20 pounds. Of course, there are also grossly overweight cats, but we won't go there, at least not now. Most cats average 9 to 10 inches in height. They are approximately 18 inches long from head to end of body, with males usually slightly larger. Cat tails average up to 12 inches in length and serve multiple functions.

Someone Said

"Even the smallest feline is a masterpiece."

—Leonardo da Vinci (1452-1519) Italian artist, architect, and engineer

Did You Notice the Cat?

The domestic cat is the only member of the feline species that can hold its tail upright. Lions, tigers, and other hunters keep their tails horizontally in line with their bodies or tucked under them.

Perhaps the tail-up position is the pet cat trademark for "Welcome home! I'm glad to see you."

The Supple Spine

Why can a cat leap more than five times her own height or jump straight backwards when startled or twist her body smoothly around and through seemingly impossible obstacles? It's not a spooky mystery; the answers are in the spine.

Cats have seven cervical vertebrae (neck area), just like most mammals. In the thorax (chest area), however, cats have thirteen vertebrae while humans have twelve. In the lumbar area (lower back), cats have seven, whereas humans have only five. At the sacrum (base of the spine) cats, like most mammals, have only three vertebrae, whereas humans have five because they walk upright. And, finally, the tail. Humans have three to five caudal vertebrae that are fused internally as the coccyx (tail bone), but cats have a functioning tail that can have a variable number of vertebrae. The bones of a cat's tail number about 10 percent of the total number of bones in the cat skeleton. The cat's flexible tail helps with balance and acts as a signaling mechanism.

So what do those extra vertebrae do? Are they the secret of cat purr-fection? Partly so, but there's another factor. The cat's vertebrae are served by an extensive and well-developed network of muscles. These smoothly functioning muscles enhance the cat's power and speed and his ability to twist at an extraordinary range. The muscle network along with the extra chest and lower back vertebrae accounts for the cat's awesome mobility and flexibility.

But there's still more purr-fection. A cat's specialized skeleton allows him to arch his back to the point where hind and front toes can almost touch. The skeleton also enables him to claim the luxury of stretching out effortlessly across (almost, or it seems so) the whole length of a couch.

An Accommodating Collarbone

Have you ever wondered how cats can squeeze into impossible places? The answer is in those purr-fectly designed collarbones. Unlike human arms, the cat's forelegs are attached to the shoulder by free-floating clavicle bones. (The human clavicle, known as the collarbone, is fixed and does not float anywhere.)

Myth, Magic and Medicine

The human body contains 206 bones. The cat body contains 230 bones. Those statistics mean that almost everything we have is in miniature in the cat, plus, plus, plus. No wonder cats can do so much more than we can. No wonder they were both worshipped and demonized! No wonder that we stand in awe of their agility!

The cat's moveable collarbone allows him to squeeze into places you never thought he could go. In fact, if a cat's head can get through a space, the whole body can get through. The cat uses his whiskers to gauge the amount of space he has to work with. Who said cats don't think!

Fame and Fortune

The Tower of London has been a place of doom for many political figures in British history. Few men or women have ever left its prison walls to resume their normal lives. But a loving and very dedicated cat saved one life in the Tower in the middle of the fifteenth century.

Sir Henry Wyatt was imprisoned by King Richard III for supporting Henry Tudor's claim to the throne. Wyatt was kept on a starvation diet in a narrow stone room with barred windows and no heat. One day a cat squeezed through the window bars and cuddled up to Sir Henry. He petted her in turn. After that day, whenever she could, she brought him pigeons that she had killed. A friendly jailor cooked them for Sir Henry. The recurring gift of roasted pigeon saved the nobleman's life. When Henry Tudor took back the throne as Henry VII in 1485, Wyatt was released.

Sir Henry Wyatt remained in royal favor for the rest of his life of almost eighty years. Cats were always welcome at his estate, named Allington. In the nearby church at Maidstone, Kent, above the choir chamber, quite near the altar, hangs a large stone memorial to Sir Henry Wyatt "who was kept in a dungeon. . .and fed and preserved by a cat."

On Little Cat Feet

Cats move precisely and silently, and they almost never stumble. Because they are hunters, their soft and silent steps are a survival advantage.

Cats can and do walk a little differently from most animals, however. Like camels and giraffes, cats walk with a pacing gait, which means they move the two legs on one side of the body then the two legs on the other side, placing each hind paw almost directly into the paw print of the forepaw on the same side of the body. . This movement is called direct registering. It minimizes both noise and visible tracking marks while providing a sure-footed placement for the hind foot.

When a cat wants to move a little more quickly, he stops using the pacing gait and switches to the diagonal. This is the most common gait of four-legged mammals. The diagonally opposite hind and forelegs move simultaneously.

CATch Words

Digitigrades are animals who walk directly on their toes (digits). The posterior of the foot is more or less raised. In other words, the back of the foot (posterior) makes up the lower part of the leg. Cats are digitigrades.

Polydactyly is the condition of having more than the usual number of toes (or fingers). It is a fairly common mutation among cats, especially around Boston and Halifax, and among the Hemingway cats of Key West. The great writer made provision for his cats and their descendents to keep living on his estate. If you go there, you'll see that some Hemingway cats have as many as seven toes.

The haunch refers to the hindquarters of an animal. Being on one's haunches means being in a squatting or sitting position.

Cat's-foot is a kind of ground ivy and pussytoes is a wooly or hoary plant with small, usually white, flower heads.

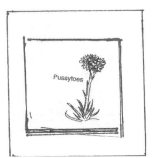

Pussytoes

The Toes Have It

The majority of cats have five toes on each forepaw and four on each hind paw. In a similar position to the human thumb, the fifth toe on each forepaw is slightly higher and off the ground. It is usually referred to as a dewclaw. Dogs have them too, but cats actually use their dewclaws to hold down prey and sometimes to help them climb trees.

Cats have thick footpads that act both as shock absorbers when they land and as insulation against hot and cold surfaces. In the footpads are sweat glands that can produce a watery sweat when a cat is particularly hot or frightened. The small pad on a cat's wrist is called the carpal, or stopper, pad. It seems to function as an antiskidding device, especially when jumping.

Claw Power

All members of the cat family except the cheetah have retractable claws. The retractable part is why the swipe of a cat's foot can be ever so soft and gentle or very formidable indeed.

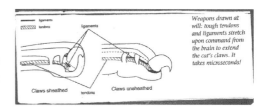

Cat claws are extended or withdrawn by tendons and ligaments in a cat's foot. When the cat is relaxed, the tendons are relaxed and the claws are hidden under the skin and held in place by a ligament. When the cat chooses to tighten certain muscles in the leg, the tendons and the ligaments in the foot stretch and the claws come forward.

The claws on the cat's forepaws are sharper than those on the hind paws. Cats maintain the sharpness by scratching (stropping) on vertical or horizontal surfaces. These exercises might be executed on both tree trunks and furniture, both concrete and carpet. Cats usually keep the claws of their hind feet in good order simply by chewing on them.

Did you know that the claws are not a part of the cat's skeleton? They are created from a substance called keratin. You'll be awed by the adaptability of these keratin cells when you realize that keratin is the same protein that forms the outer layer of a cat's skin!

What Can You Do With a Mouth?

Your cat's mouth can caress you softly on your neck or it can kill a prey with an incisive bite precisely placed on the back of the neck. Every part of a cat's mouth serves a function, whether it be tasting, smelling, grooming, "talking," or killing.

The Teeth

Cat teeth are specialized, designed to kill and eat meat. At the front outer corners of the mouth, cats have two pairs of fangs (unfortunately named canines) that grip prey and administer the killing bite to the back of the prey's neck. These fangs are also used to tear the prey's skin and muscles.

At the middle front of the mouth, top and bottom, a cat has a group of small incisors. These teeth are used for tearing and scraping food from a bone. They can also be used for carrying, and a cat can do this very gently when he chooses to do so. Have you ever seen a mother cat carry her kittens?

The rest of the teeth in a cat's mouth (premolars and a single pair of molars on each side top and bottom) are used to grip the prey. They also can help break the meat into smaller pieces before swallowing. Unlike humans, cats do not chew.

Myth, Magic and Medicine

The healing power of cats has been long-held superstitions among civilizations around the world. Licking is said to be one of the cat's healing methods. One of the oldest proverbs "To get a bad place well, let a cat lick it" was last recorded in Somerset, England, in 1923.

CATch Words

A papilla is a small protuberance on the surface of the tongue. The plural is papillae.

The cat tongue is covered with barbed papillae.

That Sandpaper Tongue

Most cat lovers agree that *sandpaper* is an apt description for the touch of even the gentlest kitty's tongue. Being licked by a cat is not an especially pleasant sensation.

But like his feet, a cat's tongue has multiple functions and it is efficiently designed for the survival of the species. It gets the sandpaper quality from the tiny barbs (almost like hooks) that cover its surface.

These papillae help feral and predatory cats clean every bit of flesh from the bones of their prey. The backward-pointing hooks also assist in the cat's grooming process. They catch and pull dead hair, dirt, and parasites from the coat.

The mother cat's papillae stimulate new life. The sandpaper quality of her tongue probably irritates newborn kittens as she licks them clean. They cry out in protest, and that cry often clears their lungs and starts normal breathing. (It's sort of like the old practice of holding a newborn baby up by its heels and giving it a slap across the backend.)

As a tasting tool, a cat's tongue seems to be both specialized and idiosyncratic. It can detect slight changes in the taste of water due to differing mineral content, but it cannot taste sweetness. Yet as every cat owner knows, somewhere in the taste buds of each individual cat are preferences for which there is no rational accounting. Some cats' tastes have been known to include cantaloupes and cockroaches, whipped cream and oysters, and of course almost anything stolen from a dog's bowl.

Myth, Magic and Medicine

Like humans, cats will often eat things that are not very good for them. The chocolates I just mentioned are an excellent example.

Among both cats and dogs, chocolate toxicity can create the need for a visit to the vet. The darker the chocolate, the deadlier. The lethal ingredient in chocolate is a substance called theobromine. Dark baking chocolate contains ten times more of this cat poison than is found in milk chocolate.

Different cats have different tolerance levels. Here's a list of the possible effects of ingesting chocolate:

➤ Increases heartbeat, both rate and force

➤ Acts like a diuretic, causing loss of necessary body fluids

➤ Causes vomiting and diarrhea; contributes to stomach ulcers in extreme or chronic cases

➤ Acts on the nervous system to cause convulsions, seizures, and, in rare cases, death

A cat's tongue acts as a portable goblet. But contrary to popular opinion, a cat does not lap up liquids on top of his tongue the way a dog does.

In November of 2010, newspaper articles running simultaneously across the country revealed new research regarding how cats drink. With the smooth tip of his tongue, a cat lightly touches the surface of a liquid and pulls a column of the liquid into his mouth. A cat laps four times a second. That's too fast for the human eye to distinguish individual movement. A cat's tongue is actually moving at a speed of more than 3 feet per second.

Skin

In comparison to most other mammals, the cat has loose skin. This is not a detriment, however, but rather another factor in the exquisite design that has preserved the species. Movement of the skin on the body allows a cat to twist and turn on an attacker, even if the attacker has a firm grip on one part of the cat.

The space between skin and muscle contributes to protecting the cat from infection. When the teeth of an aggressor pierce the cat's skin, they may never reach into body tissue and the wound, therefore, may remain relatively innocuous.

Actually, the skin of a cat contains cells vital to his immune system. It is the cat's first line of defense against microorganisms that could enter the body and do him harm. The skin makes vitamin D, which along with calcium is necessary for strong bones and instrumental in the smooth functioning of several other working systems. In most cases, the skin can also keep harmful chemicals from entering a cat's body.

Cats and kittens have loose skin on the back of their necks called scruff. It is yet another protective device. The mother cat takes hold of the scruff to carry her kittens safely from one nesting place to another.

Fame and Fortune

There are people, even cat lovers, who say the Sphynx breed of cat is the ugliest cat in the world. It is certainly the rarest and often the most expensive. Sphynx are hairless. Being hairless (OK, they do have peach fuzz) may be a claim to fame, but it's also an invitation for problems to occur. For example, each empty hair follicle still produces body oil, so the sphinx must be rubbed down daily with a soft chamois.

Having no protection from the elements, Sphynx must be kept indoors. They seek out warm places and usually prefer being with people than with other cats.

The Sphynx may also have the biggest ears in proportion to its head of any cat breed anywhere. But no one would ever dare to name one Dumbo.

People who own Sphynx say that these special cats have great personalities and are very loving. The breed first appeared in the 1960s and is sometimes called the Canadian Hairless.

Fur

Cat fur is made of keratin, the same protein that builds the skin's outer layer and the claws. It is a cat's protection against all but the severest weather, both temperature and precipitation.

Fur works to trap body heat inside the cat, even when temperatures outside the cat are very cold. In hot weather, fur works as an insulator. In response to the seasons, a cat's body tries to adjust the amount and density of fur to the conditions in which the cat lives. When average daily temperatures warm up, cats molt, or shed. This is usually an annual occurrence. Cats who live indoors where the temperature is relatively consistent, however, shed all year long.

The colors, length, and types of fur vary in the cat world from breed to breed. We'll talk more about the cat's coat in chapter 14, Cat Breeds. Right now, let's go on to some insights about how our cats "talk."

Did You Notice the Cat?

Is it the beauty of cats that has won them so many parts in modern films, or is it something more elusive? Consider:

➤ In *Breakfast at Tiffany's*, Audrey Hepburn more or less adopts a cat with no name. In real life, the cat's name was Orangey, and she played many starring roles, including Minerva in the 50s TV series *Our Miss Brooks*. In 1952, Orangey won a Patsy Award—the animal equivalent of an Oscar.

➤ A cat named Duchess terrorizes the orphaned but quite determined pig in the Universal Studios movie *Babe*. Why? She was put out in the rain.

➤ The Cheshire cat almost steals the show in the 2010 Disney version of *Alice in Wonderland*. Stephen Fry is the voice behind the grin. Johnny Depp keeps everything in control as the Mad Hatter.

➤ With an all-cat animated cast, Disney's *The Aristocats* features the song "Everybody Wants to Be a Cat" along with telling an impossible dream love story.

➤ Ginger cat Milo staked his claim to fame in the Japanese film *Milo and Otis*. The American version was released by Columbia in 1989 and was narrated by Dudley Moore.

➤ Sassy was the willful and determined Himalayan in the 1993 film *Homeward Bound: The Incredible Journey*. She was voiced by Sally Field.

➤ Virtually every child and every adult in the developed world remembers the name Figaro. Only a few know the name from Mozart's opera; most recognize Figaro as the name of the cat in the Disney movie *Pinocchio*.

➤ What adult doesn't remember Mr. Jinx, the Himalayan in *Meet the Parents* and *Meet the Fockers*?

➤ General was the name of the cat hero in the movie *Cat's Eye*.

➤ And what accounts for the popularity of Garfield?

CHAPTER 5

The Meaning of Meow

In This Chapter

➤ Cat-talk physiology

➤ The silent meow

➤ How the cat says Hi

➤ "I'm telling you something!"

You already know that cats communicate by using an extensive vocabulary of body language signals. And you know that they leave word with both humans and other animals by scent marking. But what about vocalization? Besides purring, what sounds can cats make and what do they mean?

An Introduction to *Meow*

You'd probably be amazed by the amount of research that has been done (and is still being done) on the meaning of *meow*. Most studies note between sixteen and nineteen different vocal patterns in cats. Meow meanings are differentiated by volume, pitch, length, and rhythm. Individual cats may choose to add quite a few more variations (some studies say there are up to one hundred!) to increase the vocabulary. On the other hand, some cats may choose to remain the strong-and-silent type.

Someone Said

"'Meow' is like 'Aloha'—it can mean anything."

—Hank Ketcham (1920–2001) American cartoonist and creator of *Dennis the Menace*.

CATch Words

There seems to be a word for the sound cats make in almost every language on Earth. And those words are amazingly similar in spelling and speech. Let's have a look.

Afrikaans	miaau
Albanian	mjau
Arabic (Algeria)	miaou miaou
Bengali	meu-meu
Catalan	meu, meu
Chinese (Mandarin)	miao miao
Croatian	mijau
Danish	mjav
Dutch	miauw
English	meow
Estonian	näu
Finnish	miau, kurnau
French	miaou
German	miau
Greek	niaou
Hebrew	miyau
Hindi	mya:u, mya:u:
Hungarian	miau
Icelandic	mjá
Indonesian	ngeong
Italian	miao
Japanese	nyaa
Korean	(n)ya-ong
Norwegian	mjau
Polish	miau
Portuguese	miau
Russian	myau
Spanish (Argentina)	miau
Swedish	mjau
Thai	meow meow (with a high tone)
Turkish	miyauv, miyauv

For clarity, let's group cat sounds into three types: murmurs, meows, and menaces. To the human ear, these vocalizations range from a sound we cannot hear, known as the silent meow, to the ear-piercing screams of mating season.

Cat-Talk Equipment

Cats have vocal cords just as we do, but they don't make audible sounds in the same way that humans talk. For one thing, they don't use their tongues to help form sounds. They can also inhale and exhale while making sound, while we humans simply cannot sing and breathe at the same time.

Cat sounds are made at the back of the throat. Using different speeds and intensities, the cat pushes air over her vocal cords. By changing the pressure and tension in the throat, the cat can alter the resulting sound to "say" whatever she wants. With vocal sound, your cat can express anger, yearning, a warm welcome, or a pressing need.

By the time they are twelve weeks old, most kittens can speak the full range of cat vocabulary, and their mothers know just what they want. Certainly, if you pay attention it won't take you long to learn your cat's language too.

CATch Words

The question "Cat got your tongue?" is commonly asked of a person (and especially of a child) who cannot vocalize or who simply refuses to answer a question. The silence is usually prompted by surprise or fear. Imagine a teenage boy standing with his mouth open as his father shouts, "Did you move the car?" Perhaps the saying has its roots with the cat's silent meow.

The Silent Meow

To meow silently, a cat opens her mouth as if to make an utterance but doesn't make a single sound. What is the cat doing and why? There's a lot of debate among cat experts about this kind of talk. Many believe that there is probably a sound being made but that it is pitched too high or made too quietly for the human ear to pick up.

So why do we call it a *meow* at all, if there is no sound? Think about that for a second. You've certainly heard the old adage "If you want someone to listen, whisper." Yes, that's right; our very bright cat friends got the same idea! The silent meow is usually a play for attention. And, almost invariably, we listen. It can also be a sign of affection.

Fame and Fortune

The all-too-familiar Meow Mix commercial jingle was created because of an almost (but not quite) silent meow. In the early 1970s, an ad agency was shooting a Meow Mix cat food spot. The orange tabby was cooperating beautifully, taking in and gulping down the crunchy mix until—until a piece got stuck and kitty started to choke. To get the stuck stuff up and out of her throat, she opened and closed and stretched and squished her mouth.

To the eye of the camera, the marmalade cat was delivering Hamlet's "To be, or not to be" soliloquy, but in perfect silence. A savvy ad exec took the silent footage and added a soundtrack with music. Presto! The "Meow, meow, meow" Meow Mix theme song became a time-honored memory jogger.

How a Cat Says Hello

Not all cats say hello—out loud, that is. Some cats come out of nowhere to greet you with tail held high, some twist around your legs, some open their eyes to look down at you from the top of the bookcase and give you a blink and maybe a yawn. But occasionally, in each of those situations and in lots of others, you'll be greeted with a short meow. It's like a kiss, a hug, a nod, or a pat on the back. Just think of the short meow as a hi and consider it another show of affection.

The cat's greeting meow always sounds upbeat and affirmative. Sometimes, however, it's shortened to a sound unique to the cat called a chirrup. Don't worry; you won't confuse it with a bird chirp. The cat chirrup is made with the mouth shut. You can put it into the murmur category. It is used for greeting beloved people and is murmured between friendly and familiar cats, especially after a period of separation. After a return to the nest, for example, mother cats often use the chirrup to greet their kittens.

Someone Said

". . .it is a very distinct tribute to be chosen as the friend and confidant of a cat."

—H. P. Lovecraft (1890–1937) American horror, fantasy, and science fiction author

Meow Meanings

Of the three forms of communication used by cats—body language, scent marking, and vocalization—cats among other cats consider vocalizing the least important. But domestic cats are very tolerant of their human companions and understand that sometimes we just don't get it unless they say it out loud. So they have developed cat language, often including sounds and meanings that are unique to their particular household.

Many ailurophiles state categorically that they can hold conversations with their cats. In addition to their sensitivity for reading human body language and responding to human emotions, cats do understand many words. Studies have shown that with just a little training, most cats can respond to up to fifty words. (They may not always respond the way we want them to, but they do respond!)

Myth, Magic and Medicine

Can cats be taught to speak our language—that is, to mimic sounds that we identify as words? One South Carolina couple thought so and took their cat's right to speak freely all the way to the United States Court of Appeals for the Eleventh District.

Blackie was a very compliant kitten. His owner worked with him using tape recordings and face-to-face mouth observations. At the age of six months, the young cat could utter a number of recognizable words and phrases. The media were attracted and Blackie (and his owners) began charging a fee for his radio and television appearances. He even made it to the national program *That's Incredible*.

But like all things media related, interest died away, and Blackie and company began performing on street corners with an up-turned hat on the ground for donations. Someone complained. Local authorities said the group needed a business license at a cost of $50. Blackie's owners claimed that he had the right to speak on any street corner or soap box just like any other American. They sued.

The owners lost their case in district court but wouldn't give up. The Court of Appeals then turned their case down, saying, "The Court will not hear a claim that Blackie's right to free speech has been infringed: First, although Blackie arguably possesses a very unusual ability, he cannot be considered a 'person' and is therefore not protected by the Bill of Rights. Second, even if Blackie had such a right, we see no need for appellants to assert his right jus tertii [as a third party]. Blackie can clearly speak for himself."

Did the U.S. Eleventh District Court of Appeals really acknowledge Blackie's ability to speak? It certainly reads that way. Hmmmm....It seems that even lawyers and judges can recognize the awesome wonder of the cat's brain!

I'm Hungry! Or. . .

Probably one of the most frequently used meow sounds means "I'm hungry." Most cats have it perfected so that it will get your attention and perhaps be just a little annoying when repeated enough. The meow sounds like a whine, quite different from the short, happy "hello" meow.

This demanding meow can start out quietly, almost a murmur, perhaps best described as a subtle reminder. But if you don't listen, don't pay attention, or don't stop whatever you are doing, that soft sound can be intensified into a grating intrusion on your hearing, not to mention your time.

If you live with a cat, you know the sound of this meow. Besides hunger, it can indicate a desire for attention, the need for some playtime, or just plain loneliness. This meow might even say, "Move over! I want to sit on the couch too."

CATch Words

The sounds a cat can make are not always pleasant to human ears, and our perception of them has had an influence on the English language.

A catcall is a raucous cry, whistle, or other vocal sound made to show disapproval at a theater or sports event. The use of the word was first recorded in 1749. Theater catcalls reached their heyday in early twentieth-century vaudeville, where expressions of audience evaluation were never discouraged. On television in the 1950s, catcalls at wrestling matches seemed to be a part of the show.

Caterwauling means making a loud, harsh, annoying cry. For many people, the word is associated with the belief that cats howl to each other as love calls. This is simply not true. Tom cats caterwaul when discussing territorial rights. (That does, however, include possession of a ready, willing, and able female.)

A cats' chorus or cats' concert refers to a discordant din. The term is meant to bring up an image of cats caterwauling in the night.

Please, Oh, Pretty Please!

While the demanding meow can sometimes become irritating, the imploring meow is always ingratiating. It is softly vibrating talk that is difficult to answer with a negative word or gesture. The meow seems to come from the whole cat body and, of course, it's loaded with love.

Your cat will say please when she wants something you can quite easily give but haven't yet offered. It might be the opportunity to lick your finger coated with the sour cream and shrimp dip. (Dips are for sharing, you know.) Or it might be a request that you put aside your book, make room in your lap, and spend a little time petting.

Fame and Fortune

Since the 1920s, the phrase *the cat's meow* has been applied to something that's very attractive or exceptionally good. For example, "Your new hat is the cat's meow." In 2001, Peter Bogdanovich picked up on the phrase and directed the film *The Cat's Meow* based on the mysterious death of film mogul Thomas H. Ince. The action takes place in November 1924 on board William Randolph Hearst's yacht. There are no starring cats in the film, unless you count the American "fat cats" that are being portrayed.

What's This?

Most cats have an almost insatiable curiosity. They love to discover and try out new things. Nevertheless, they also like everything in its proper place and complain about unexpected changes in routine or furniture placement. And they have a meow to voice their attitude.

Sometimes when we hear this meow, we seek out the cat just to see what she has found or gotten into. The meow starts out low, almost a hum, and then rises in pitch and loudness to a short meow, similar to the greeting meow. It's almost as though the cat is saying, "OK, what's this? Hello?" The sound is not aggressive, but the cat reserves the right to become aggressive if the situation demands.

CATch Words

In American and later in British slang, *the cat's pajamas* and *the cat's whiskers* came to be used in the same way as *the cat's meow*. "He thinks he's the cat's pajamas" might be said of someone strutting around a bit too proudly. "Well, ain't she the cat's whiskers!" might be said of a woman dressed to impress.

The phrase *fat cat* in America refers to a big shot or a person who thinks he is one. It is also used to denote a wealthy contributor to a political campaign or the person who bankrolls a risky venture. In the general population, a fat cat might be a lethargic and complacent person.

The Chatter

The chatter is a closed-mouth sound. It seems as if the jaws are hitting against each other. You'll hear it and wonder what is going on in the cat's brain. Hint: it is most often used on a windowsill.

To a cat, looking out the window is a lot like watching television. There's always something to watch out there. The cat chatters when that something is exciting, like a bird at the bird feeder or a squirrel in the backyard. While the sound is not aggressive, many cat studiers believe that the cat is imagining the capture and killing of the prey with a bite to the back of the neck.

On the other hand, the chatter can also be interpreted as a sound of anticipation. Toms approaching potential girlfriends often do it. Do you think there may be a parallel activity somewhere in human behavior?

Someone Said

"After scolding one's cat one looks into its face and is seized by the ugly suspicion that it understood every word. And has filed it for reference."

—Charlotte Gray (1948–) Canadian journalist and author

Intense Feelings

Life for cats can have both good and bad times. And they have sounds to tell us so. Cat voices change to express anger, aggression, fear, stress, pain, and frustration. And although you may not think so, you'll recognize the meaning of your cat's call.

Stress

Cats feel psychological stress just as humans do, and it affects their bodies and their behavior in much the same ways. Many situations can cause stress, including loneliness, the death or departure of a family member, and illness. But the most vocally objected-to situation is usually traveling in the car. Many people believe that being cooped up in a cat carrier while traveling adds to the unpleasantness—and to the intensity of the cat's response.

The cat's stress call is a continuous series of long moans. These cries are distinctively different from any other vocalization you may have heard from your cat. Be aware that the sound does not indicate pain; it is the voicing of intense displeasure and frustration at the inability to do anything about it.

The Cry of Pain

When in pain, a cat's cry can be piercing and shrill. Probably the best example of the pain cry comes from the female in season who has just been penetrated by a tom. The scream slices through the night and everyone knows what has just happened.

That female cat's cry is pure pain. Toms also cry out in pain, usually from being wounded while fighting or perhaps caught in a trap. But the sound is a little different: the cries are mixed with aggression and frustration.

Don't Tread on Me!

Most animals give some warning signal before attacking when they are being threatened or annoyed. Cats are no different. A cat's growl usually starts with a low rumble, but this is a rumble that is never to be confused with a purr. The rumble can increase in volume and usually ends in spits and hisses.

If an unfamiliar cat is showing fear and aggression with a low rumble, move away quietly. A cat who feels threatened might lash out at you with her claws or even bite. Under certain circumstances, such an attack could be initiated by a cat who is normally friendly or timid. Fear, whether it is justified or not, causes both people and cats to act in unexpected ways.

Did You Notice the Cat?

Every MGM (Metro-Goldwyn-Mayer) film is stamped with the roar of a lion. In the 1970s, those lions got a little competition. Mary Tyler Moore created her entertainment company, MTM. Having such a similar acronym, she couldn't resist a little dig at the giant movie corporation.

An orange kitten named Mimsey was rescued from an animal shelter and brought to the MTM set. With the camera rolling, she uttered a squeaky, tentative meow. And the trademark image was made. Mimsey's meow graced the credits at the end of every Mary Tyler Moore production.

Right after that first filming, the real Mimsey was given to a staff member to take home and keep as a pet. She lived happily, unaware of her fame, until 1988.

CHAPTER 6

 **Clean and Beautiful**

> ## In This Chapter
>
> ➤ How your cat keeps himself clean
> ➤ Combs and brushes
> ➤ Dealing with cat hair, fleas, and hair balls
> ➤ Bath time

Global generalizations are difficult to substantiate, at best. But cats seem to be a global phenomenon, so maybe a few generalizations will be insightful as we start this chapter. For example, in medieval times, cats were thought to be allies of the devil and therefore symbols of evil, but in most twenty-first-century cultures, cats typically represent cleanliness, sensuousness, and refinement. Just think of the number of cat images used in advertising!

Because of their grace and beauty (among other qualities), cats are often associated with women. Certainly their careful grooming is a factor in this pairing. (Right now, we won't talk about caterwauls in the night or the metaphoric use of long pointed nails.) Another positive association with women and grooming is the behavior of the mother cat. She takes excellent care of her kittens and keeps their living quarters clean.

And, finally, the cat's cleanliness and self-care is one of the many reasons that cats have become the number one household pet in America and in most other developed countries. The instinct to keep clean has contributed to the long survival (over 8,000 years) of the cat species. And today, we humans keep our pet cats cleaner still, even though they don't always appreciate our efforts.

Clean Cats

Here's a little story that has been enacted a thousandfold in American households: A child, a dog, and a cat come into the house on a rainy March afternoon. The child stands there dripping mud circles around his boots. The dog shakes (at least twice) and splatters the mud/water mixture from his coat onto the walls, the furniture, and any persons foolish enough to be standing nearby. The cat disappears.

After the muddy mess is cleaned up with rags, towels, and warmly tolerant love, the person who did the cleaning wonders, "What happened to the cat?" She looks about and finds her answer. There is the cat, sitting atop the coffee table as pristine as a porcelain statue.

Would any other pet perform so politely? Not unless you kept a tiger in the house. All members of the cat family (even the biggest hunters) groom themselves every day. No one has to tell them to wash their "hands." And after their paws are clean, cats use them to wash their faces; they even clean behind their ears.

The order in which a cat washes is random. It is estimated, however, that cats spend up to 30 percent of their waking time grooming themselves. Does that figure surprise you? Did you think of eighteenth-century fops and courtesans powdering their wigs and ruffling their fills? Don't be concerned. There's no connection at all. Grooming for a cat is a reflex reaction that is locked into his DNA. It is not motivated by pride or pleasure; it is, in fact, a survival tool.

A cat usually grooms himself when he is feeling relaxed. Cats seem to luxuriate in the slow, methodical, and carefully attentive process. Sometimes, however, a cat resorts to preening when he is nervous or anxious. Perhaps cats think of the process as something to do that will help the time pass, just as a person might pace the floor, have a cup of coffee, or read the newspaper.

The Tongue as a Tool

The tongue is the cat's grooming tool. As mentioned in chapter 4, it is covered with hooklike papillae that can pull dirt and debris out of the fur. You may be surprised where the cat tongue can reach. Because of his flexible spine and ability to turn his head almost 180 degrees, a cat can clean most body parts with his tongue. The exceptions, of course, are the head and face and the back of the neck.

To clean their faces, cats apply saliva to a paw and then use that paw like a wet washcloth. They rub each area in need of attention in ever larger circles until they are satisfied that it could meet the harshest inspection of a sergeant major.

The tongue as a tool has another function. Licking stimulates the oil glands deep in the hair follicles. The oil that comes up not only contributes to the sheen of the coat, but also protects the outdoor cat against the weather.

Private Parts

The tongue and licking process not only cleans but also helps with scent marking. By lifting one hind leg and turning back to lick the inside of both legs and the lower abdomen from the anus outward, the cat spreads his body scent in a wider arc and reinforces his identifying odor.

Sometimes when a cat has been in contact with unfamiliar objects, animals, or people, he will return home and begin extensive grooming, often starting with the areas under the tail and continuing carefully to go over the body areas that have been in contact with the "other" (whatever that happens to be). In this way, the cat reestablishes and reinforces his own scent identity. As a bonus, the cat also tastes again whatever it was that he met up with.

As cats grow older, this type of fastidiousness falters perhaps because cats get arthritis, and it may become impossible (or at least painful) to turn one's head 180 degrees or to bend every which way to clean back end parts. With age-related aches and pains setting in and perhaps a little dementia too, older cats may need extra help with their grooming. A

Myth, Magic and Medicine

Cats are sensitive to certain chemicals found in fertilizers, insecticides, paints, automotive products, and even the salts thrown on sidewalks and roads in winter. These substances can be ingested when a cat is licking himself during grooming and can cause dental disease. Poisons can also be absorbed through the paw pads. If your outdoor cat suddenly becomes ill, check to see what's happening in your neighborhood and call your veterinarian.

damp paper towel can do wonders to clean up the areas they can't quite get to, and a gentle brushing afterward to fluff up the dried hair is usually found tolerable even by a proud and sensitive cat.

Cleaning Where One Can't Possibly Reach

Your cat particularly appreciates having the top of the head and back of the neck rubbed or petted because these areas are not reachable by his tongue. Mother cats with partially grown kittens and cats who live with companion cats have solved this problem: they groom each other.

Mutual grooming, called allogrooming, is usually centered on the head, face, and back of the neck. Besides keeping hard-to-reach areas clean, this habit also creates a kind of communal scent marking. This shared scent enables fellow members of a cat community to recognize one another and to strengthen the bonding of the group.

But mutual grooming is also dependent on cat personalities. A friend who was born in Lithuania told me recently about her first two cats, Tigritza and Veruschka. The two cats were adopted at the same time and from the same shelter, but they were not related. "Veruschka would lovingly groom Tigritza many times a day. Tigritza accepted this very willingly indeed, but somehow saw it beneath herself to reciprocate. It seems Tiggi had a princess complex from day one in our house. It remained a wonder to us how a kitty from the SPCA could have learned to see herself as feline royalty."

Even as young as six weeks, a kitten will climb on his mother's back and begin licking the back of her head, especially behind her ears. Most mother cats really enjoy this special bonding with their offspring.

CATch Words

Allorubbing refers to the rubbing behavior of cats to transfer scent from one cat to another. These activities establish a kind of community scent which helps identify accepted members of the group. Humans might think of it as wearing a uniform that is unique to a particular organization.

Saliva is a slightly alkaline mixture of water, protein, salts, and enzymes that is secreted into the mouth by the salivary glands.

The Importance of Saliva

Cat saliva is very much like human saliva. It is secreted into the mouth by the salivary glands to start the breakdown of ingested food and to help lubricate the passage of that food into the digestive tract. But cats, being among the most efficient of animals, have still more uses for their saliva.

By spreading saliva onto to their coats, cats are helping themselves keep cool. While the cat is lying in the sun, the saliva evaporates and creates a kind of air conditioning. So it's no wonder that cats can be seen grooming more and more often when the weather is hot and after they have been hunting or playing hard.

Saliva also assists in the renewal of a cat's coat. Besides licking, the cat can sometimes be seen chewing on his coat with the small teeth along the front of his mouth. The hair being chewed is moistened by saliva. Effective chewing removes dead hair, picked-up particles stuck in the fur, and often parasites from the coat. It also stimulates the growth of new hair.

Fame and Fortune

More than 3,000 years ago, Egyptians saw cats as divinely beautiful. Many people still think so. A lovely 5 1/8-inch bronze statue created during the Ptolemaic period (circa 1069–30 BCE) conveys the ancient and still ongoing awe of the cat's symmetry, cleanliness, and balance. It recently sold for $32,957. You can view it at www.christies.com/LotFinder/lot_details. aspx?intObjectID=4974274.

Allergies to Cats

More people are allergic to cats than to dogs or other animals. The allergen is usually the cat's saliva, not his fur or dander.

When a cat grooms himself, the saliva is transferred to his fur. The saliva particles then float in the air settling on furniture, draperies, even your hands. The results in the allergen-sensitive person could be watery eyes, an itchy nose, and sneezing—even welts similar to mosquito bites can appear on arms or legs.

People used to think that bathing a cat would keep the loose dander down. That's simply not true. Vacuuming doesn't always help either because it will just stir up the particles of cat allergen, causing you more distress in the end. So what is there to do?

You don't have to get rid of your pet. Any medical doctor will tell you that the allergen problem can now be treated successfully. For some people, over-the-counter antihistamines and decongestants work well. Others may need shots or other treatment from an allergy specialist. But with proper treatment even asthmatic people can keep cats. An exception might be a child who suffers from severe asthma.

Fame and Fortune

While still a preschooler, Caroline Kennedy acquired a pet cat whom she named Tom Kitten. But, alas! Her father, President John F. Kennedy, proved to be allergic to the cat.

Tom Kitten was placed in another home, but he was not forgotten. When Caroline's mother, Jacqueline Kennedy Onassis, died, her estate was sold at auction. A framed photograph of Tom Kitten sold for $13,000.

People Grooming Cats

If cats are so clean and beautiful, why should humans interfere in their care? Why not just leave them alone and admire them from afar?

Someone Said

"The greatness of a nation can be judged by the way its animals are treated."

—Mohandas Gandhi, (1869–1948) Indian philosopher and prominent leader in the Indian crusade for independence

Let's put the questions in human terms. Why do we shower, brush our teeth, shave, shampoo, and blow-dry our hair? Certainly the human race could survive without all that. Why do we take vitamins? Why do we go on vacation, celebrate important dates, and decorate our homes? Most of us could keep going without these extras. So why do we bother?

We humans don't just want life, we want life to be the best it can be. Those of us who love cats want a better life for our feline friends too. *Better* always feels good, and making something better is its own reward. You can improve your cat's lifestyle with just a small commitment of time and care.

How Often Should I Groom My Cat and Why?

How often you should groom your cat depends upon the type of cat you have and how much grooming you want to do. Long-haired cats are usually groomed almost daily to prevent matting and tangles. Semi-longhairs can also be groomed daily, but many owners prefer to do so every two or three days. The fur of short-haired cats can be groomed once a week, or the task can be left to the cat himself.

When grooming your cat, always brush in the direction of the hair growth, not against it. And brush gently, you do want to take out dead hair and debris but you do not want to pull out healthy hair. You and your cat should actually enjoy your grooming sessions together. It is a great time for bonding, and most cats like the attention and the stroking. To add to the pleasurable experience, carry on a conversation with your cat in a soft and musical voice.

Besides cutting down on the amount of shed cat hair floating around the house, the important reason for brushing your cat are to prevent mats, tangles, fleas, and hair balls. It's important, however, that you don't think of grooming as an obligation or another bothersome chore. The world won't end if you miss a few days now and then. On the other hand and for everyone's health and happiness, you should think of grooming time as relaxation time.

Mats and Tangles

If you come up against mats or tangles anywhere on your cat, stop combing. Pulling at mats will hurt your cat and do little or no good. Instead, have a pair of scissors with rounded ends, the kind used to cut a baby's fingernails, handy. Mats and tangles can then be cut out without pain or risk of injury to the cat or your fingers.

Some experts recommend electric cat-hair clippers for removing this tangled hair. If your cat will tolerate them and you feel comfortable using them, they work well. But you might have to do a little soft talking to get Cleopatra to sit still while listening to the buzz and feeling the tingle.

A cat who is severely matted may have to be anesthetized by a veterinarian in order to have the mats removed one by one with surgical efficiency. Some owners elect instead to have the severely matted cat shaved by a professional groomer. If you choose that option, expect to wait three to four months for the coat to grow back in.

Fleas

Grooming your cat with a fine-tooth metal flea comb dislodges any debris in your cat's coat, including dead fleas, if there are any, which look like black specs in the hair. On a cat's skin, flea eggs and flea feces show up as white spots that look like dandruff, but cats don't get dandruff as humans know it.

Don't shrug off fleas as another of life's annoyances. They are the cause of disease and discomfort, and they move quickly from one animal to another. If there are no convenient cats or dogs around, they will even bite humans. And they breed exponentially! Once fleas establish a foothold, a house can actually become flea infested and require the services of a professional exterminator.

If you think your cat does have fleas, talk with your vet. Don't use the sprays and powders available at the dollar store, pharmacy, or mall. Many contain substances that are actually toxic to cats and even small children. Your veterinarian can recommend the newer flea-prevention medications that work very well without doing harm.

CATch Words

Fleas are wingless parasites that live outside of the host animal's body. They survive by biting and feeding on the blood of their host. A flea can jump up to 6 feet in the air and can easily transfer from one animal to another. (Cat fleas can move to dogs and dog fleas can move to cats.) A female flea can produce up to fifty eggs a day. The eggs can remain dormant in carpeting and upholstered chairs for up to two years. (More about fleas and the problems they cause in chapter 16.)

CATch Words

A hair ball (sometimes called a fur ball) is a matted wad of hairs that a cat swallows while grooming himself. A hair ball usually forms in the stomach and is later vomited up.

Hair Balls

If you see a cat vomiting, don't panic. Most often the problem is caused by a hair ball. A hair ball usually comes up as a brown mass, often tubular. It can be regurgitated as a single piece or it can be accompanied by a clear or sometimes foamy fluid. Hair balls can also be evacuated with the stool.

If you see a vomited hair ball on your carpet, pick up as much as possible with a paper towel, and then sprinkle some baking soda over the remaining liquid on the floor. The baking soda will absorb the liquid, and when the area dries, you can vacuum it up.

Occasionally hair balls can lead to serious obstructions in the intestines that will require surgery. Lack of appetite and/or constipation can be symptoms of such a problem. The best prevention methods are regular grooming, adding some insoluble fiber (grass or rye grass, for example) to the diet, and feeding a hair ball prevention product such as mineral oil to the cat. But consult your veterinarian for advice on what products and how much to use. Do not rely on printed product labels. Like humans, cats are individuals and respond differently to medications and foreign substances.

Eyes, Ears, Nose, Teeth, and Claws

Grooming involves more than just brushing and combing a cat's fur; it provides maintenance for the whole body. Following are maintenance tips for various parts of a cat's body.

➤ Eyes: Unlike humans, cats do not cry tears when sad. But their eyes do have the ability to produce tears for moisture. Excessive tearing, however, usually indicates a medical problem and should be reported to your vet.

➤ Sometimes small scraps of debris will collect at the corners of your cat's eyes. You can remove them by wiping gently with a moist cotton ball or facecloth. Some cats of Persian ancestry with flat faces are prone to tearing and may develop tear stains that run down toward their noses. These stains can usually be wiped away.

➤ Ears: A cat's ears are extremely sensitive and most cats do a fine job of keeping their own ears clean. Earwax is a yellow-brown substance that can collect at the base of your cat's ears. The wax is produced by the cerumen glands and it is perfectly normal. If the wax builds up excessively or if your cat's ears become dirty from his outdoor adventures, you can clean them with cotton balls dipped in warm olive or mineral oil. Do not put cotton swabs down into your cat's ear canal.

➤ Nose: A cat's nose is also very sensitive and generally needs no special care or human tampering. A runny nose or a particularly dry nose, however, usually means something isn't quite right. Watch your cat closely and if anything else seems amiss, do give the vet a call.

➤ Teeth: It is becoming fashionable to brush the teeth of our cats and dogs. But still, many cat owners, even the devoted ones, object to the idea of cleaning a cat's teeth. After all, they say, cats have survived without toothbrushes for, ahhh, has it really been 8,000 years or so?

Myth, Magic and Medicine

Experts suggest brushing the teeth of a pet cat daily with a soft child-size toothbrush. You can use plain water or specially formulated cat toothpaste. Do not use human toothpaste on your cat because some of the brands contain detergents that could do harm to cats.

Nevertheless, modern science has identified potential tooth problems some of which, experts say, are certainly the result of the cat's modern diet. Like humans, cats can get cavities and periodontal disease. They can also develop cat halitosis if the teeth and gums are not kept clean. Halitosis is not exactly something you will want to deal with. The condition produces a horrible urinelike smell from the cat's mouth. That odor is a red flag for help.

> ➤ Claws: Some outdoor cats and all indoor cats need to have their claws clipped from time to time—once a month is usually a good routine. Unless your cat is particularly docile, it is generally best to clip only a few claws at a sitting.

If you're a nail-clipping novice, you might feel some trepidation when you first take clippers in hand, and your cat will sense your fear. Speak quietly to your cat, go slowly, and be conservative. It's better to err on the side of too little clipping than too much. You can always clip more often if necessary.

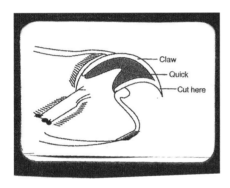

Where to trim your cat's claws

To clip a cat's claws, hold a paw in one hand and press gently on the top of the "toe" so that the claw comes forward and is exposed. Except when cutting black claws, you will be able to see a pink area called the quick. Cut the nail just in front of the quick. Be careful not to cut through the quick because the nail will bleed and the cut will be painful to the cat. If your cat has black claws, you will need to learn by trial and error where the quick is. Begin conservatively by cutting only the very tip of the claw.

Bath Time

Most cats are quite certain that water is intended only for drinking. They just can't understand why any self-respecting animal would want to douse its fur with it. So why should we humans periodically put our favorite, fastidious, self-aware, and self-cleaning pets through the "torture" of a bath?

Some cats (notably outdoor toms) actually like to get dirty once in a while, and they aren't always pleasant to have in the house afterward. Baths are a means of controlling fleas, some other parasites, and some skin problems as well.

Many owners, though, even wealthy, particular, and well-informed owners, proudly say that their cats have never needed or had a bath. And for many other owners, not bathing cats is a manifestation of the "if it ain't broke, don't fix it" philosophy.

If you choose to bathe your cat, always use a shampoo prepared for cats. Some human shampoos leave residues that can prove toxic to a cat who licks himself after the ordeal is over. If you can't get cat shampoo and the bath must be given immediately, use baby shampoo.

Myth, Magic and Medicine

Oh agony! Your cat has come home after being sprayed by a skunk. Don't dawdle—get the cat shampoo, get help, get some old towels, get the cat in the sink, and make plenty of bubbles. Rinse, damp dry, and then tell Captain Courageous that he will feel much better after a soak. Pour either milk or tomato juice directly onto the cat, rub it in, and try to get him to stay still for ten minutes or so. Then rinse thoroughly, dry, and hug.

If you were once a Boy Scout or a Boy Scout mom and believe in the motto Be Prepared, you might want to buy a commercial skunk odor remover product. These are available in many pet stores. You can tuck the container into the back corner of a cabinet, but don't forget which one!

The First Time

Unless your cat was introduced to baths as a kitten, he may object (with varying degrees of force and fury) to the idea of being bathed. The process of giving a bath, therefore, may require two people at first, one to hold the cat, and one to do the washing.

This may strike you as funny—two adult humans for one little cat. But be assured, it's good advice. Confinement is stressful to cats; add soap and water and it's very stressful.

Try to talk reassuringly to your cat to keep her as calm as possible through the bathing process. Cats do listen even in times of stress, and the voice of a loved one can be a comfort. But if your cat objects fiercely, do not hold tighter and force him down. That kind of action will make an issue out of having a bath that may never be resolved. Instead, tell your cat that you love him and try again another day.

Someone Said

A cat's rage is beautiful, burning with pure cat flame, all its hair standing up and crackling blue sparks, eyes blazing and sputtering.

—William S. Burroughs (1914–1997) American author

Preparation

When preparing for your cat's bath, place a rubber mat or a cloth bath mat at the bottom of a sink, human bathtub, or plastic baby bathtub. This will give him something to dig his claws into if he should feel the need to hold on.

About 4 inches of water is adequate for most baths. Be sure the water is warm enough by testing with your wrist or elbow. A cat's body temperature is higher than ours, so the water should feel quite warm to your touch, but not hot. (About 90 to 95 degrees Fahrenheit is good.)

Be sure that you have everything you will need set out and within easy reach. Your cat will not sit still in the tub while you go to fetch something you forgot. Top of the list: shampoo, a washing cloth, towels.

Procedure

Gently wet the cat. Work in the shampoo with a massaging motion while telling your cat how beautiful and wonderful he is. Be especially careful when soaping the cat to avoid his sensitive eyes, ears, and nose.

Rinse thoroughly after the shampoo, and then towel dry. Many professional groomers suggest using a hair dryer that is set at a low speed to dry a cat before releasing him. Most cats won't object to a dryer.

Professional Grooming

In this age when hardly anybody mows his or her own lawn anymore, it's not surprising that cat grooming is a growing industry. When I wrote my first book on cats in the mid-1990s, the only trade association for cat groomers was called The National Dog Groomers Association of America, Inc. Only a limited number of members, however, groomed both dogs and cats, and specialized cat groomers were hard to find. Today, a person who is squeamish about cutting claws or giving baths can access at least two national cat groomers trade organizations to obtain the names of members in a given local area.

The National Cat Groomers Institute of America (NCGIA) claims that it was the first feline-specific groomers association ever to be formed. It began in the spring of 2007 for the purpose of setting and maintaining cat grooming standards, providing training and education, and awarding certification when training requirements are met. Find them on the internet at www.nationalcatgroomers.com.

The Professional Cat Groomers Association of America (PCGAA) calls itself an international organization that was formed exclusively by dedicated cat grooming professionals who have extensive experience, continued education, advanced certification, and business savvy. The PCGAA has implemented a whole approach to the grooming of cats. Find it on the internet at www.professionalcatgroomers.com.

Did You Notice the Cat?

The whole world recognizes the beauty of the cat. And every cat seems to agree.

Who's The Fairest of Them All (1887) **is the most famous oil painting done by British artist Frank Paton.**

CHAPTER 7

A Day in the Life of Your Cat

In This Chapter

➤ About sleep

➤ Eating and drinking

➤ Playtime

➤ Loving time

The beginning of retirement is often a stressful time for humans. Suddenly the daily rhythm of life has evaporated. Many men and women simply don't know what to do with their time each day. Not so for cats, who, after all, never retire from being cats. Time management is simply not a cat problem.

From kittenhood to old age, cats seem at ease with the unfolding of each day. They do like patterns and security, however. Cats like things kept in certain places, they like meals at certain times, they like to know when you're coming home, and they like plenty of sleep. Other than that, each day is an adventure in seeing and doing whatever can be seen and done.

To Sleep, Perchance to Dream

Sleep! There are those who say it's what cats do best. Most healthy adult cats sleep away 50 to 60 percent of each day, while some manage

Someone Said

"Cats do not have to be shown how to have a good time, for they are unfailingly ingenious in that respect."

—James Mason (1909–1984) British film and stage actor

70 percent. Senior cats and very young kittens can get that figure to 80 percent quite easily. How do they do it?

Research has shown that in both cats and humans, sleep is induced by melatonin in the brain. The amount of this chemical and the timing of its release are probably controlled by the gene that determines each individual's circadian rhythm.

Many experts say that a cat's circadian rhythms are quite different from those of a human. In the wild, cats are nocturnal animals. But even feral cats don't sleep all day or stay up all night. A cat is naturally most alert and active at dawn and dusk, when hunting is at its best. Most cats are sleepiest at midday and in the middle of the night.

In general, cats prefer many short periods of light sleep and a few periods of deep sleep over the human pattern of one long sleep in a twenty-four-hour period. This can sometimes cause small problems like being pounced upon at 3 a.m. by a creature who wants to play or express affection.

A cat's sleep pattern is very hard to change because it is deeply embedded in the feline DNA. Some owners have resorted to keeping a water-filled squirt gun on the bedside table and using it ruthlessly until Mephistopheles gets the message that jumping on the bed in the middle of the night is not an approved activity.

CATch Words

A catnap is a very short, light sleep during the day.

Circadian rhythm is a twenty-four-hour cycle common in most animals. It dictates when the animal is most and least active.

Myth, Magic and Medicine

The cat sees through shut lids.

—English proverb

During periods of light sleep, cats are pretty much aware of what's going on around them even though their eyes appear to be shut. They can move either from light sleep into deep sleep or from light sleep into instant awareness. In fact, when startled out of a light sleep, they are immediately ready to take whatever action is appropriate to the situation that woke them. It's as though they were sleeping but awake at the same time— another cat puzzle!

Two Kinds of Sleep

By studying brain waves, modern science has determined that cats, like humans, have at least two different types of sleep: slow-wave, or quiet, sleep, and REM, rapid eye movement, sleep. During slow-wave sleep, the cat's muscles relax and her brain activity slows to a rhythmic pattern. REM sleep is deeper but lasts for considerably less time. It's estimated that REM sleep occurs during only 30 percent of a cat's total sleeping time.

In humans, scientists believe that REM sleep is the time that we dream. Most experts think that cats dream too. Almost every cat owner can remember seeing his or her sound asleep cat begin to move her feet, twitch her tail, and perhaps even make aggressive sounds. But the cat will never tell what she was chasing or, for that matter, who won.

Someone Said

"Cats are rather delicate creatures and they are subject to a good many ailments, but I never heard of one who suffered from insomnia."

—Joseph Wood Krutch (1893–1970) American essayist and critic

Waking Up

Just like us, cats yawn, but there's a bit of a difference. We tend to yawn most often when we're getting sleepy; cats yawn when they are waking up. They also yawn in greeting. If you come home and inadvertently wake your sleeping cat, your greeting may be just a yawn—and then your cat might just go back to sleep.

If your cat decides to actually get to her feet after the wake-up yawn, she will go through a waking ritual that exercises many of the muscles that are essential to maintaining her flexibility and the length of her stride. First, however, the yawn may be repeated. The cat will open her mouth as far as possible and curl her tongue between the lower incisors.

Next Kitty will stretch out her paws, sometimes even exposing the claws as she gets up to stand on all four feet. But be aware, she's not done yet. You'll see her draw her body together by tightening her body muscles and arching her back.

The next step in the waking dance is a long stretch forward. The cat's rear end will stays high while the spine now curves downward. Kitty's head will be lower than her back and her front legs will be stretched. You may think she's now ready to walk, but not quite yet. Your cat is still aware that the muscles of her hind legs need to be stimulated. You'll see her legs stretched out behind her one at a time, almost as if she's pushing away from a wall.

This combination of yawning, stretching, standing, arching up, and stretching out again, (both front and back) helps the cat stay in shape. After all, if you take seven naps a day, and then do a wake-up routine after each one, or even after just most naps, it's almost as good as doing tai chi.

Finding the Perfect Place

Some cats can and do sleep anywhere; others have very distinct preferences. Many owners even make extensive provisions to assure cat relaxation. Unfortunately, it's not always easy to get it right. Sometimes Kitty will ignore the perfect place you have just installed.

Did You Notice the Cat?

Slippers lived in the White House during Theodore Roosevelt's administration. He was a large blue-gray polydactyl who demonstrated his position as First Cat with dignity and self-assurance.

In 1906, Roosevelt was hosting an important state dinner. Slippers joined the party while appetizers were being served. But it was all so, well, boring, so he stretched out on the carpet that led to the dining room and fell sound asleep. When it was time for the dinner to begin, President Roosevelt and representatives of the world powers of the early twentieth century all yielded precedence to the sleeping cat by walking around him.

Did anyone complain? Take a guess. And remember: he was a very fine cat indeed.

CATch Words

Catnip is a member of the mint family of plants, which are related to familiar kitchen herbs like sage and thyme. It contains a chemical called nepetalactone, which gives most cats a delightful high. The buzz is activated through the sense of smell and affects the cat's nervous system. It is safe and nonaddictive, and it is available in pet stores.

Buying a Cat Bed

Cat beds come in many shapes, sizes, and colors. Most cats prefer those with high sides because they feel more protected. For a cavelike bed, search for a high woven basket with an entry hole in front, or an upholstered bed that has a high semicircle for a headboard.

Be sure that any bedding you provide is washable, but don't wash it too often. Cats feel comfortable when they can detect their own scent on things they consider their own.

But what if your cat doesn't like the cat bed you bought? This happens more often than most of us want to admit. Should you put in toys or catnip, or perhaps put the cat bed in a closet, bathroom, or other small enclosure, and then close the door and just wait for Puss-in-Boots to get used to it? No, not usually a good idea. Cats are independent thinkers, and once they have made up their minds, even passive torture is unlikely to force a change.

Fame and Fortune

In 1975, a graduate student named Leon Seidman wanted to get some catnip to make his pet, WB, happy. WB, however, looked down his nose at all the brands that Leon brought home from the marketplace. The best rating that he would give, and only infrequently, was four stars.

The next summer Seidman was on vacation in West Virginia and saw fields of catnip growing everywhere and available for the taking. He filled his car with it and headed home. WB approved the fresh catnip without reservation. Leon went back for seeds and began growing it in his backyard. At first he gave it away to his ailurophile friends so they could make their cats happy too. But then he started a catnip business.

Today, his product, Cosmic Catnip, is a world-favorite brand. Cosmic Pet Products, Inc., of which Seidman is president, packages over 140,000 pounds of catnip annually. That's more than any other company, anywhere. The company is also the largest manufacturer of cat toys in the United States.

When the Cat Prefers Your Bed

Most ailurophiles let their cats sleep wherever they choose. Favored places are almost always warm. And among the favorite of favorites is usually your bed—which isn't so bad if your cat sleeps at the foot of the bed and on top of the duvet. But Kitty might have different ideas.

Cats like pillows, and they like to get under the covers and between two humans—which isn't too bad if the cat sleeps curled up in a space-saving circle. But there are stories of cats who sleep in the center of the bed, on their backs, in a star shape (the six points are four legs, tail, and head). This leaves the devoted owners each hanging on to an edge and never able to cuddle without a furry interference.

What to do? Use your cat-training imagination. But if all else fails, close the bedroom door before you retire. (Be sure the cat is on the other side of the door and not hiding under the bed.) Or put the cat in another room (perhaps even the unoccupied guest room) and close that door. Some "discussion" might ensue for a few nights, but your cat will eventually settle for what she decides is second best.

Warm and High, or Deep in a Cave

A warm spot can be anywhere; the owner's lap is a favorite sleeping place. In some older homes, cats like to sleep on top of radiator covers or near the hearth of a crackling fireplace in winter. Some owners install "cat sills" that extend out from a sunny windowsill. Others find their cats sleeping in corners, perhaps under the bed but almost always right next to a forced-air heating duct.

Myth, Magic and Medicine

If a cat sits with its tail toward the fire, we will have a hard frost.

—British saying, first recorded in March, 1775

Cats sitting with their tails to the fire. . .are said to foretell change of weather.

—British saying, about 1790

If you are having trouble finding your cat one day, look up. Cats like high places, probably because they feel safer there (especially if the household has a dog) and they can enjoy a panoramic view of their surroundings. It's advisable to remove the Ming Dynasty vase from the top shelf of your bookcase, and you might leave the space unoccupied for your cat. How will she get up there? You can spy on her, but be aware that the ways of cats are both devious and determined.

On the other hand, many owners report that their cats carefully move around the collections of pottery, crystal, or porcelain displayed on their bookshelves and other high locations. One couple with an awesome collection of American Indian pottery reported being amazed to witness the graceful ease with which their sweet Heishi wiggled her way among these artifacts without ever once knocking anything over. It's not that she appreciated the value of the pottery; for her, being careful was just second nature.

On the floor level, cats love to climb into empty boxes and empty paper bags. Again, being surrounded gives them a sense of security. Your cat may also look for a space where nobody goes. My daughter's cat, Freckles, likes to sleep behind the table where the guinea pig cage is located.

The Couch or Chair

Cats like to be near familiar smells, including yours. You will often find them sleeping in "your" chair or stretched out on the couch where you routinely watch football games on Sundays in autumn.Cats also make themselves at home in your dirty laundry (it doesn't smell dirty to them). Some cats have been known to climb into an open dryer or front-loading washing machine. Always check before starting these appliances. There have indeed been reports of cats meeting their end in this way. And, finally, your cat may feel comfortable in an open dresser drawer or the back corner of your closet. If you close up the drawer or closet, accidentally, you'll hear her calling.

Eating and Drinking

In many homes, mealtime is the high point of a cat's day. Food is a major interest of all cats, especially those who spend their lives indoors. And with pet food aisles getting longer and longer in the supermarket, there's no reason dining should be boring or that a cat should be malnourished.

Myth, Magic and Medicine

In a cat's eyes, all things belong to cats.

—English proverb

Most cats like to know they can find their meals in their own dining area (in the same spot, that is) when the dinner bell (can opener, container cover, or rattle of dry food) sounds. The dining spot should be out of the path of household traffic, away from strong odors, including the litter box, and, if there's a dog in the family, in a place where the dog can't reach.

Most folks feed their cats twice a day, a morning meal and another late in the afternoon or early in the evening. With both men and woman working nowadays, few owners try to do three meals a day for their cats, but many leave some dry food out all day, just in case Cleopatra wants a snack.

Be certain that both food and water bowls are wide enough so that the cat's head and whiskers can fit inside. Whiskers are very sensitive, and feeling them rubbing against the side of a bowl can be off-putting even to a hungry cat. Always try to serve the food at room temperature.

Myth, Magic and Medicine

Be especially careful to put fresh water out for your cat every day. A cat who loses up to 50 percent of her overall weight by not eating can still survive. But if she loses just 15 percent of her water weight, she will die.

More about the cat's diet, nutritional needs, and multibillion dollar pet food industry in chapter 15. For now, be sure to go easy on snacks and creative feeding. Many cats are allergic to cow's milk, and all cats react negatively to chocolate. Dog food, while appealing to many cats, may not have enough protein to satisfy a cat's needs. Cats, by the way, cannot survive on a vegetarian diet.

Most important of all, be careful to watch what Kitty gets at the dinner table. Most cats learn to like human food a lot, and there is always the temptation to slip your silent beauty a bite or two. Too many treats can contribute to feline obesity, which for cats as well as for humans can prove a serious health risk in later years.

Did You Notice the Cat?

Being that they consider themselves part of the family, cats like to hang around at the dinner table. They've been doing that for hundreds of years, all around the world.

CATch Words

Cat salt is finely granulated salt formed from bittern. Bittern is the bitter water solution of salts that is left after ordinary table salt (sodium chloride) has been crystallized out of the brine.

Cat thyme is a European plant in the mint family. It has an aromatic leaf.

Catfish is the name generally given to a large class of fish characterized by having no scales. These fish also have long barbells, or feelers, around the mouth. That, along with the habit of lashing their long tails as they swim is probably the association with felines. Most catfish are freshwater fish found in North America and Europe under a variety of local names.

Catlap is a derogatory term for a weak drink.

Catmint is an herbaceous plant with aromatic leaves. Its young shoots can be used, although sparingly, in green salads.

Cattail millet (Italian millet) is a species of grain-bearing grass first grown in prehistoric times and still in use, especially in parts of Asia and Europe. The best variety to eat is golden millet, which is, of course, yellow in color. It is used to make coarse bread and porridge. It is also used in the preparation of the North African dish couscous.

Oh to Scratch!

There's a sound that might be heard in your cat-loving household that will make you stop whatever you're doing, guaranteed. It's the r-i-i-i-i-p of upholstery. A ripping done, of course, by your cat. Hearing a cat scratching on bare wood, especially if it's Granny's heirloom rocker or something equally valuable, is just as dismaying. Hearing your cat scratch at, or even climb, draperies also makes one's blood run cold. Some cat owners even forego draperies in favor of blinds, shades, or valences.

Why Scratch?

Cats have a need to scratch that's embedded in their genes and their physiology. They have scent glands in their feet, and scratching helps cats mark their territory. It also sharpens their claws and helps shed old or loose nails.

Scolding cats for doing what comes naturally will only confuse them. It's better to provide acceptable scratching places and to make unacceptable places less desirable. For example, cats don't particularly like smooth surfaces. When decorating your home, you should consider using leather, imitation leather, marble, granite, or lacquer-finished pieces. Avoid, if possible, nubby fabrics. Hardwood floors are advisable, but give up on the idea that any carpeting will remain untouched. "The saggier the better," says the sagacious cat.

The Scratching Post

You'll need a scratching post, or maybe two, so that your cat can be happy clawing away at will, and you can be happy that she's not clawing at your furniture. (Don't think, however, that a scratching post will absolve you from the chore of nail clipping. That still has to be a regular part of grooming.)

A scratching post is just that, a chunk of wood or other sturdy material covered by a rug. Make sure the underside of the rug is exposed so as not to reinforce or even encourage carpet clawing.

Scratching posts can also be made of sisal rope, burlap, corrugated cardboard, or some equally sturdy fabric that has cat appeal. Your scratching post doesn't have to be beautiful; its only purpose is to provide your Caesar, Cleopatra, or Mark Antony with an outlet for the urge to scratch.

At least three feet is usually a good height for most posts. Be aware, however, that a workable scratching post should be higher for a larger cat. In fact, it should be longer than the length of the cat because it also acts as a stretching post.

Scratching posts are available at virtually all pet stores, or if you're handy, you can make your own. A common place to put them is near the cat's favorite sleeping spot so she can scratch and stretch right when she wakes up. If possible, the scratching post should be anchored to the floor to prevent tipping. When your cat gets going on a good scratching post, she will feel very much like she's scratching at a tree trunk.

Someone Said

"Those who'll play with cats must expect to be scratched."

—Miguel de Cervantes (1547–1616) Spanish novelist, poet, playwright, and soldier

To help accustom your cat to using a scratching post instead of the conveniently located furniture, you might smear the surface of the post with catnip to make it more alluring. Guide Caesar's paws over the post in a scratching motion. You can also regularly place a treat at the top of the post. Be sure to praise your cat lavishly each time you see her clawing away. It won't happen instantly, but with a little time and patience your cat will seek out her post whenever the urge to scratch becomes her dominant desire.

How to Encourage No Scratching

Posting signs won't help a bit to discourage your cat from scratching. You need to make the off-limit objects that your cat might scratch as unappealing to her as possible. Call it a situation of negative reward, if you will. Here are some suggestions:

➤ Take a sheet of contact paper (sticky side up) or a strip of two-sided tape and run either one along the area where you don't want your cat to scratch. Tack down the ends to keep it in place. When Puss stretches up to scratch, she won't stay long and most likely will not come back because cats don't like sticky feet.

➤ Place crunched-up aluminum foil over a surface where you don't want the cat to scratch. Foil makes a crinkly tinny sound that cats do not like.

➤ Take a can or plastic container and fill it with coins or pebbles. Tie or tape a piece of string to the can and attach the string to a favorite scratching area. When the cat scratches, the can will fall near her, and the noise will startle her. She'll be less and less likely to return after each time she encounters the "magic" noisemaker.

➤ Spray your cat with a water spritzer if you catch her in the act of scratching something that you want to be off-limits. Cats do not like to be sprayed.

➤ Spray a citrus- or menthol-based spray (sold in pet stores) on off-limit items as a preventive measure to discourage cats from coming near. Cats find the odor offensive and the spray is guaranteed not to harm the furniture. Eucalyptus oil is also a turnoff for cats.

Playtime!

Like humans, cats love to play. Everyone has seen kittens chasing their tails and young cats chasing each other for no other reason than for fun. Charles Dickens' cat would jump on his desk and bat the pen out of his hand whenever he wanted to play. Many times, the French writer Michel de Montaigne wondered if he was playing with his cat or if perhaps, in reality, the cat was playing with him!

Outdoor cats release the energy that prompts the need to play by hunting or simulating the hunt. Indoors, they invent games and sometimes they let us help. Pouncing, chasing, and batting are of course high on every cat's play list, but before we get much farther let's just stop to say that play should really be defined by your cat. In other words, the activity should suit her age and disposition.

As you know, there are shy cats and outgoing cats, cats who play well with other cats, and cats who prefer human companionship. There are immensely imaginative and inventive cats, and there are cats who prefer to limit their playtime to batting their paws at a bauble hung on a string.

Most cats enjoy chasing a thrown ball and even a wadded-up sheet of paper. But don't expect Cinderella to bring it back to you. That's a dog thing, after all. Cats will also chase a piece of string dragged along the floor and jump at and attack the circle of light shown on the wall by a flashlight. By moving the circle of light around, you can choreograph your own cat ballet.

Myth, Magic and Medicine

A cat bitten once by a snake dreads even rope.

—Arab proverb

Someone Said

"Do you see that kitten chasing so prettily her own tail? If you could look with her eyes, you might see her surrounded with hundreds of figures performing complex dramas, with tragic and comic issues, long conversations, many characters, many ups and downs of fate."

—Ralph Waldo Emerson (1803–1882) American essayist

Cats enjoy hiding in paper bags or cluttered corners, and then jumping out at whatever passes by. One of my own cats (Emily Dickinson Kat) used to hide under the open stairway between the patio and the deck. When our two mini dachshunds ran down the stairs, she would jump out and "attack" them. She scared them every time and she loved it.

There is really no need to buy cat toys. Look about your house. Think what you might do with a feather, a cork, an old wooden spool from thread, or even a pine cone. If you're good at sewing, you can make little fabric squares and fill them with catnip, which will prompt action like that of a human having had a few drinks and then dancing atop a bar.

Myth, Magic and Medicine

Be very careful about offering your pets balls of string, yarn, or ribbon, or even nylon stockings. Cats love to play with them, tear them, and string them out all over the house. The tearing, stripping, stringing, and strange deposits may not bother you a bit, but be aware that many a cat owner has made a fast trip to the nearest veterinary clinic after the cat has swallowed a mouthful or two (or three) of those playthings. Tangled string can cause serious intestinal damage. And one of the worst offenders is Christmas tree tinsel.

It's Loving Time

Despite their associations with witches, the devil, superstition, and evil since medieval times, cats came into their own as loving and social house pets in the western world by the middle of the nineteenth century. Probably the most important marking date of this change of attitude was the first international cat show held at the Crystal Palace in London on the 13th of July 1871. Today in the twenty-first century, both purebred cats and moggies alike are loved around the world.

Someone Said

"It is difficult to obtain the friendship of a cat. It is a philosophic animal, one that does not place its affections thoughtlessly."

—Théophile Gautier (1811–1872) French writer

Your cat shows her love for you by wanting to be close to you. You can show your love for your cat by petting, massaging, and talking to her. Cats love the sound of their people's voices and the touch of their hands. A cat's love is unqualified, nonjudgmental, and everlasting. Love is the very essence of a cat's day, every day.

PART THREE

Your Cat and Your Home

CHAPTER 8

How to Choose a Cat

In This Chapter

➤ What kind of cat person are you?

➤ Choosing a cat

➤ Where to get a cat

➤ Visible signs of a healthy cat

Why do you want a cat? That may sound like a silly question to a person who is reading this book, but if you are about to get your first cat, it's a very important question. Cats have personalities just as dogs and, of course, people have personalities. But equally important, different people have different lifestyles and different reasons for wanting a pet. This chapter will help you choose a cat who will best fit your needs and wishes.

If you are replacing a cat you have lost or adding to your cat family, you should ask yourself why you want another cat. Of course, you can't really replace a cat whom you have loved and lost, but you can replenish your sense of companionship and unconditional love of a cat or cats in your life. Ask yourself what you are seeking at this pointing your life, and then consider the points made in this chapter as a reminder check list. Let's start with a quiz on cat ownership qualifications.

Someone Said

"One of the oldest human needs is having someone to wonder where you are when you don't come home at night."

—Margaret Mead (1901–1978) American anthropologist

Some Questions to Ask Yourself

I can hear you wondering about the idea of qualifying for cat ownership. You're probably thinking anyone can have a cat.

That's true. But if potential owners were a little more aware of their own needs and wishes regarding their pets, there would be fewer cats dropped off in shelters, fewer feral cats, and fewer starved kittens. There would also be happier cat owners and cats. The answer to the following questions will help you choose a cat who will be just right for you and your family.

> ➤ Is companionship a factor? Coming home to an empty house is no fun. If you wish for the warmth of a companion, a furry face can welcome you and be there when you need someone to hug or complain to or take care of.

Someone Said

"There are two means of refuge from the miseries of life: music and cats."

—Albert Schweitzer (1875-1965) German Nobel Peace Prize winner

> ➤ Do you want to teach your children to care responsibly for a pet? Children can learn how to be responsible by caring for a cat. Cat chores can include feeding, keeping the water bowl filled, grooming, sweeping up shed hair, and litter box duty. Be sure to assign age-appropriate duties to your children and always supervise young children when they're with your cat.

Perhaps the real value of keeping cats and children can't be taught but can only be learned: the love that can develop between the two.

> ➤ Are mice a factor in your life? Every autumn, field mice try to find their way into the shelter of garages, cellars, and attics. A cat living in the house will discourage mice from invading your home.

Or perhaps you own a business and you want to keep the customers from coming upon bags or boxes with chewed corners. If this is your reason for getting a cat, remember that cats have social needs that are as real and demanding as their instinct to hunt. Be sure that you can take some time to give a working cat the love and attention he needs.

Cats have been working to keep mice out of kitchens since the kitchen was invented.

> ➤ How long can you keep the cat? The life expectancy of an indoor cat in America is now fifteen to twenty years. Will you be able to care for your cat for that long? If you think not, are you willing to make provisions for your cat's future care?

Also consider the projected stability of your life. Are you leaving for college in a couple of years, hoping for a foreign assignment at work, or perhaps even thinking that divorce might be a possibility? Major changes are stressful to cats because they dislike change and because they feel your emotions too. If your life is about to be turned upside down, or perhaps 180 degrees, you might want to delay getting a pet until things settle down a bit.

➤ How much of each day will your cat be alone? Despite their reputation as solitary hunters, cats need company. If your cat will be the sole pet in your apartment, think of his day in relation to yours. If your work day keeps you away from home for most of the day or if you travel frequently for your job, a cat can get pretty lonely. Even if you hire a cat and even if your cat-sitter follows the visiting schedule you set up, your cat will feel deserted.

➤ One solution to being away from home a lot is to get two cats. Two cats will keep each other company, and they are really not much more work than one, but an additional cat is a bit more expensive. On they other hand, you get double love, and often double laughter.

➤ Can you afford the cost of cat ownership? The cost of food is a running tab, of course, but there is also cat litter, some toys, regular veterinarian checkups, and the always-present possibility of a major veterinary bill in the event of a serious illness or accident. As keeping pets goes, cats are relatively inexpensive and medical insurance is available, but money and affordability should be a consideration when determining if a cat is right for you.

➤ Do you just want more? Perhaps the loss of a cat is not the reason you are looking for cat number 3 or even number 4. Perhaps you just want another cat. Well, why not? There's no quota of cats, but there are a few practical considerations such as whether or not your landlord or homeowners' association has set limits, and whether or not you have the time and financial resources needed to provide adequate care and space.

Oh, and one other thing. Will your present pet(s), the ones you already love, accept the newcomer? You can read more about introducing a new cat into your household in chapter 11.

Fame and Fortune

Vanna White, the world-famous letter turner on *Wheel of Fortune* since 1982, is an ailurophile as well as a health advocate, crocheting expert, and ongoing contributor to St. Jude's Children's Hospital. She has owned two cats, Rhett Butler and Ashley, who have been mentioned often on the show.

Choosing a Cat Who's Right for You

Your first concern when choosing a cat is personality. You want a match. Not necessarily the same kind of personality that you have (opposites do attract, you know), but a personality that will be a complement to your lifestyle and your heart; a personality that will fit in with the other members of your household. Some major considerations are age, gender, and pedigree.

Myth, Magic and Medicine

"A cat has nine lives, Ben," Barney retorted. "You're a very cool cat, so that leaves you with eight more."

— from *Doctors* by Erich Segal (1937–2010)

The myth that a cat has nine lives was first recorded in print in 1546.

Kitten or Adult

Who can resist the antics of a kitten, a tiny ball of fluff whose face seems to be all about his wide, bright eyes? Not many people! If you opt for a kitten, you will be assured of moments that will make you laugh out loud as Fluffy explores the house and everything in it. Two kittens together are as good as a circus or an old-time vaudeville comedy show.

But very, very quickly kittens grow into adult cats. Cute kittenhood lasts for nine or ten months at the most. During that time period, your little cats are rather fragile and subject to illness or injury. And for some people, kitten antics are just a bit too much. You should also remember that when you get a kitten, you're making a long-term relationship commitment.

So for some people, adopting a grown-up cat works out better. Grown-up cats can be as youthful as one or two years old.

CATch Words

Cool cat is American slang that has spread around the world. Since the 1950s, a cool cat has been an extraordinarily hip, or hep, person, usually a man. In the 1920s, a cool cat was someone who kept up with all the latest fads and trends. Today, *cool cat* can mean someone who is unworried, calm, and relaxed, and it can also refer to a person who is slick, up-to-date, and popular.

The advantages of getting an older cat can be summarized by four points:

➤ You can evaluate the cat's temperament now by observing how he interacts with you and with others. Kittens can be observed also, but temperament can change during the maturing process.

➤ The mature cat has passed through the illnesses and fragility of kittenhood.

➤ You won't have to live through the hyperactivity of a kitten on the go.

➤ The cat may already be spayed or neutered.

If you're thinking that you are going to miss out on a lot of fun and laughter by getting an older cat, don't worry. Cats of all ages from young adults to the elderly will still make you laugh and smile and celebrate the joy of living with their own special quirks and sometimes outrageous, sometimes insightful behavior.

The older cat might already have some health problems and almost surely others will come up sooner than if you had a kitten or very young cat. Some mature cats may have been neglected or mistreated in past years, and they may need extra time to settle into a new home. However, many more oldsters have been given up because of an owner's developing health problems or allergies, or because of an impending move or similar circumstances that are not in any way related to the cat's behavior.

Which is better, kitten or cat? There are felines of every age who need loving homes. The decision is yours to make.

Male or Female

Altered males and females (those who have been spayed or neutered) both make good house pets. Many people say you cannot tell the difference in temperament between the two. Some say that neutered males are actually more affectionate than those who are intact.

CATch Words

Spaying is the surgical procedure that removes the reproductive organs of female cats and dogs.

Castration is the surgical procedure that removes both testicles of male cats and dogs.

Neutering can refer to either procedure.

Both male and female cats who are not sexually altered can cause problems as house pets. The males tend to be more aggressive and more territorial with other pets in the house. They often mark furniture and draperies leaving a rather unpleasant odor that is difficult both to tolerate and to remove.

Unaltered female cats struggle to get outdoors during each estrus in order to find a mate. They may also spray in the house while in heat, and they usually walk about "calling" to let the world know of their condition. The indoor calling and the scent of estrus may attract outdoor males. Even if you are successful in keeping your hot little girl indoors, your house could be the center of a cat concert that may not be appreciated by your neighbors.

Purebred or Moggy

As it is with choosing a dog breed, choosing a purebred cat gives you a more accurate prognosis of temperament, size, and coat. You'll know what both the mother and father cats look like. And you'll know the personality profile of the breed. This information can cost you a good deal of money, however. Purebred cats are anything but cheap, although occasionally one does turn up at a shelter. The entire next chapter is devoted to profiling the most common purebred cats in the developed world.

Temperament in a mixed-breed kitten can also be somewhat evaluated by observing the kitten among his littermates and by getting to know the mother, but the father is usually an unknown entity. Among cats, however, temperament is still very much an individual matter. As with people, qualities of temperament depend upon a kitten's early experiences as much as it does upon his genetic makeup.

Where to Get a Cat

If you have your heart set on a Ragdoll who will be laid back and easy or on a Siamese who will carry on philosophical debates with you or on any other particular purebred characteristic, a cattery is your shopping place. But you won't be going to the mall! The best catteries, like the best kennels, are run by people who keep their cats or dogs in their homes.

CATch Words

A cattery is a house where purebred cats are raised to be sold. They are usually categorized and priced by their intended role: pet, show cat, or breeder. The cats' owners usually live at the cattery. Many cattery owners advertise that their cats are raised underfoot or are hand raised to separate them from the kitten mills that do still exist, just as puppy mills still exist.

A cathouse is American slang for a brothel.

Most Americans, though, prefer just "regular" cats with no particular breed identification. Research done by the Humane Society of the United States shows that less than 20 percent of cat owners get their pets from private breeders.

By far the most common means of getting a new cat or kitten (or two) is from a friend or relative. Strays on the doorstep and animal shelters are the source of about 30 percent of new cat arrivals in American homes. (Chapter 10 covers the special concerns of adopting strays.) Pet stores and newspaper or Internet advertisements are the least common sources.

Your Local Animal Shelter

Even smaller American towns usually have an animal shelter, and bigger cities usually have several that are operated by a variety of sponsoring organizations. Most do a fine job of trying to find homes for animals who have been lost or discarded. But almost all experience a constant financial crunch.

So should you be worried about the cat you might get at a shelter? Not usually because most shelters take back a pet who is not working out, for whatever reason and a good working shelter screens out animals who have serious behavior problems or incurable illnesses.

The rules and regulations for adoption vary from one place to another. Expect some screening questions upon application. The most common questions concern:

➤ Your current housing (house, condo, apartment)

➤ Children in your home (number and ages)

➤ Other pets in your home (type, number, ages)

➤ Your veterinarian (name and contact information)

➤ Your activity level (time away from home, travel expectations, why you want a pet)

➤ Your previous experience with pets

Please don't feel as though your personal space is being invaded by these inquiries. The shelter employees or volunteers are asking the questions to help match pets and prospective owners successfully. They want to avoid returns and, even more important, prevent situations where cats are turned out onto the streets again.

Fame and Fortune

Morris the cat is known internationally as "the world's most finicky cat" (a very fine advertising line for 9 Lives cat food for which he is the brand logo). Since he first appeared on television in 1970, there have been many cats who played Morris. The first Morris was discovered in 1968 at the Hinsdale Humane Society Animal Shelter near Chicago by a professional animal handler named Bob Martwick. All the cats who have played Morris have been rescues.

Besides his film debut in *The Long Goodbye* with Elliott Gould, Morris starred in *Shamus* with Burt Reynolds and Dyan Cannon in 1973. He has "authored" three books: *The Morris Approach*, *The Morris Method*, and *The Morris Prescription*.

You can usually expect to give a donation when you adopt a cat from a shelter. The amount often varies according to your means, but some shelters require a fee for neutering. (The amount is always considerably less than you would pay at a private veterinary hospital.) There may also be a charge for various vaccinations. Call ahead and ask for information on adoption.

There is usually an animal history card either attached to the cage or available in the office or online. It usually includes information on how and why the animal got to the shelter, his medical history, and behavioral assessments. Don't hesitate to ask questions! Remember you are about to acquire a new member of your household.

Did You Notice the Cat?

Some prospective cat owners avoid going to shelters to look at cats for possible adoption. Why if they really want a cat do these people avoid going to places where cats are available?

Motivating factors are hard to categorize, but I would bet there's some fear of embarrassment and more than a little self-doubt involved. *What if I don't like any of the cats that are available? How do I gracefully tell the staff "not this time"?*

On the other hand, some people are afraid to trust their own judgment. *What if I can't choose one? Will I take home more cats than I should? Will I choose the right cat?*

And what does one say to the attendant who asks, "Did you notice the calico in the last cage?"

My advice is don't be afraid to talk with the staff at a shelter. Ask that attendant why he or she mentioned that particular cat? Talk about what you are looking for in a pet and ask for recommendations.

Answering Advertisements

Answering an ad may not be a bad way to go. Cats born in a home usually begin their lives well adjusted to people and will be comfortable around people all their lives.

If you visit a litter and like what you see (who couldn't like a kitten?), take particular notice of the cat mother and her temperament. She represents 50 percent of each kitten's genetic makeup. Ask the owners if they know who the father is and if he's an outdoor house cat or a feral cat. Remember, however, that there may be more than one father for a litter.

Ask if the kittens have been seen by a veterinarian and if they have received any vaccinations. Then watch the kittens play for a while. Does one seem to be the leader? Does one seem shy? Is one a clown? Or perhaps there's a snuggle lover. Think beyond the adorable appearance and let your personal needs and preferences determine your decision.

It is wise not to take a kitten younger than eight weeks from his mother. She is a teacher as well as a provider of nourishment, and there are some things one can only learn from one's mother. And ideally the kittens should be litter box trained before you take yours home.

Someone Said

"The really great thing about cats is their endless variety. One can pick a cat to fit almost any kind of décor, income, personality, mood. But under the fur, there still lies, essentially unchanged, one of the world's free souls."

—Eric Gurney (1910-1992) Canadian-American cartoonist and illustrator

Pet Stores: Thumbs Down!

The Humane Society of the United States takes a strong stand against buying a kitten from a pet store:

"Don't buy kittens from pet stores. Pet stores are notorious for selling unhealthy or poorly bred purebreds, and even irresponsibly bred non-purebreds. Kittens sold in pet stores are outrageously expensive, often two to four times more expensive than the same type of kitten bought from a private breeder. They are often obtained from "kitten mills," where animals are poorly treated and bred (and bred and bred) for profit. By buying from the store, you are supporting these mills and adding to the pet overpopulation problem."

There is, however, an exception to this general rule. The national franchise PetSmart works with local shelters to help place cats and kittens. It may not be the very best way to bring available cats to the attention of the pet-loving public, but it does work. With the adopted cat, new owners are given health certificates for the pet and all the available information on his background.

Signs of Good Health

Whether your choice is a kitten or an adult cat, you want to choose a healthy pet. When you take in a mature cat, there may already be some health problems, but you should know about them and know how to manage them.

The signs of good cat health are in many ways similar to the signs of good human health. Eyes should be bright with no watery discharge. The nose should be cold and moist, the tongue and mouth vibrant shades of pink. Teeth should not be yellowed or chipped. The coat should have a sheen and it should be even all over the body, with no bare spots. It is better for the cat not to be overweight. The cat should move about easily and be interested in what is happening in the world around him.

Very young cats should be playful. Kittens start playlike behavior as early as two weeks after birth and it's ever-upward from there. Kittens pounce, bite, chase, and bat at things with their paws. Sometimes you may see them walking sideways with their backs arched like a Halloween cat. They also cuddle up with their littermates and even wash each other.

Even when everything you can see about a cat wins your heart, however, don't leave the final decision to your untrained eyes. Take your new pet to a veterinarian for an initial checkup as soon as possible. Most responsible cat breeders will agree to take the cat back if the examination comes up with unsolvable problems. Part Four, Feline Health Care, discusses what you and your vet can and cannot do for your cat.

Myth, Magic and Medicine

If you choose a cat whose markings include a cross on his back, you may be interested in an ancient Italian legend. It is said that a cat gave birth to her kittens in the stable at exactly the same time that Jesus was born. The descendents of those kittens all have a cross on their backs.

Some art historians speculate that the legend perhaps (at least partially) explains why so many paintings and sculptures of the Annunciation and of the Madonna and Child include a cat. Other critics say that the cat represents the devil who is always lurking.

The Madonna of the Cat was painted by Giulio Romano (ca 1499-1546), an Italian student of Raphael. The painting can be seen in the Museo di Capodimonte, Naples, Italy.

In this painting, the only living thing looking directly at the viewer is the cat. The intensity of the cat's gaze conveys a sense of vigilance that contrasts with the playfulness of the Holy family.

CHAPTER 9

Purebred Cats

> ## In This Chapter
>
> ➤ How selective breeding got started
> ➤ Standards of quality
> ➤ About longhairs
> ➤ About shorthairs

If you want a purebred dog, you can choose between a Pomeranian who will weigh 3 pounds when full grown and a mastiff who may well exceed 180 pounds when full grown. And just about everything in between. Not so with cats.

> **Someone Said**
>
> "The cat is a character of being, the dog, a character of doing."
>
> —Michael J. Rosen (1954 —) American author and editor

Cat breeders have not succeeded in changing the cat very much. Some experts say that is because selective cat breeding started much later than dog breeding, as did the growth of cat organizations and cat shows. I don't think so. The domestic cat hasn't changed much in 8,000 years and it probably won't for the next 8,000. In this chapter, however, we'll take a look at the special appearance, characteristics, and personality traits that have been established within the purebred cat breed list. But first we'll take a look at how people have depicted cats throughout the years.

Attitudes through History

Although the cat breed hasn't changed much throughout history, attitudes toward cats have varied considerably. Cats have appeared in the arts of many of the world's oldest civilizations, sometimes as gods and sometimes as demons, and sometimes as household pets. Even in the most culturally influenced and the most stylized visions, however, we can still recognize the essence of the cat we know now.

In Persian mythology, Akwan was a demon who tried to kill Rostam, a culturally esteemed hero, by throwing him into the sea while he slept. Even in this demonized form, the cat features are there for all to see (figure 1). The essence of the cat is even more obvious in this *Demon Playing an Instrument* from a Persian drawing dating about 1500 CE (figure 2).

Figure 1

Figure 2

Figure 3

Figure 4
Even pre-Columbian folk art from the Andean Mountains has left us a stylized embroidery design that is unmistakably a cat!

On the other hand, about 950 BCE, Bastet (or Bast) was a beautiful Egyptian cat goddess who loved music and dance. She was the protector of pregnant women and also protected men against evil spirits. She was generally considered the personification of the beneficial fertilizing power of the sun.

By the thirteenth and fourteenth centuries in Europe, cats roamed both streets and palaces and were the models for many appearances in art. Here's a cat (you can tell by the way the animal is sitting) with a sheeplike head and a unicorn horn from a thirteenth century French illuminated manuscript (figure 3).

A Brief History of Selective Cat Breeding

In more recent history than we've just explored, specifically in the mid-nineteenth century, scientific work by Austrian monk Gregor Johann Mendel (1822–1884) on the importance of genes in determining all living beings coincided with the beginning of selective cat breeding and, in fact, the very first cat show. It was held in London in 1871 and organized by Harrison Weir, an English gentleman and artist who wrote the standards for each breed to be exhibited. He is generally known as the father of cat fancy.

In North America, the first major cat show took place in Madison Square Garden in New York City in 1895. It was organized by James T. Hyde, and the winner was a Maine Coon, the first breed to be developed in the United States.

Soon afterward, associations began to form around the world to register purebreds, create rules for shows, and set standards for the cats in competition. In 1887, the National Cat Club was started in Britain; in 1896 the American Cat Club became the first North American cat registry. In 1906 the Cat Fanciers' Association (CFA) was founded. It has become international and is now the world's largest registry. It is purist and strict.

The second largest registry is The International Cat Association (TICA). Founded in 1979, it is more liberal and accepts new breeds more rapidly than any other association.

Each registry sets its own standards for judging and its own rules for membership. Cat shows are usually organized and supervised by these individual cat associations. Some breeds that are recognized by one association may not be recognized by another.

What Makes a Fine Show Specimen?

So if breed standards vary from one group to another, how can anyone know if they have a really top-notch cat? For many cat people, a top-notch cat is the one you love, but there are some general aesthetic guidelines that are more or less universal. Let's take a quick look. American and British standards focus on five elements of the cat: head, eyes, body, coat, and color.

➤ Head: The standards for each breed cover the size and shape of the head. Also taken into account are the ears and how they are set, the nose, and the cheeks.

Photo credit: Clark Lambert

The wedge-shaped face is most common among cats, but each breed differs slightly, and each individual differs too.

Myth, Magic and Medicine

Whether we like it or not, height, weight, and bone density are determined genetically in cats and humans (and most other animals). In other words, you and your cat are probably going to have a body type resembling at least one of your respective parents. But because of the power of recessive genes, there's always the outside possibility that you or your cat might take after some distant relative with a different body type.

Predictions regarding probable body weight, size, and share are much more accurate for purebred cats than for humans or cats without a pedigree, because there are far fewer unknown recessive genes in the pool.

➤ Eyes: The size, shape, color, and spacing of the eyes all contribute to the judges' scoring.

➤ Body: Consideration is given to the general build of the cat (the American judges include the tail length and at what angle to the body it is carried; the British do not). The length, straightness, and sturdiness of the legs, the depth of the chest, and the straightness of the back are all factors in this evaluation. And, finally, the paws are judged for their shape and structure.

➤ Coat: The length of the coat as it applies to the breed standard is important. The judge evaluates its denseness and condition and will take notice of any tufts on the ears or toes. British judges include coat color.

> ➤ Color: Only American judges consider color as a standard separate from the coat. In the United States, color is specified in the standards for the breed. Color is also considered for lips, chin, nose, and paw pads.

Body Types

Although they are all part of the breed standards, outside the show ring, body type, color, and length of coat are the most distinguishing features from one cat to another. Cats, like people, can come in sturdy and stocky or lithe and limber types. Let's look at the terms most cat fanciers use to discuss their cats' body types.

> ➤ Cobby: Sturdy cats who have a compact body, a deep chest, and a broad head. We would call a human with this body type stocky.

> ➤ Semi-cobby: Somewhat longer but not quite so sturdy as the cobby cat. The American shorthair is a good example. We'd say a human with this body type is of average or medium build.

> ➤ Muscular: Usually quite long but with good sturdy bones. In terms of humans, this is an athletic build.

> ➤ Foreign: Long, elegant cats like the Abyssinian are an example of this body type. Their bodies are slender and their tails are long. We might call a woman with this type of body svelte; a man would be called wiry.

> ➤ Oriental: Very long and elegant like the Siamese. *Sinuous* might be a good descriptive word for a human of this type.

> ➤ Substantial: Big cats like the Maine Coon have a substantial body type. A human of this body type might be called big and tall or perhaps plus size.

Color

Artists think of color as the three primaries, red, yellow, and blue, plus black and white and all the other colors that can be made by mixing. In the world of cats, color also means coat pattern. You'll see many of the same colors and patterns in purebreds as in moggies. Let's look at some common terminology.

The Tiger Trait: Tabby

Striped and spotted is one of the most common coat patterns in both purebred and un-pedigreed cats. These markings have been inherited through thousands of years from the cat's wild ancestors. Today we know the how and why of this pattern development. Research has pinned down the agouti gene.

CATch Words

Agouti is a color of fur that is caused by each hair having alternating light and dark bands. The agouti gene is responsible for determining whether a mammal coat is a banded, agouti, color or a solid, non-agouti, color.

CATch Words

Pointed, when referring to a cat's appearance, means a change of color on the nose, ears, tail, lower legs, and paws. Most Siamese cats are pointed.

Photo credit: Linda Reimer

We see cats who have the agouti gene as either striped or spotted because each of their hairs is banded with alternating light and dark color. The form of the banding and the amount and intensity of pigment (think of a sliding scale between the palest yellow and black) determine the pattern we perceive. In simple terms, the banding pattern determines whether your cat resembles a tiger or a leopard.

Shades and Smokes

Many cats look as though they are a solid color until some movement allows our eyes to catch waves of white coat close to the skin. The individual hairs in the coats of such cats are not banded in patterns like the tabby, but change color only once at some point along the shaft.

When only the outer 25 percent or so of each hair is colored (leaving most of the hair shaft close to the skin white), the cat's coat is called a shade. When 50 to 80 percent of the shaft is colored (leaving from 20 to 50 percent of the shaft close to the skin white) the cat's coat is called a smoke.

Shade and smoke coats come in most colors, even black. They do not, however, come in red or cream, which always have an underlying tabby pattern to some degree.

The One-Color Cat

The solid-color cat is the result of a mutation that people manipulated through breeding. Cats of one color do not have the agouti gene. Some solid-color cats, the Siamese for example, are pointed.

Cats who are pure white carry a dominant color-blocking gene that keeps pigment out of the skin and hair. This gene can also cause eyes to be blue, green, or copper, and sometimes even odd colored (each eye a different color). In blue-eyed and less often in copper-eyed cats, the gene can cause deafness in either one or both ears.

White Patches

Another gene, commonly called the white-spotting gene, results in coats of various colors that are marked with various degrees of white. The colored furs may be marked with tabby patterns or they can be shades, smokes, or solids. The white areas are pigment-free.

Do you know a cat named Boots or Mittens? Then you've seen the white-spotting gene at work in a special manifestation that scientists call mitted. Less then 25 percent of a mitted cat's fur is white, and it's most often the feet. A cat somewhere between one-third and two-thirds white is called a bicolor, and a cat more than two-thirds white is called a harlequin or van.

Tortoiseshell and Calico

What's the difference between tortoiseshell and calico? The generally accepted

Fame and Fortune

Chelsea Clinton brought a mitted manifestation of the cat white-spotted gene with her to the White House in 1993. The black-and-white Arkansas un-pedigreed tomcat was named Socks.

Myth, Magic and Medicine

Calico cats are considered lucky in many parts of the world, including in the United States and Canada. In England and Ireland, they are called money cats.

Calico Cat Photo credit: Merle Allshouse

differentiation is that the tortoiseshell is a black cat with red and/or orange markings and some white, whereas the calico is a white cat with patches of red, orange, and black. More important, however, is the way the colors are mixed. The tortoiseshell has a mottled coat coloring (colors run together); the calico has distinct patches.

Most tortoiseshell and calico cats are female. When the rare male with these colorings is found, he is usually sterile.

Selected Long-Haired Cat Breeds

Sometimes long-haired breeds are looked upon as the pampered aristocrats of the feline world because they require careful grooming by their owners. Most owners, however, will tell you that the time is both well spent and relaxing. They say their cats are worth every single minute!

The Persian

Some say that the Persian is the earliest of the long-haired cats and the ancestor to them all. Persian cats first appeared in Europe early in the sixteenth century. Today there are more than sixty varieties and color variations in cat registries around the world. The Himalayan variety looks like a long-haired Siamese. The red peke-face is bred to look very much like a Pekingese dog.

The Persian is a cobby cat with a flowing and very full coat. It has a large head with small ears and large round eyes. Its placid but fun-loving nature make it a popular choice for apartment living. But busy owners should remember that each Persian in the house will need about fifteen minutes of grooming each day.

The Angora

The Angora originated in Turkey before the sixteenth century when it began to spread through Europe. It is sometimes called a semi-long-haired because its coat is silky and much shorter than the Persian's. The fur has a tendency to wave and is easier to groom than the Persian's dense fur.

Unlike the Persian (with which it was indiscriminately interbred in the nineteenth and early twentieth centuries), the Angora has a body that is slim and athletic. Its gentle and friendly personality and intelligence contribute to its desirability as a pet. In the UK, Angoras were interbred with Siamese to create a more "talkative" breed, and the standards for the breed are different in the United States.

The Maine Coon

The Maine Coon was the first cat breed to be originated in the United States. It is believed that Angoras brought to New England by British sailors during the nineteenth century were bred with semi-wild Maine forest cats until a very distinct breed evolved.

Fame and Fortune

Britain's Queen Victoria may have been a little straightlaced ("We are not amused.") but she loved horses and small animals. Prince Albert brought home many cats. Her Majesty's favorite was a black-and-white longhair named White Heather. Some reports say the cat was a Persian, some say an Angora. It is most likely that the cat was a mix of the two since the crossbreed was extremely popular in late nineteenth century Britain. The Queen willed that the cat be kept and royally cared for in the palace after her death, and her son, King Edward VII complied.

The Maine Coon is one of the largest cat breeds, but it is a gentle giant and a good family cat. With long legs and large paws that are used almost like hands, the Maine Coon is an excellent hunter. Some say it looks a little like a raccoon, but there is no relationship at all, except perhaps that both animals are excellent survivors.

The Norwegian Forest Cat

The Norwegian forest cat is similar to the Maine coon in size, appearance, and temperament, but it is a separate breed of European origin. It has a top coat of long, shiny, water-shedding hair, and a wooly undercoat that acts as an insulator.

Norwegian forest cats have long legs, bushy tails, and very sturdy bodies. Outdoors, they are very good at climbing because they have particularly strong claws. Indoors, they are friendly but also quite independent.

The Norwegian forest cats is probably descended from long-haired Persians and Turkish Angoras mixed over the years with short-haired cats brought home by Viking sailors.

The Ragdoll

The Ragdoll is an all-American breed developed from the culture of 1960s California. Probably the most laid-back of all cat breeds, Ragdolls can and will relax completely, whenever, wherever. They will actually go limp when picked up, which is probably a factor in their breed naming.

Ragdolls are nonaggressive and uncomplaining. They also have a high tolerance for pain, so much so that you may not know when they are hurting. Because they usually refuse to fight for any reason, they do better as indoor cats, where they have some protection from other cats and wild predators.

Many experts believe there is some white Persian and some Siamese in the Ragdoll background. It is just about the same size as the Maine coon, with blue eyes and semi-long fur.

The Turkish Van

The Turkish Van loves to swim and will seek out water whenever it can. In fact, it is sometimes called the Turkish swimming cat. And quite naturally, it originated in the beautiful Lake Van area of Turkey.

The breed is a semi-long-haired, medium-heavy build, and athletic. The body fur should be creamy white, with red or auburn, or sometimes black and white, patches of color on the head and tail.

Vans are socially well adjusted, bold, and very affectionate. Besides swimming, they have another unusual trait: in summer the Van loses much of its long fur and becomes a short-haired cat. This is an adaptation to the climate in Turkey.

Selected Short-Haired Cat Breeds

Short-haired cats far outnumber their long-haired cousins. Virtually all cats born in the wild

Myth, Magic and Medicine

There is a legend in Turkey that explains the distinctive thumb-sized spots of color on every Turkish Van's forehead. The story goes that Allah was so impressed with the cat's beauty that he bent down to kiss it. He held the cat in his hands as he bestowed the kiss of blessing, leaving the sacred impressions as marks for all the world to see.

are short-haired because the gene for short hair is dominant. There are, however, a great many varieties of short-haired cats among purebreds, not to mention the many kinds of moggies.

The American Shorthair

The purebred American shorthair can be traced across the Atlantic to a British red tabby named Belle who was sent by an English breeder to get the Americans started with a fine

purebred line. Belle was the first cat in the twentieth century to be registered with the newly established Cat Fanciers' Association. The breed was first called the domestic shorthair, but the name was soon changed to American shorthair. Canadians still call these cats domestic shorthair.

So where did Belle find appropriate mates? Other British citizens sent specimens, and we know that there were cats on the *Mayflower*, and even on the *Niña*, *Pinta*, and *Santa Maria*. So the American shorthair evolved, and by 1966 a set of standards accompanied the breed name.

How are American shorthairs different from British shorthairs today? First of all, the Brits have a lot more subcategories determined by coat and color. The American version is also more muscular and athletic. It has a well-developed chest and strong shoulders and legs. One can almost see the heritage from the American working farm cat, who had to survive some pretty tough weather using its own resources.

American shorthairs make a good showing in the ring, but at heart they are companion cats. They are tolerant and good with children. And they can be almost any color or pattern that you can think of.

The Scottish Fold

True to its name, the Scottish Fold originated in Scotland. Some say the breed was first seen in London in the 1880s (a few probably jumped ship). But its first real recognition as a distinctive breed came in 1961 in Perthshire, Scotland. The kittens with this unusual mutation were born on a farm.

As you might expect, the breed name came from the folded ears, which make these cats look a bit like they're wearing a hat! Scottish Folds have a dense coat, a short tail, large green eyes, and a broad, almost round face. They are generally friendly, loving, and intelligent, but they usually pick only one person to love loyally and forever.

The Chartreux

The Chartreux is a popular French domestic cat. Legend has it that the breed is descended from cats brought to France by Carthusian monks. Another legend says that the breed is

descended from feral mountain cats from what is now Syria. Supposedly these gray-ghost beauties were brought back to France by the Crusaders in the thirteenth century.

To all the families who love this breed, it doesn't matter one bit where it came from. Unlike Siamese, Chartreux are quiet cats, rarely uttering even small meows. In fact, some are mute. But they are extremely observant and intelligent and good with children and other animals. They tend to pick a favorite in the family and will even move from room to room with that person.

The Egyptian Mau

Mau is the Egyptian word for "cat." The origin of this breed is not clear, however, although we suspect there may be some kinship with cousins of the cat goddess Bastet. Some historians claim that the breed bears a remarkable resemblance to the cats depicted on ancient wall paintings and scrolls.

Fame and Fortune

Just as the French poodle is the dog breed most often associated with France, the Chartreux is the cat-breed pride of the French people. President Charles de Gaulle chose one as his pet, and the famous author Colette kept two with her in Paris, where she resolutely chose to stay throughout the German occupation.

The Egyptian Mau's first official appearance was at a cat show in Milan in 1953. There is considerable controversy over the breed among cat registry organizations, but it is being included in this sampling because of registry recognition in the United States and because it is such a beautiful specimen of a spotted cat.

The breed is small to medium in size and weight, with muscular legs and a streamlined body. The face of the U.S. Egyptian Mau is moderately wedge-shaped with pale green round eyes that give it an expression of intense inquisitiveness, perhaps even worry. Its coat is silky and dense. The Mau is intelligent, loving, playful, and gregarious.

The Siamese

The Siamese is the extrovert of the cat world. It greets everyone, demands its due attention, and expresses its opinion on everything. Some people are bothered by its rather loud voice, others love the ongoing conversation.

Despite being a small, graceful, and slender cat, the Siamese usually dominates other cats in the household. Most Siamese cats love children and do well in family situations,

Someone Said

"Siamese Cats [sic] have a way of staring at you. Those who have walked in on the Queen cleaning her teeth will know the expression."

—Douglas Adams (1952–2001) English writer and dramatist, author of *The Hitchhiker's Guide to the Galaxy*

even though they often consider one particular person as their own true love. They are extremely intelligent, but like other aristocrats can sometimes be moody.

The Siamese has a wedge-shaped head, large pointed ears, and almond-shaped blue eyes. Despite breeder efforts to eliminate a kink in the tail, some Siamese still have this trait.

How the first Siamese got to America is up for debate. Some sources say David Sickels, an American diplomat at the U.S. consulate in Bangkok sent one to Lucy Hayes, wife of President Rutherford B. Hayes. The female cat arrived at the White House in 1879. Other sources say that the breed was made popular when the King of Siam gave two cats to Owen Gould, who was the British consul general in Bangkok. He took them to London and put them in the Crystal Palace show. Soon after, Siamese cats were being bred in the United States, and kittens were bringing in top prices. (One report says $1,000 per and that's in dollars at the beginning of the twentieth century!)

Siamese cats were all the rage in the Roaring Twenties, less so during the Depression and the World War II years, but the fads and fables don't really matter. This oriental breed has not only endured, it has become one of the most popular cats in the whole world.

The Abyssinian

Many people believe that the Abyssinian breed is the ancestor of all others. Although *Abyssinian* refers to Ethiopia, genetic research shows that the cat probably originated near the coast of the Indian Ocean. The breed was developed in Egypt.

The most striking feature of this ancient cat is the ticked (agouti) fur, where each hair has bands of darkening colors along its length. Ruddy (a reddish tone) was the original and still the most popular primary color.

The Abyssinian has a medium-sized body and long legs that combine with excellent musculature to produce the look of a fine athlete. The breed also has abundant energy and needs space to exercise. And, it loves to play in the water!

Abyssinians are intelligent, affectionate, and interact well with their owners. They will learn tricks, and they usually enjoy showing off and being praised. They do not like to be left alone for long periods of time, and they do not like to be crowded.

The Singapura

The Singapura is the smallest of the registered cat breeds. As adults, females may weigh as little as 4 pounds; males are usually closer to 6 pounds. They have oriental, lithe, and musical bodies. Their eyes are hazel, green, or yellow, and they have rather large and moderately pointed ears.

Singapuras are quiet, affectionate, curious, and intelligent pets. And they like to play fetch and join in on human games and activities.

The Japanese Bobtail

Japanese bobtail sounds a bit like a breed that someone made up for the 60s hep culture. But that's just not true. In fact, the bobtail is the result of a genetic mutation created by the expression of a recessive gene. The gene must be present in both parents for them to produce bobtail offspring. And it's been around for a very long time. One theory asserts that the breed arrived in Japan from the Asian continent at least one thousand years ago.

How did the Japanese bobtail become so popular in Japan? In 1602, Japanese authorities declared that cats should be free (not owned and uncontrolled) throughout the country. (Cats, you see, were helpful in controlling the vermin that were destroying the silkworm industry.) So buying or selling cats in Japan became illegal, and cats roamed both the city streets and the farms.

Japanese Bobtail #1   Sm Guidos p. 128

Already in the country when the law was passed, bobtails may have become the dominant cat of Japan because so many of the people believed ominous superstitions about what the tail of a cat might do. And "somehow," long-tailed cats diminished in number.

The Japanese bobtail can be any color in the cat show ring, although van and calico patterns seem to be favored in judging. The bobtail has a short, fine coat and is of small to medium build. It has large round eyes and is friendly and playful. All members of the breed have a similar habit of raising one paw as if in greeting, which has made this cat the symbol of hospitality and good luck in Japan.

Your Moggie

The vast majority of cats in homes around the world have no pedigrees. Some people may be able to recognize traits in their cat's physical makeup or personality that align the pet with one of the established breeds, but nothing can be proven without registration papers.

Someone Said

"You haven't lived until you've lived with a cat."

—Doris Day (1924–) American actress and singer

Myth, Magic and Medicine

In Japan, the beckoning cat, *maneki neko,* is an auspicious symbol. You can find one near the entranceway or somewhere within many Japanese business establishments throughout the world. Either the left paw or the right paw may be raised. The significance of the choice of which paw varies from area to area and even from person to person. Among the most common superstitions is that the left paw raised brings in customers while the right paw raised brings in good luck and wealth. But some people believe exactly the opposite! And some cat figures are being made with both paws raised.

CHAPTER 10

 # Strays and Rescues

> ## In This Chapter
>
> ➤ When a cat chooses you
> ➤ Rescuing abandoned cats or kittens
> ➤ Cat identification tools

They are everywhere: the lost, dumped, and deserted kittens and adult cats looking for food and shelter—for a home. Perhaps one will choose you and turn you into a first-time cat owner. Or perhaps you already have a cat or two at home, and you find yourself inviting one of these "orphans" to join your family. Truly, there's always room for one more.

Even if you think your cat family is at maximum capacity, you might want to read this chapter anyway. Because, if you love cats, you will find it very difficult to leave a starving cat in an alley. You will feel called to the rescue, yes, like Mighty Mouse or the Lone Ranger.

Be aware, however, that there are risks involved in rescue. You will need to know some very important information before you try to pick up, help, or take home a cat who has grown up in the wild. This chapter will help you make informed decisions both with cats who come to you and cats who you rescue.

When a Cat Chooses You

Kittens looking for a home might be found cuddled in a corner of a porch (or under it), in a garage, or in bushes near a home. Some of them may have been born wild but are now hungry and/or ill and feel the need for shelter. Others, even a whole litter, might have been abandoned by irresponsible owners.

Someone Said

Stray Cat

Oh, what unhappy twist of fate
Has brought you homeless to my gate?
The gate where once another stood
To beg for shelter, warmth, and food
For from that day I ceased to be
The master of my destiny.
While he, with purr and velvet paw
Became within my house the law.
He scratched the furniture and shed
And claimed the middle of my bed.
He ruled in arrogance and pride
And broke my heart the day he died.
So if you really think, oh Cat,
I'd willingly relive all that
Because you come forlorn and thin
Well. . .don't just stand there. . .come on in!

—Francis Witham

Did You Notice the Cat?

Czech playwright Karel Capek was grieving for the loss of his poisoned female cat when he opened his front door one day and found a female kitten. He felt the cat had been sent to him in consolation. He took her in and named her Pudlenka. She bore twenty-six kittens in her lifetime.

Most experts agree that a feral kitten between six and ten weeks old will adapt to living with humans and become a good house pet. Once they are a little older, however, kittens have a harder time becoming tame. Even when they are adopted by caring owners, some never completely settle down or interact well with people.

If you find a kitten near your house who is obviously familiar with people and comes to you willingly and without fear, you may want to check available resources to see if he belongs to someone and is just lost. If the kitten seems fearful, however, and needs soft talking and coaching before letting you approach and touch him, you can probably assume that he has not been raised in a home. Don't spend too much effort trying to find an owner.

An adult cat who chooses your house as his own may show up frequently near your doorways, garage, or carport. He may even jump into the house through an open cellar window or run in unnoticed with one of the children, and, voila, you may find her sitting on your kitchen countertop. Most often these friendly cats have been abandoned. One of the many problems in cities with highly mobile, corporate-employed citizens and in resort areas during the off-season are the pets that are left behind when the family moves or returns home. Again, if a cat who is particularly friendly to people chooses you, you should make some inquiries to see if anyone has lost a pet before you give your heart away.

Checking For Previous Owners

To try to find a cat's previous owner, start by checking your newspapers to see if anyone is advertising a lost cat. Call your vet's office if it is located nearby to check for a posting on its bulletin board, and check local supermarket, church, condo community, pet groomer, hairdresser, and boutique bulletin boards.

Call all the local shelter organizations to see if anyone has made inquiries on a cat who sounds like the one you found. Some humane and rescue organizations will even let you post a photo on their website. You can also find national pet-finder services on the Internet. Among the largest is HomeAgain.com, where you can enter information about a lost or found pet.

If you don't immediately find any possible owners, try doing your own advertising. Many weekly or bi-weekly newspapers and newsletters will allow you to run a found pet ad in a few issues free of charge. You can also put the cat's photo on your local Craigslist or other Internet shopping and exchange site. And you can post your own bulletin board notices.

Searching for a cat's previous owners has some potential pitfalls you need to avoid. To prevent scheming persons from claiming a cat and then selling him into medical research or to a kitten mill, take some notes on identifying features of your found cat and don't reveal everything in the ad. When you get phone calls, ask the callers questions such as what name the cat answers to, how many toes he has, if the cat has any unusual marks, and the color of his eyes. Don't be too anxious to give the cat back without some identifying information.

Keep copies of your ads. It happens more frequently with dogs, but some unscrupulous cat owners have actually claimed that their cat was stolen. Returning such a cat may start off a hurricane of paperwork and issues.

Myth, Magic and Medicine

A lot of prophecies surrounding cats have been bandied about throughout the world. Here are a few.

A strange black cat on your porch brings prosperity.

—A Scottish superstition

A cat sneezing is a good omen for everyone who hears it.

—An Italian superstition

A cat that is bought is never good for much.

—A British superstition

Where Should I Put this Cat?

Trying to find a cat's owner takes time. Even if you don't think you'll ever find anyone to claim the cat and have more or less decided to keep him, you'll have to secure him in a safe place before you fully introduce him to the free run of your home and the resident cats, if there are any. At least as an experienced cat person, you will already have all of the equipment and paraphernalia that owning a cat requires.

If this is your first cat, you'll have to go to the store to buy a litter box and cat litter, and feeding and water dishes. To start, paper plates will do for cat food, and margarine or whipped-topping plastic containers will serve well for watering. You should also consider buying an inexpensive cat transporter, because a trip to the vet is imminent.

CATch Words

Cat litter is a manufactured substance used to fill litter boxes for the purpose of indoor capture and disposal of cat feces and urine. Before cat litter was invented and marketed in the 1950s, cat owners used sand and sand mixtures in indoor cat lavatories or more often let their cats go outdoors.

Today, cat litter is a loose, granular sandlike material that absorbs moisture and masks odors such as the ammonia smell in urine. The most common base is clay, although recycled paper pellets and sometimes silicon-based crystal variations are also used. The sandlike texture appeals to a cat's natural instinct to eliminate in material that is easy to dig into.

No matter how well equipped you are, you still have to decide where to keep the newcomer until his fate is determined. First and most important, keep him separate from any other animals in the household. A stray cat may be carrying serious cat diseases such as feline leukemia and feline immunodeficiency virus. He may also have fleas or worms or even ringworm, which is a fungal infection contagious to humans.

The safest bet is to take the cat to the vet for an all clear before bringing him into your house. But life doesn't always follow the safest pattern and many, maybe most, people take in a stray cat before being able to take him to the vet.

So what's a good place for Kitty's first days? Choose a small room with no other animals present and no access to the outdoors. Many rescuers use a bathroom. (It also helps that there isn't much to scratch or chew on there!) Give the cat some old blankets or even rags to sleep on. Put the litter box in a corner and the water and food dishes as far from it as possible. And visit Kitty often.

Rescuing Abandoned Cats and Feral Kittens

There are statistics about homeless cats available everywhere: from national and local government agencies, from animal control authorities, and from humane societies and ailurophile support groups. The numbers vary somewhat depending on who is doing the research, but the bottom line is that there are many, many more cats in the United States, and in the world, than there are available homes. Most groups say that neutering will solve the problem, but to neuter a cat, one must catch the cat. Catching feral cats and even abandoned cats is often a more difficult job than most people expect.

Did You Notice the Cat?

If you live in an area where feral cats are relatively numerous and you have small children, you will need to deal with the sandbox problem. Children love to play in the sand, but cats see a child's sandbox as a luxury lavatory. Be sure to cover the sandbox whenever it is not in use. Cat feces and urine can breed bacteria that are harmful to children. Fleas and worms may also turn up in sand used by cats.

Many people begin their capture strategy by leaving dry food out in the garage. This works because cats come back to the place they know they can find food. The practice is a little risky for the homeowner, however, because the food can also attract raccoons and squirrels.

If you choose to leave dry food out for the neighborhood cats, you can work on persuading them that you are friendly by talking to them and slowly getting closer and closer when they come to feed. Once a cat develops trust, he will come closer and often he will eventually allow petting.

From the gentle strokes stage, it's usually a short time before the cat can be invited in your house—if, that is, he was once, even though it may have been long ago, raised in a house with humans. Feral cats raised in the wild are usually not much interested in going indoors.

If you want to keep the cat overpopulation problem down by neutering your visiting friends, you will have to capture them individually in a humane cat trap, and then take a trip to a cat shelter for neutering. You should not pay full neutering price for this procedure on a feral cat. Most cat rescue organizations and many veterinarians offer highly discounted prices or do not charge for the service when someone brings in a feral cat or kitten.

After neutering, a cat can be released into the wild again and continue the life he knows. He may or may not decide to remain friends with you.

So why bother with all of this? A neutered cat lives more peaceably among other cats, with less risk of fighting or pregnancy. You benefit because the cat will continue to control the vermin population around your home. Oh, and you don't need to feel deprived; you can still set out food and watch and talk with your feline visitors.

Fame and Fortune

One of the greatest art museums in the world, the Hermitage in St. Petersburg, Russia, was and still is patrolled by cats! Yes, cats were the custodians who once kept mice from chewing up priceless manuscripts and paintings. Today, the cats must live in the basement and are only allowed to patrol the outskirts of the building because they can set off sensor alarms inside.

Cats at the Hermitage Museum are mostly strays. Their food and medical care are provided through donations made by the employees and visitors and the proceeds from an annual sale of children's artwork.

Handling a Frightened Cat

Whenever on a cat rescue mission, be sure to wear heavy work or gardening gloves. Even the most docile cat may scratch and bite if suddenly picked up.

Most cats carry bacteria called *Pasteurella* in their mouths. This bacteria is not harmful to cats but can be harmful to humans. Bites and scratches can become infected and should be treated with antibiotics by a doctor.

Someone Said

"A cat is a lion in a jungle of small bushes."

—old American saying

Most feral cats distrust humans, sometimes with good reason. Food, the smellier the better, is the best pacifier and friend maker. Once a cat is eating right next to you, you may be able to pick him up. Don't try to take him into your lap. It is best to pick the cat up around the middle and put him quickly into a cat transporter.

Most local animal shelters have more sophisticated tools for capturing strays and many lend them to anyone willing to leave a deposit, which is given back upon the return of the borrowed tools.

Among the tools is the cat net, which gives you the advantage of distance for the capture. But if your first attempt at netting fails, don't expect to see the cat again anytime soon. Another tool is the cat grabber, a pole with tongs, which works better when there are two cat capturers: one to keep the cat's attention and the other to approach from behind. And, finally, humane cat traps can be borrowed or rented.

While in the process of capture, always talk quietly and soothingly to the cat. Remember, cats have extraordinary hearing and a person who is shouting increases their anxiety. Try to think like a cat: *I am being taken over by a giant; I don't know what will happen next; I don't know how to escape.* Once you understand where the cat is mentally, you'll quite naturally behave more appropriately.

Identification

Cats are treasures we certainly don't want to lose. But even as recently as the early 1990s, cat identification usually consisted of buying a cat collar and hanging a metal heart from it engraved with your phone number and maybe the cat's name. Most cat advisory groups suggested using breakaway collars that would release if the cat became caught by a tree branch or other hazard. These collars are still available today in pet stores and even in some supermarkets and big-box stores.

But the dawn of the twenty-first century has brought about a better way to equip your cat with identification. Microchip technology works to provide identification that is nationwide. A veterinarian injects a pellet the size of a grain of rice under a cat's skin in the vicinity of his shoulder blades. The procedure is no more painful than an inoculation.

Someone Said

"Like a graceful vase, a cat, even when motionless, seems to flow."

—George F. Will (1941–) American Pulitzer Prize–winning columnist, journalist, and author

With the microchip insertion, a cat has permanent, lifelong identification based on passive radio frequency identification (RFID) technology. A veterinarian or other provider registers the owner's contact information in a nationwide database. The owner is provided with paperwork so that ownership information can be updated (change of address) or transferred.

If a cat is lost or if ownership of a cat is in dispute, a microchip reader is used to retrieve the ID number in the microchip. This unique number is used to retrieve the owner's contact information from the database.

Many shelters today microchip every cat before being placed in a private home. The cost is included in the adoption donation fee. Microchip fees at a private vet's office vary in different areas of the country but are never very high.

Pet ID can be particularly important in times of natural disasters, such as earthquakes, hurricanes, or tornadoes, that force residents from their homes. Lost cats with identification have a much better chance of being returned to their owners.

Did You Notice the Cat?

Upon his death, Sultan El-Zaher Bebars, (1223–1277) the ruler of Egypt and Syria at the time, demonstrated his love for cats to all the known world. He bequeathed a piece of land near his mosque in Cairo for the support of homeless cats. It was known as *Gheyt-el-Quoltah* (the orchard of the cats). Today, eight centuries later, meat is still brought to the center of the garden at the time of afternoon prayer each day. Feral cats come together to feed.

CHAPTER 11

Household Tranquility

In This Chapter

➤ Introducing a cat to your home
➤ Introducing a new cat to the other cats
➤ Cats and children
➤ Cats and the elderly

Since the early 1990s, cats have been the most popular household pet in the United States. And no wonder—they are beautiful to look at, small, quiet, calm and calming, clean, loving, and loyal. Most of the time.

But cats are not miniature people in a furry form. They have their own world view, even if that world is six rooms and one and a half baths. For maximum cat happiness and tranquility in your household, it's important that you understand cat stress factors and cat emotional stabilizers.

Someone Said

"Happy is the home that shelters a friend."

—Ralph Waldo Emerson (1803–1882) American philosopher, essayist, lecturer, and poet

Introducing Your Cat into Your Home

Each cat has her own way of coping with the stress of finding herself in a new place. When you put your feline friend down on the floor for the first time, she might scurry under the sofa and stay there for hours, maybe even days. (Even Cleveland Amory had a terrible time getting Polar Bear to come out where he could be seen, fed, and touched.)

Cats have even been known to leap out of an open window in an attempt to escape the new surroundings. Of course you will have your windows closed or at least have them protected by screens when you bring your fur face home.

Myth, Magic and Medicine

For generations, people have said that a cat always lands on her feet. This is true most of the time, but not always.

The cat's highly developed sense of balance located in the inner ear contributes to an amazing cat instinct to right herself and land on her feet. Cats, like most creatures, base their movements on what they see, but they also subconsciously correct and augment vision with lightning-fast balance messages from the inner ear to the brain.

You can watch a slow-motion video of a cat falling on the Internet at video.nationalgeographic. com, where you can enter the key phrase Cat's Nine Lives. The film also discusses the high-rise syndrome that explains why cats can sometimes survive falls from tall apartment buildings.

Sometimes a new cat hides herself so well within the house that her owners think she has been lost. Don't worry. The cat will eventually become hungry and thus be forced to come out to explore for food. She will probably choose the nighttime hours for this adventure. If this is your first cat or the first one in your house, you can leave an open can of cat food on your countertop. You'll know that kitty is still with you, somewhere in the house, when you come into the kitchen the next morning, groggy-eyed and craving coffee, and you find the cat food gone.

It's really hard to forecast how your particular new cat will be affected by your surroundings. Yours may be the cat's first real (safe) home after wandering the streets or being confined in a cage. Or yours may be just the latest in a series of foster homes, some of which were not so great. The best way to help your pet become acclimated to your home is by starting the introduction in a limited space (a small room, for example) and by keeping your home quiet while she gets used to life at your place.

But that may be easier said than done, especially if you have children, because everyone will want to see and pet the new kitty. Sometimes the best method is to bring the cat into the house in a cat carrier. Then let everyone look at her through the mesh, perhaps even throw in a treat or two. Then Kitty goes into her own room for a few days. Gentle, quiet people should visit often, one at a time.

Some new cats, however, are quite brave and curious. Even if your new cat is acting nonchalant and walking about with well-controlled curiosity, try to allow her to wander at her own pace. Don't allow children or dogs to chase her. Talking to the new cat, however, is definitely a plus. Especially if you keep your voice low and musical.

Myth, Magic and Medicine

"When moving into a new home, always put the cat in through the window instead of the door. Then it will not leave."

—American superstition

How much should you handle a new cat? A friend who lives with and loves four cats, all of whom have been adopted from the streets, gave me some very fine advice: when a cat needs to be petted, she will come to you. Don't worry if your new cat seems to be sleeping all of the time. All cats sleep a lot, but your home may be the first place that Kitty ever felt safe while sleeping. Sleeping safe feels so, so good!

Naming Your Cat

Some cats come with names attached and you can avoid an identity crisis by not changing the name. But if you just can't stand calling your cat a name like Pyewacket or Little Witch or even Beelzebub, be assured that you can teach a cat to respond to a new name. Start out by calling both the old name and the new name together. Gradually leave off the old name.

But what will the new name be? There are those persons who take one look at their new white cat and immediately call, "Here, Kitty! Here, Milkshake!" And that's it! The cat is named. No problem. For others, deciding on a name is a tortuous process that may take days or even weeks.

Some owners select names referring to food (Marmalade, Cookie, Brownie, Peaches, Gumdrop, and even Sara Lee). Others let the place they found the stray influence the cat's name (Freeway, Ally, Chelsea, Treetop). The cat's personality is another name determinant (Sunny, Tiger, Rowdy, Terminator). And a lot of cats are named after famous people or places in history (Dante, Chopin, Westminster Abby—called Abby of course—Orlando).

Did You Notice the Cat?

Did you notice any cats in *Huckleberry Finn*? How about *Tom Sawyer*? The famous American author Mark Twain, whose real name was Samuel Clemens (1835–1910), never wrote much about cats, but he considered himself an authority on the subject. He loved cats and lived with them and gave them all kinds of names. Some of the names he chose for his cats were Abner, Apollinaris, Beelzebub, Blatherskite, Buffalo Bill, Fraulein, Satan (and her kitten named Sin), Sour Mash, Tammany, and Zoroaster. He once wrote to his wife, "Next to a wife whom I idolize, give me a cat—an *old* cat with kittens."

Fame and Fortune

T. S. Eliot (1888–1965) was an American-born English poet and Nobel Prize winner who wrote very serious poetry and amusingly characterized cats. A book he wrote for children is called *Old Possum's Book of Practical Cats*.

It was published in 1939, but it became world-famous when it was adapted to the stage in the musical *Cats*.

Old Possum's Book of Practical Cats is filled with amusing poetry and wonderful names for cats. In fact, the first poem is titled "The Naming of Cats." If you've read the book or seen the play, you'll recognize Old Gumbie Cat (Jennyanddots), Growltiger, Rum Tum Tugger, Jellicles, and Skimbleshanks.

T. S. Eliot ends the book with a poem titled "The Ad-dressing of Cats," and then in 1952 added another poem, "Cat Morgan Introduces Himself."

Introducing a New Cat to Other Cats

When you introduce a new cat to your resident cat, will the fur fly? Some say all it takes is one new cat in the house to assure a fight or two. Sometimes that's true. Cats do form close communities or "families," and they are not always welcoming to strangers. But there are steps you can take to make the introduction go more smoothly.

Usually the resident cats' anti-welcome attitudes can be worked out within a week or two. The established residents sort themselves out into a new pecking order that includes the new cat. During the adjustment time, however, you can expect some degree of hissing, growling, fighting, and chasing. If you go out, separate the newcomer, for the sake of everyone's safety.

CATch Words

Clowder, cludder, and *clutter* are all English words for a group of cats. Their origin is in the first decade of the nineteenth century. The terms are rarely used today.

A kendle, or kindle is properly a group of kittens. But if you Google the word today, you'll get electronic book information.

In American slang, a cat fight refers to an intense argument or fight between two women.

A cat fit is an emotional outburst or expression of anger, again usually by a woman.

It's wise to keep your newcomer separate from the others for the first forty-eight hours or so. As with introducing the first cat into the household, you can use the bathroom or other small room where the door can be kept closed and all necessities kept inside. On the third day or so, position the door so that it is open a crack, wide enough for the cats to meet, sniff, even touch noses, but not wide enough to allow a cat body through. On the fourth day, open the door and allow the newcomer freedom. But still don't go out and leave your cats together unsupervised.

Another approach is to keep your new cat in a large metal cage (you can probably borrow one from a friend who has a large dog) with all the necessities inside. Because there is space between the bars, the animals can see and sniff and become accustomed to each other. On the other hand, some owners in two-story houses, keep the resident cats on one floor and the new cat on another with the stairway blocked off. This is something of a bother for humans, but it does work.

Some new cats are accepted easily into a multi-cat household without any fuss. This is particularly true when the new member is still a kitten. In other households, one of the cats may decide to tolerate the newcomer, but the two

Someone Said

"One cat just leads to another. "

—Ernest Hemingway (1899–1961) American novelist and writer

will never become friendly. Infrequently, the new cat is never accepted by the other cats in the household.

If after about four weeks of attempted introductions it still looks as if there will never be peace and tolerance, never mind goodwill, in your home, you have four choices:

➤ You can call in an animal behavior therapist to help with everyone's adjustment (see chapter 18).

➤ You can keep the cats separated forever, which requires considerable attention.

➤ You can learn to live with the occasional hissing or fighting.

➤ You can return your new cat or take her to a shelter to find a new home.

Many times in this book I've given examples of how cats are a lot like people, and I must do so again. Just like some members of the human race, some felines prefer to be alone or at least in a one-cat household. They never do adjust to or even become accepting of another cat sharing their living quarters.

Myth, Magic and Medicine

In some parts of Asia, it is said that if you are afraid of cats, you must have been a rat in your last incarnation.

CATch Words

"Fight like cats and dogs" is an American colloquialism. A cat-and-dog couple usually means the couple is in a quarrelsome relationship.

Introducing a New Cat to the Family Dog

The results of bringing a cat into a household that already includes a dog or two are not entirely predictable. Cats and dogs can and do live together peacefully, and many even become friends, sleeping and playing together. A lot depends on how they are introduced and treated, the breed of the dog(s) involved, and the temperament and age of the cat.

When you first bring your new cat into your home, introduce her to your dog gently and slowly. Keep the dog on a leash and hold the cat securely, perhaps even wrapped in a blanket. Talk quietly to both animals. Let them sniff each other. Don't just put the cat down in front of the dog and expect them to be friends. Dogs have an instinct to chase anything that runs; cats have an instinct to run away from larger animals and climb. It's not a good way to start.

Both dogs and cats do better when introduced as young animals or when both or either has already been living in a household with the other species. But remember each dog and each cat is an individual. If your cat seems afraid or if there is any hissing or growling, put your cat in a large cage, as described above. The cat will be protected and the dog will eventually accept her as part of the household (usually).

There are some dog breeds and temperaments, however, that put a cat at more risk. Be more careful if your canine house pet is a prey-oriented breed such as a dachshund or a highly territorial dog such as a rottweiler. With a few exceptions, most herding breeds, working breeds, and sporting breeds will not kill or even intentionally injure another animal. Most toy and small dogs eventually accept a cat as an equal.

Virtually all of the hound breeds should be watched until you are quite sure that the dog looks upon the cat as a household member. The same is true for all terriers; they are bred to seek out and kill prey. Be aware that most of the dogs we call pit bulls in the United States are related to the Staffordshire bull terrier. The terrier heritage of pit bulls means they also need to be supervised when a new cat enters a household.

Among the herding dogs, the one to watch is the Australian cattle dog because it herds by nipping at the heels of the animals being herded.

Someone Said

"Cats are smarter than dogs. You can't get eight cats to pull a sled through snow."

—Jeff Valdez – Latin American comic, writer, producer

"If animals could speak, the dog would be a blundering outspoken fellow, but the cat would have the rare grace of never saying a word too much."

—Mark Twain (1835–1910) American author

Myth, Magic and Medicine

In Norse legend, four cats, not dogs or horses, pull the chariot of Freyja, the goddess of youth, beauty, sexual love, and fertility. Friday was a sacred day of the week to the goddess and is named after her. Scandinavian people used to set saucers of milk outside their doors at night for Freyja's cats and, of course, Freyja's favor. Farmers left saucers of milk in their fields to ensure a good harvest.

Cats and Children

Many cat breed standards include the phrase *good with children*, and indeed most cats are good with children. They particularly like to play chase and to bat hanging toys with kids, but cats will also sit quietly while a child does his homework. Cats usually run away rather than fight when they are intimidated or threatened.

Artists over the centuries have drawn or painted cats and children together. In American and English literature, the cat seems to be the prominent animal of children's fable and fiction. And in modern media productions, cats often take a starring role. In most cases, these imaginary cats are having fun, but they also teach moral lessons such as loyalty, perseverance, focus, watchfulness, cleanliness, courage, and fortitude.

Did You Notice the Cat?

The list of cats in children's literature is very long, from the three little kittens who lost their mittens, to the Cheshire cat in *Alice in Wonderland,* to *The Owl and the Pussycat,* to Dr. Seuss' *The Cat in the Hat.* In the UK, no self-respecting citizen would let a child grow up without knowing the success story of *Dick Whittington and His Cat.*

In the art world, Mary Cassatt's painting *Children Playing with a Cat* (1908) still stands out among the many paintings of kids and cats.

I need to stress that children, especially young children, should be taught not to hurt a cat. Most breeds of dogs will withstand a child pulling their tails or ears and even sitting on them with stoic good humor. That is not always the case with a cat who cannot escape. If a child is intentionally or unintentionally cruel to a cat, the child is likely to be scratched, and then the cat will run and hide. Children should also be taught that it is unkind to wake a cat suddenly from sleep.

Cats seem to have a sixth sense about babies and rarely hurt them. Nevertheless, many superstitions and old wives' tales persist about cats in the house with a newborn. In 1825 this warning appeared in a publication in Scotland: "It is reckoned highly improper to leave a cat alone with an infant; as it is believed, that it has the power of taking away the life of the child by sucking out its breath."

Of course the superstition is untrue, but as late as 1987 a woman in London was recorded as saying, "Be sure to shut the door of the baby's room when she's asleep. I don't want the cat to jump into her cot. I don't think he'd do her any harm, but better be on the safe side."

Not so long ago, people even believed that if a cat passed over a pregnant woman, harm would be done to the fetus. In 1988, a woman in London said, "I'm sixty-four. Had seven children, two dead. One went under a bus, two and a half he was. The other was born dead. Cat went over me."

An indoor cat coming up close and even sleeping next to a pregnant woman can do no harm. Sometimes outdoor cats can carry bacteria from eating infected prey. There is one particular danger from cats during pregnancy: sometimes emptying the litter box can cause a disease called toxoplasmosis.

If you are a woman who might be pregnant, it is best to arrange for someone else in the

CATch Words

Toxoplasmosis is a disease that can be contracted by a pregnant woman while she is scooping and changing the litter box of an infected cat. More often, however, it is caused by the mother eating undercooked and infected meat. It can affect the brain and nervous system of a fetus during the first trimester of a pregnancy. A pregnant woman can have a blood test to find out if she already has an immunity to toxoplasmosis, and cats can also be tested for the disease.

household to take on the chore of cleaning the litter box. If this is not possible, use a surgical face mask and disposable gloves when cleaning the litter box, and frequently disinfect it with a cleansing wash.

The best way to prevent toxoplasmosis is to keep your cat indoors. If you feed her fresh meat, be sure to cook it thoroughly. And be sure to keep your children's sandbox securely covered when not in use. If there are feral cats in your area, use gloves while gardening. Remove solid waste from the litter box daily, since it takes more than one day for the source of infection to shed from the stool to the litter.

When you do bring a new baby home and everyone is fussing over the addition to the family, don't let your cat become jealous. Give her a little extra attention. Perhaps even rub some baby oil on your hands and let the cat sniff it. You want your cat to become accustomed to the scents around the baby and to associate them with you and the family. You should also let the cat sniff the baby's blanket and even his diapers. Remember, smell is an important identification credential to a cat.

Cats and the Elderly

Should you get a cat when you have an elderly relative living with you? Or how about if you yourself are getting on in years and perhaps are less active than you used to be? My suggested answer is yes!

There couldn't be a better pet for an elderly person. Cats are affectionate, clean, warm, and comforting. They ask for very little. You'll never see a cat holding a leash in her mouth waiting for you to take her for a walk. You'll never see a cat acting disappointed because you can't throw the ball for her at the moment.

And cats, being cats, are always a source of pleasure. You may find yourself laughing at their antics or being calmed by stroking their fur while you listen to (and feel) the contented purr. And once you know and love a cat, they're fun vicariously too, in books, in movies, and in comic strips. There are no machine guns or revenge schemes in the cat's world, but they surely do mimic human life in many ways. The similarities are what cartoonists use to make us laugh.

Fame and Fortune

Garfield, his owner Jon Arbuckle, Arbuckle's dog Odie, and their friends have been making people laugh since 1978 when they were created by Jim Davis. At the end of the first decade of the twenty-first century, *Garfield* was syndicated in over 2,500 newspapers and estimated as the world's most widely read comic strip.

A good part of its success lies in the mirror that it holds up to everyday life in our society. Common topics are obsessive eating, dieting, Mondays, Garfield's distaste for work, and troubles with dating. Controversial topics and politics are avoided.

CHAPTER 12

Unmentionables and Other Challenges

In This Chapter

➤ About that litter box

➤ Unappreciated spraying

➤ Behavior problems

➤ Traveling with a cat

Do you remember potty training your child? How about housebreaking a puppy? Did you buy puddle pads? Did you get down on your knees with rug cleaner and paper towels more often than you'd like to admit? Cats are easier, much easier.

Nothing is perfect, however. There are definitely some challenges when living with this beautiful animal. Challenges like dealing with the manifestations of raging hormones, loneliness, and aggression. And there are decisions too. For example, will your cat be an indoor cat or will he be allowed to go out to play? Who will care for him if you're away on a business trip or vacation? What if you have to relocate to another part of the country?

Let's take the problems one by one.

Someone Said

"A cat sees no good reason why it should obey another animal, even if it does stand on two legs."

—Sarah Thompson (1979 –) American actress

The Litter Box

I think cats are the easiest of all animals when it comes to training for proper elimination behavior. Cats have a strong instinct to bury their waste. This probably developed in an effort to hide their presence from possible predators, long before they became domesticated.

The hiding-and-covering instinct passes from one generation to another. Most cat breeders put a litter box near the nesting place when the kittens are a few weeks old. The mother cat does the rest.

When you bring home your eight-week-old kitten (even if he came from a shelter), you need only to place him in a litter box for about fifteen or twenty minutes after he has been fed. With a few tries and one or two successes, he'll know where the box is and use it regularly. Adult cats just need to be shown where the box is located.

Where to Put the Litter Box

Place the litter box in a spot in your home that affords the cat some privacy. The kitchen is not usually a good location. You want the litter box away from food. Under something (perhaps a soaking tub in the laundry room) or behind something (perhaps the couch on the porch) is often a good choice because other animals (particularly larger dogs and, of course, children) can't get to it.

Basements, if you have one, are also a good location. You can install a cat flap (otherwise known as a cat door) in the lower portion of the door to the cellar. You then must teach your cat how to use the door by taking him through it several times. Once he gets the idea, he can slip through the door, go down the stairs, and relieve himself in private!

Once you've found the right place for the litter box, don't move it if you can help it. Cats might complain about a series of new locations.

Fame and Fortune

It is believed that one of civilization's greatest thinkers, Sir Isaac Newton (1643–1727), invented the pet door. Why was he distracted from calculus, light spectra, gravity, the speed of sound, and the philosophy of religion? He owned (and loved) a cat who wanted both sunshine and a comfortable bed. The requests for egress and ingress interrupted the scientist in the midst of thought. So he solved the problem!

The Shape of the Box

Most cat litter boxes are rectangular and made of plastic with sides usually about 4 to 6 inches high. They are available in supermarkets, pet stores, and big-box stores. Or you can make your own. Those plastic wash basins they give you when you enter a hospital are great for cat litter once you're back at home and getting well. The high sides, however, may not be appropriate for an older or arthritic cat.

While scratching at the litter, cats sometimes kick it out of the litter box. The bits of litter thrown outside sometimes travel through the house and can end up in laundry, beds, or even shoes. Some fastidious owners buy litter boxes with hooded (and removable) tops and a hole for entry at one end. If your cat doesn't mind the confined, dark space, these enclosed "toilets" can work out well. If he does mind, he may find other places to do what's necessary.

Kinds of Cat Litter

There are so many kinds of cat litter on the market today. Some are wood based, some sandy, some recycled materials made granular, but the most popular type (preferred by over 80 percent of cat owners) is called clumping litter. And, yes, it clumps up when used and, yes, that makes removal easier. But easy identification and removal of used litter is not an excuse for not cleaning out the litter box regularly.

Besides differences in composition and texture, cat litter comes scented and unscented. You get to choose, but remember that most cats don't like change. If you find a cat litter that your cat likes, stick with it. He may object to a new texture or even a new smell. Some of the scented litters are appealing to humans but almost repulsive to cats. Usually, an unscented litter is best. Even though it's unscented, it still absorbs odors.

Cleaning the Box

A litter box should be cleared of solids and clumps daily. A small amount of new litter should then be added. Slotted plastic scoopers are sold in the pet-supply areas of markets for the purpose of clearing out a litter box. If you choose to buy one, be aware that they snap in half easily. My recommendation: leave the pet area and buy a metal slotted ladle in the housewares section of your market. Wrap some iridescent tape around the handle and dedicate the ladle to your cats. It will last forever and only need a rinsing after each use.

The litter box ought to be emptied and washed with soap and water or better yet, a disinfectant solution about once a week. It should then be refilled with fresh cat litter to a depth of about 2 inches. As I said, some litters are scented but the best way to control odor is through frequent cleaning.

So what happens if you forget to clear out the litter box and then it becomes overloaded and too dirty? Don't be surprised if Kitty begins to eliminate just outside the box or even picks some cleaner (although unapproved) place for toiletry purposes.

Did You Notice the Cat?

Believe it or not, some cats can be trained to use a toilet. Yes, a human toilet. If you don't believe this, go on the Internet and search for cats using a toilet. I found over a million results with those key words.

But remember, cats won't flush and they don't give a care in the world about dribbling on the seat. Personally, I think a cat litter box works better.

Unappreciated Spraying

As we've discussed, cats spray to mark their territory. That's quite fine outdoors. Indoors, the odor can be more than a little off-putting, not to mention hard to get rid of.

Once a cat decides to relieve himself on a place other than the litter box, he will probably use the same place again, and the practice may become habitual. (Believe me; you do not want this marking!) So try to discover the cause right after the initial deviation.

Besides objecting to an overly full litter box, there are several medical reasons for a cat to begin urinating in strange places. It can be a sign of kidney disease, bladder infection, diabetes, emotional stress, or another disease. Rubbing your cat's nose in the soiled place and spanking accompanied by harsh words, as is often done with dogs, will not have any effect on a cat's behavior.

The first step in response to FUS is to have the cat checked by a vet to be sure there is no underlying physical cause. Then you must look for a psychological cause. Is the cat particularly anxious or perhaps lonely? Is he urinating near

CATch Words

FUS is the acronym for frequent urologic syndrome. You usually discover the problem soon after a cat begins to urinate in unacceptable places.

a window where he might be watching prey that he can't possibly catch or neighboring cats trespassing?

Is there a female cat in heat in the neighborhood? Unaltered toms who are confined indoors find this excruciating. Even neutered cats sometimes are stimulated. Is there a new animal or even a new person in the house? Is there family stress, perhaps an unusual amount of shouting, perhaps an impending divorce? Cats are very sensitive to the affairs and feelings of their humans. Spraying is an instinctual response resorted to in many different situations.

While working on the spraying problem, try to make your cat feel as comfortable as possible. It is often a good idea to make the places that your cat has already used inaccessible, or at least unappealing for spraying and elimination purposes. Some cat owners block off such places; others even put mats down and place the food bowls there. Keeping a cat away from a place that still carries the odor of urine (even if humans can't smell it) will make the formation of a new habit at that place less likely. Some owners dealing with FUS stress add another litter box in a different location in the house, giving the cat a choice.

CATch Words

Not all the images of cats depicted in words and phrases in our language are positive. Here are some not-so-nice colloquialisms:

➤ She's a cat: a malicious woman

➤ She's catty: spiteful and often conniving

➤ Cat-farting around: fussy actions that have the effect of being irritating

➤ Cat-witted: not teachable, even not trainable, and having a closed mind

➤ Sourpuss: grouch

Other Behavior Problems

Many of the cat behaviors that humans find undesirable such as scratching at the doorjamb and indoor spraying are greatly intensified by sex-related hormones. Besides spraying and scratching, both male and female cats dealing with reproductive hormones may display bad temper, impatience, restlessness, and verbal complaining. Some, especially males protecting their territories, will get into fights. If you want to avoid these behavior problems, the best decision is to have your cat neutered.

Like humans, cats also respond to many of life's other stress situations (those not related to sexual activity). The response is usually a change in behavior patterns. Again like humans, some common changes in behavior are overeating, undereating, over-grooming to the point where the licked spot becomes bald, and restlessness. Among the most common cat stressors are:

➤ death or extended absence of a loved family member;

➤ introduction of a new human into the household;

➤ introduction of a new cat or other pet into the household;

➤ long hours of being left home alone;

➤ changes in the behavior of a beloved owner or owners;

➤ moving to a new home; and

➤ loss of a companion cat in the household.

Cats do get depressed, and the symptoms of depression in cats are almost exactly like those of humans: listlessness, a lack of interest in life, lack of grooming resulting in an uncared-for appearance, changes in eating habits, changes in sleep patterns, and personality changes.

In the not-so-distant past, people who could not cope with their cat's behavioral changes took extreme means. The cats were either delivered to a shelter or abandoned in some remote area. Today, both everyday people and veterinary colleges are recognizing that problem behavior often has a source that can be treated.

Myth, Magic and Medicine

Animal or pet therapist is a growing field. Although a license isn't required, some veterinary colleges offer courses in animal behavior, some college and university programs have behavioral advisors associated with their clinics, and some private veterinarians keep a referral list of individuals who have worked successfully with behavior problems of cats or other animals.

Books are being written in this field, and professional groups, both local and regional, are being formed. But the job is not an easy one. Trying to understand the behavior of an animal who does not speak our language and trying to help that animal and his human owners adapt to life together takes love and tremendous patience. And as the French naturalist and writer Georges-Louis Leclerc (1707–1788) said "Genius is patience."

Indoor, Outdoor, and Indoor-Outdoor Cats

The typical cat living exclusively or mostly outdoors has a life expectancy of about three years. Many are killed in auto accidents; others are poisoned, either accidentally or intentionally; some are captured and sold to research organizations. The indoor pet cat can be expected to live fifteen years or more.

A cat can live a happy life within the confines of an owner's home. In fact, indoor life is now a very frequent recommendation being made by professionals who are interested in cat welfare. Yes, there are non-feral country cats (farm cats and barn cats) who are actually relatively safe hanging around on the property and interacting with humans. But in highly populated areas, there are more perils than benefits to the great outdoors.

Dr. Franklin Loew of Tufts University School of Veterinary Medicine once said, "There are four keys to longevity in cats. One is luck; two is proper nutrition; three is health care, including appropriate vaccinations; and four is keeping out of harm's way." Harm's way can be defined as "outdoors" for most cats. In urban areas with maximum high-rise and mid-rise apartment buildings and minimum open land, it may not even be a choice.

On the other hand, if you live in suburbia and you are feeling badly that your indoor cat will never feel the sun on his back or a warm breeze through his whiskers, you might consider a cat fence to confine your cat to your backyard. You can install a cat-sized pet door to the fenced yard, and your cat can then have the best of both worlds. Check out national cat magazines or the Internet for specific information on cat fencing and other protection products.

Did You Notice the Cat?

The effective use of this cat's claws steals the show in the painting *Old Woman Praying* by Nicolas Maes (1634–1693). The painting can be seen in the Ruksmuseum, Amsterdam.

There are, however, some dangers to having a pet door in your home. If you have a toddler or other children, be sure that the opening covered by the flap is not large enough for a child to get through. And be aware that if your cat can get through, so can most other cats in the neighborhood and even some small dogs who have been "let out to play." The smell of food might just bring you some unexpected guests or even unwanted guests such as a raccoon or a possum.

Cat doors can be locked when you and your pet are away from home for more than a day or two. In some cases the flap can be secured. Most often, however, a metal sheet can be inserted over the opening. It fits into grooves built in along the outer edges of the installation. Another safety measure is to be sure that the cat door is installed far enough from any locks so that an intruder could not reach up through the cat door and open the locked door from the inside.

Myth, Magic and Medicine

Declawing a cat is a surgical procedure called an onychectomy. It removes not only the claw but also the first joint of each toe. Declawing is legal and can be performed on indoor cats in North America, Japan, Korea, and China. In many other parts of the world, however, it is considered an act of animal cruelty.

If a declawed cat happens to wander outdoors, he is essentially helpless. He cannot defend himself or even climb a tree for safety. Kept indoors, a declawed cat's feet heals over time and the cat will play at "pouncing on prey" and batting at things again. And, of course, there will be no furniture scratching or drapery shredding.

Hire a Cat-Sitter or Board Your Pet?

As we progress into the twenty-first century, extended time away from home for humans is almost inevitable. Many of us travel for our jobs; most of us take vacations from time to time. So what do we do with our cats?

Of course, you can ask a friend or relative to take in your precious beauties. But will those beauties approve of the new environment? Will they show their disapproval with problem behavior? Will they try to escape and find their way back to their own places? Cats are very territorial and they either want to stay home or go home.

So when you have finally saved enough for that twenty-one-day cruise to Antarctica, what are your options for Troilus and Cressida? You can ask a neighbor to drop in perhaps twice a day to feed, fondle, and check the cat litter. (But how will you know that your instructions are being followed? And does your neighbor have a backup plan in case he can't make it?)

For many people, especially those on shorter business trips, enlisting a neighbor to check on their cats works out just fine. And you can always return the favor! If you have no close relative or good neighbor available, however, you can hire a professional pet-sitter or board your cat at a vet clinic or nearby cattery.

Someone Said

"A cat is an animal which has more human feelings than almost any other."

—Emily Brontë (1818–1848) English novelist and poet

What Does a Cat-Sitter Do?

Hiring professional pet-sitters has become an increasingly popular alternative to boarding pets, especially for multi-cat households where boarding fees can add up to more than the room rate at, say, Days Inn. Although some pet-sitters actually stay in your home and become de facto house sitters, most practice their trade by stopping by once or twice a day to check on your cat(s), feed and water them, change the cat litter when necessary, and pet and play with them for a while. The fee is usually the same whether there are several cats in the house or only one. The lone cat, however, may need more human contact time.

Most cats, even shy cats, adapt quickly to these new caretakers. The pets usually approve of them and form affectionate relationships because most pet-sitters are just about always genuine "animal people." Cats are more likely to accept a cat-sitter because the cats are not being stressed by a new residence and life pattern.

Before you entrust your cats (and your home) to a visiting stranger, however, you will want to get some reliable information. Here are some questions to ask a potential cat-sitter:

➤ How long have you been in the pet-sitting business?

➤ Do you have references? May I call them?

➤ Have you had any previous experience with. . .(name any problems your pets might have)?

➤ Are you bonded or insured? What company? (Note some states require pet-sitters to be bonded.)

➤ Do you know (name your vet)? Do you know where that office is?

➤ Do you have an alternative sitter who will take over for you if you are unable to meet your commitments? (Some owners arrange for a friend to take over in the event of an emergency.)

➤ What do you do in inclement weather?

➤ Can you be contacted daily either by cell phone or e-mail?

Be sure that you and the pet-sitter agree upon exactly what is to be done during each visit. Some owners leave a written checklist; others make arrangements to call at regular intervals, usually when the pet-sitter is scheduled to be there. Some sitters agree to send a daily e-mail summing up the state of the "family."

No matter how experienced your pet-sitter is, no matter how well she knows the neighborhood, be sure to leave specific instructions for an emergency. (Many owners also leave instructions with their vets.) It's also a good idea to leave the name and phone numbers for a friend or relative who can make a medical decision if you cannot be reached. And prearrange credit with your vet.

Fame and Fortune

When Cleveland Amory's book *The Cat Who Came for Christmas* was published in 1987, the marketing people told him that they could sell more copies (and make more money) if he would take Polar Bear along on the publicity tour. Mr. Amory declined. The book was still a top-ten best seller.

You can find national pet-sitter organizations listed on the web. The two largest are National Association of Professional Pet Sitters (NAPPS) and Pet Sitters International. Each organization can provide the names of member pet-sitters in your local area.

Boarding

Although the American Humane Society has advised that most pets are happiest and least stressed when cared for in their own homes during their owners' absences, there are times and situations when boarding is essential or even preferable. This is especially true with special needs cats. Some owners also do not feel comfortable giving a cat-sitter total access to their homes.

Many cats are frightened at first by the new environment of a boarding facility. The vast majority, however, get over their discomfort within a few days and do quite well as long as the boarding facility is well designed and well run.

What are the standards for boarding facilities? Check these points for your cat's comfort and safety:

➤ Required vaccinations for feline distemper, rabies, and feline leukemia

➤ An inspection for fleas on every cat before admission, and a requirement for flea treatment for those cats who are infested

➤ A separate run for each cat that prevents nose-to-nose contact with other boarded cats, unless the owner requests the family cats to be boarded together

➤ Adequate lighting, fresh air, and comfortable temperature maintenance

➤ Allowance for your inspection of the boarding facility

➤ Drinking water available at all times

➤ Willingness to feed a special diet or give medication, if necessary

➤ Record keeping that includes your contact information and your vet's address and contact information

Car Travel with a Cat

Haven't we all seen at least one dog hanging out the window of a moving car, mouth open, tongue out, and ears flying in the wind? You'll never see a cat doing that! Some cats who are introduced to car travel as kittens do learn to enjoy it, but rarely enthusiastically. To prevent accidents, most authorities recommend that cats be kept in a cat carrier, or at the very least restrained firmly by humans. (It's usually best to use a blanket.)

Relatively new to the pet supply marketplace are pet seat belts. (Yes, you can have them installed in the back seat of your car.) The best models consist of a harness that fits comfortably on the cat's body, and then attaches through an anchor belt to the car's human seat belt fasteners. The anchor belt should be long enough for the cat to move around, lie down, and perhaps even look out the (closed) window. It should not, however, be long enough to allow the cat to leave the seat during travel time. Some anchor belts can even be adjusted to allow greater length during stopovers so you and the cat can get out of the car without danger. The length can also be adjusted to allow your cat to use a litter box on the floor. The recommended interval for travel without stopping for a break is three to four hours—just as with humans.

It is better not to feed your cat for about three hours before the beginning of a trip. For longer trips, of course, water and small bits of food should be offered at regular intervals. The total amount of food offered should be slightly less than the cat normally eats. Many owners elect to feed their cat the main meal after they arrive at a motel.

Myth, Magic and Medicine

Never leave your cat for significant intervals in a closed car on a hot day. The interior of a closed car heats up very quickly, and the resulting extreme temperature can be fatal.

Flying Cats!

Cats just don't take to airline travel. For most of them, it's a once-in-a-lifetime experience that they would prefer not to have. If you must fly your cat somewhere, however, let's go over some recommendations.

Federal regulations govern which crates are permissible for handling animals by commercial carriers. These rules change from time to time, and they may be augmented by the particular airline that you choose. Get printed guidelines from the carrier several weeks before the intended departure date and be absolutely certain that your crate complies. If it doesn't, the airline may deny boarding. Getting your money back will be difficult, if not impossible. Some airlines and airports sell acceptable animal transports.

Find out what health certificates are required and when you must present them. Some airlines allow the carrier for a small cat to be placed beneath the seat in front of you. There is inevitably a charge for this privilege, however.

Whether your cat is in the cabin with you or in the live cargo area, be sure that your name, address, and phone number are printed on the cat carrier and on a tag that the cat is wearing. Print LIVE ANIMAL in large letters on both sides of the carrier and use an arrow to indicate which way is up.

Did You Notice the Cat?

At the end of September 2005, Emily, a not quite one-year-old tabby, accidentally got herself sealed up in a transport container. She traveled by truck, airplane, ship, and truck again from Wisconsin in the United States to Nancy, France. The crate was pried open on October 24th, her first birthday. Emily was discovered, thin and thirsty, but still alive. With the help of modern Internet communication, the whole world instantly knew about her trip.

After a required month-long quarantine in France, Continental Airlines awarded Emily a complimentary business class flight home.

Well before the departure date, discuss with your veterinarian whether to tranquilize your cat for the trip. If yes, be careful to administer the recommended dose. Cats respond differently than other animals to medications. An inappropriate or inaccurate dose could cause serious problems or even death.

When You are Selling Your House

With the confusion of real estate agents, potential home buyers, and movers traipsing through your house, special cautionary steps need to be taken to keep your cats safe when you decide it's time to move.

Showing Your Home

Real estate agents almost never open a door with a barking dog behind it. But just put a sign on an interior door that reads Cat Inside—Please Do Not Open, and most house hunters and their guides forget how to read. It can be pandemonium. The cat gets out and finds a place to hide (the best possibility). The cat is descended upon by the house hunters' children or sometimes one of the adults and someone gets scratched. The cat gets accidentally locked in a closet. Or, worst possibility, the cat runs outdoors.

If you are selling your home and will often be out of the house when it is shown, you must take some time to make safety arrangements for your cat or cats. Some handy people actually build a cage for the cats with a padlock on the door. Some sellers put the cats in a room with a door that can be locked and post a sign that reads Cats Inside. This room will be shown only on a second showing. Other sellers take the cat with them whenever the house is shown. Some home owners are lucky enough to be able to leave their pets with friends or neighbors for short periods of time, perhaps a room can be set up with a litter box and water available during these showing visits.

Those sellers who have indoor-outdoor cats usually hope the cats will stay outdoors. Usually they will, but arranging a temporary placement elsewhere is safer.

Moving Day

If you think that moving day is a stressful occasion for you, try to imagine it from the perspective of looking up from about 9 inches off the floor or finding the thing you are sleeping on suddenly moving. Many a cat has been lost at one end of a move or the other.

Moving companies are most appreciative when owners make provisions to keep cats safely out of the way. A small animal underfoot can be extremely dangerous to people carrying heavy or cumbersome items. For cats, there is also the danger of entrapment. There are many stories about cats who have been packaged and sent off in wardrobes!

Probably the best place for a cat on moving day is in a confined area (even a crate) at a neighbor's house. If you don't have a place that you feel comfortable with, however, arrange to board your cat. He probably won't like it much, but at least your cat will be safe.

At the other end of the move, allow your cat to explore his new home only after the movers have left and all the doors and windows are closed. Cats have a strong instinct to return to their home territory and will try to slip out at any opportunity.

Some cat owners confine their pets to a single room for a day or two to help reduce their cat's transition anxiety. After Mr. Thomaskat seems to have accepted the new room, they leave the door open so that he can begin to explore the rest of the house. Being a cat, he'll probably return to the now-familiar room for a few days at least.

If you allowed your cat to go outdoors in your old home, you should suspend the privilege for a while in your new home. For how long depends on when you think your cat is finally feeling that this is really his home. Many owners actually buy a cat leash and walk outdoors with their cat in order to keep total control for some time.

Someone Said

"I love my cats because I love my home, and little by little they become its visible soul."

—Jean Couteau (1889–1963) French poet, novelist, and filmmaker

It's also important to establish contact with a veterinarian at your new location and to change your address and contact information with the microchip identification company before you allow the cat outdoors overnight. You may need that vet sooner than you think because your cat will be the new kid on the block and will have to fight for territory and a place in the local hierarchy. No wonder many owners prefer to transform the outdoor-indoor cat into an exclusively indoor pet after a move.

PART FOUR

Feline Health Care

CHAPTER 13

Sex and the Pregnant Feline

In This Chapter

➤ How and why do cats "make love"

➤ How to know if your cat is pregnant

➤ The newborn kittens

➤ The caring mother

So far in this book we've talked quite often about the similar responses cats and humans have to many aspects of life. Sex is not one of them. Cats don't do it for fun; in fact there's very little pleasure in copulation for either males or females. So why the caterwauls? Why the fights? Why all the fuss?

Hormones. In all animals, there are some things the rational brain simply cannot control. In cats, procreation (the continuation of the species) is definitely one of them. In this chapter you'll learn why there are kittens.

Someone Said

"No matter how much cats fight, there always seems to be plenty of kittens."

—Abraham Lincoln (1809–1865) sixteenth president of the United States

Love in the Cat World

Two cats can love each other, and they can choose to be lifelong companions. But admiration, friendship, respect, helpfulness, playing together, even sharing have absolutely nothing to do with sexual activity in the feline species. However, the weather does.

Male cats are ready to mate at any time, but they will do so only with a female cat who is "in season." The estrus (or season) of a female cat is dependent upon daylight and warm weather. In the northern hemisphere, female cats do not come into season after the days become shorter, from late September through December. As daylight hours begin to increase in late January, more and more queens come into heat and more and more toms are stimulated to seek them out. Some indoor cats and some cats who live in warmer climates, however, do continue the estrus cycle throughout the year.

CATch Words

A tomcat is an unaltered male cat. When *tomcat* is applied to the human species, it is usually slang for a promiscuous woman chaser. Sometimes *tomcat* applies to a man who lacks a sense of responsibility for his children. In rural North America, a dysfunctional person might be said to be "as useless as tits on a tomcat."

A female cat kept for breeding is called a queen. When a human male is called a queen, however, he is being designated as effeminate.

Estrus is a regularly occurring state of sexual excitability during which a female animal will accept a male and is capable of conceiving. Colloquially, a female cat or dog is said to be in season or in heat.

When a Cat is in Season

If you live with an unaltered male or female cat, you may be wondering how to tell when and how the mating instinct is driving behavior. Each gender has its own symptoms, and you don't have to be extraordinarily sensitive to pick them.

Tomcat Traits

A tom will mate whenever he can with any female cat who will have him. His sex drive is stimulated by the scent of the female estrus and by her wailing cries.

When a tom becomes aware of a queen in season, he begins to declare his territory more vehemently than usual by spraying and scratching more often indoors as well as outdoors. He begins to roam, possibly quite far from home, and he fights with other cats who cross what he considers his turf and with the cats whose turf he crosses. Usually the fights are between male cats, but occasionally a female who is not in estrus does get involved.

The sexually stimulated tom may also become aggressive toward people and other animals. Do not be frightened by the strange behavior and do not blame your normally docile pet.

He really can't help himself; hormones spread throughout the whole body, from end to end, including the brain.

The Behavior of a Queen

A queen's behavior while in heat is not exactly what might be expected of her majesty. A queen coming into season wants to let other cats know she is definitely ready for sexual activity. Like the toms who react to her scent and calls, she is not really responsible for her behavior. Almost everything that she does is influenced by her raging hormones.

The queen's estrogen levels are high throughout her estrus and estrogen is even excreted in her urine. As she comes into season, she will begin to urinate and spray much more frequently in order to leave scent markings by which toms can find her. She will also begin to call, both day and night, (We do notice it more at night, however.) These wailing sounds are extremely attractive to unaltered males and can be heard for quite some distance. (If you're a literary person, think of the siren's irresistible enticements in *The Odyssey*.)

People who have never before owned an unspayed cat may mistake her callings for cries of pain. Quite the opposite is true; she is signaling need and desire. There are also other puzzling signs. When inexperienced owners see their Annabelle Lee rolling on the floor indoors or on the ground outdoors, stretching frequently, raising her hindquarters, and even dragging herself around by her forepaws as though her hind legs aren't working, they may think she is ill and rush her off to the vet. That's the last thing she wants.

Myth, Magic and Medicine

Throughout the world there are many superstitions that link cats with human mating. Here are just some samples:

➤ The girl who cherishes a cat is sure to marry.

➤ Keeping a black cat in the house will ensure that all of your daughters will find appropriate husbands.

➤ If you step on a cat's tail, you will not marry during the coming year.

➤ Should a girl say yes or no to a suitor? The decision might be left to the cat. In some European countries when an eligible man proposes, three hairs from the cat's tail are carefully folded into a piece of paper and left on the girl's doorstep at bedtime. In the morning, the paper is unfolded. If the hairs are crossed, the girl should marry the suitor. If they are not crossed, she should reject him.

➤ In northern Europe, young girls are told to feed the cats well so that the sun will shine on their wedding day.

➤ If two young women shake a cat in a quilt, the one closer to the end where the cat runs out will marry first.

➤ If a bride feeds the cat before she goes to the church, she will have happiness throughout her married life.

➤ A black cat as a wedding present means good luck.

➤ In Thailand, the breed of cat we call Korat and the Thai people call *si-swat* is considered a bearer of good fortune. A pair of them is traditionally presented to a bride and groom to ensure a happy marriage.

➤ If a cat or cats turn up at a wedding celebration, it is considered very good luck.

➤ In eastern European countries, family members present the newlywed couple a cradle with a cat in it to ensure children.

Some owners don't realize that their cat is ready to mate, because they are looking for the wrong evidence. Female dogs (bitches) in season leave telltale stains on carpets and on any furniture where they are allowed to sit. Queens do not leave red stains.

Cat Mating

Despite her calling and acting out, the female cat will fight off prospective mates until she is ready for copulation. When she decides to accept the suitor, she allows him to mount her and grab her by the scruff of the neck. The act of mating takes less than a minute (some say as little as ten seconds!) and it hurts.

The penis of a cat is small but it is covered with hooklike barbs facing back toward the tail. It goes in quite easily; the tomcat ejaculates quickly, and he immediately tries to withdraw. The problem is that the barbs scrape the female vulva.

There's no doubt that Annabelle's scream this time is really a scream of pain. In fact, she will often try to turn on the male and bite him or scratch at him. If her tom is experienced, he anticipates the aggression and maintains his hold on her neck until she calms down a bit. Then he releases her. They both go off to separate places to rest and relax, and of course clean up a bit.

Cats do not ovulate until copulation actually occurs. It is the abrasion of the vulva that is believed to stimulate the hormone that causes the release of ova (eggs). Often, however, two or more matings are required to stimulate enough hormone to release the eggs. So after one try, both male and female wait a bit and then do it again. After two or more successful couplings, many males get tired and move aside for another male to take over. This can go on several times a day for several days, which means, of course, that the kittens in one litter can have different fathers.

If kittens are not conceived during the estrus stage of the queen's cycle, there is a brief interval of from two days to two weeks called diestrus when ovulation cannot occur and the queen is not interested in mating. Diestrus is immediately followed by another heat cycle. No wonder there are always plenty of kittens! And seriously, no wonder responsible owners should consider spaying.

Fame and Fortune

Among purebreds, male cats may be highly prized, very productive, and an excellent source of income, especially if the breed is rare and in demand. For example, in 1999, a long-haired Turkish Angora named Antonio B. Pinardin (Toni for short) was one of a few eligible, healthy, intact males with top-notch bloodlines. His stud fees approached $1,000 a breeding.

Pregnancy

Feline pregnancy lasts between sixty-three and sixty-eight days. During that time, progesterone becomes the predominant hormone in the queen's body. About four weeks into the pregnancy, some owners will notice behavior changes, weight gain, a swelling of the mammary glands, and an enlargement of the nipples with a color change from pink to rose.

In the early days of pregnancy, however, changes are virtually unnoticeable. The cat might stay closer to home, rest more, and become a little quieter. She will probably lavish more affection on you than you have been accustomed to. Or she may not change at all. By the fourth week of the nine-week pregnancy, a veterinarian can usually palpate the cat and feel the kittens.

During the last three weeks of her pregnancy, a female cat will probably spend more time lying on her side to relieve the weight of carrying the developing fetuses. As she approaches her due date, she will try to find a suitable nest. In the days just prior to delivery, she may experience loss of appetite and some anxiety. You may catch her shredding the newspapers or other materials lining her birthing box or the nesting place she has chosen.

Myth, Magic and Medicine

It is important to avoid bathing a queen before delivery and for some time afterward (usually until after weaning). You do not want to wash away the particular scent associated with the cat and with each teat. If each kitten cannot find her own teat through scent, the littermates may become confused and uncomfortable. Older kittens may even fight.

A Pregnant Cat's Diet

A normal amount of food is usually adequate for the first few weeks of pregnancy. After about the fourth week, however, the cat's appetite will increase gradually until she is eating almost double her normal ration of food as her due date nears.

Over the term of the pregnancy, the cat will need extra high-quality protein and some extra minerals such as iron and calcium. You might want to consult with your veterinarian before choosing from among the many commercially prepared cat foods designed specifically for pregnancy.

False Pregnancies

Sometimes when a cat does not mate during estrus or when a mating does occur but is sterile, a false pregnancy will occur. In this case, the hormones of pregnancy will make the queen act and feel as though she is pregnant. This condition will last from thirty-five to seventy days. Some cats even go through milk production and false labor.

False pregnancies usually end of their own accord and the cat resumes her normal cycle. When false pregnancies recur again and again, however, you should consult a veterinarian. Although there are hormone therapies available to relieve the uncomfortable symptoms of repeated false pregnancies, many owners prefer to have their cats spayed.

Someone Said

"Nobody who is not prepared to spoil cats will get from them the reward they are able to give to those who do spoil them."

—Compton Mackenzie (1883–1972) Scottish writer and naturalist

Cat Menopause?

Menopause doesn't happen with cats!
Cats stay beautiful and capable of producing offspring throughout most of their lives. If they could speak, they would proudly proclaim, "We're never too old!"

Although litter size may diminish, cats can easily continue to get pregnant and give birth right through their teens (which in human terms equates to early old age). There have even been documented reports of healthy litters delivered by twenty-five-year-old queens (in human terms, that's very old age—almost time for a birthday card from the US president).

Did You Notice the Cat?

If you should be in the Musée d'Histoire Naturelle in Cherbourg, France, don't miss the wonderful statuette of the cat goddess Bastet suckling her kittens. The bronze sculpture dates from the eighth century BCE. It is 23 inches wide.

Giving Birth

The female cat gives birth alone. The tom is usually nowhere to be seen. In fact, if he were to show up, the queen would chase him away. This behavior is probably as ancient as the cat species itself. Male felines seem to be unreliable with kittens. Even today, male lions are known to kill their cubs, especially if they suspect that another male has been lurking around. Occasionally, there are reports of a male cat killing kittens.

Hours before delivery, a pregnant cat spends most of her time in the nesting area she has chosen so that it will be covered with her recognizable scent for her kittens to identify. She may start frequent licking of the genital and abdominal areas. Sometimes there is discharge from the nipples and some bloody discharge from the vagina. The cat may move around frequently, trying to get comfortable. All of this is part of the first stage of labor and can continue for up to six hours, sometimes more for a first litter.

The queen breathes faster, often through her mouth, during this first stage of labor. Don't be surprised if you also hear the cat purring during labor. (It is said that purring is associated with happiness, and despite the pain of delivery, the cat may be truly feeling contentment as she brings new life into the world.)

During the second stage of labor, the contractions get stronger and the cat will begin to push to expel the new birth. Cats in labor often lie on their side and lift one hind leg to ease delivery.

Each kitten is born wet and messy. The mother severs the umbilical cord by biting it. When the placenta is expelled, she eats it. For feral cats, this nourishment enables a mother cat to spend all of her time in the nest during the crucial first days.

The mother cat devotes herself to each kitten as she is born. She takes particular care to wash the new kitten's face and head to clear away membranes and fluids and to stimulate the first breaths. She also washes the kitten's entire body and then aligns her fur appropriately to give her maximum insulation. During the washing process, the new mother becomes familiar with the scent, shape, and appearance of each new member of her family.

After attending to the kitten, the mother cat cleans her genital area before the next kitten is born.

A cat's labor can be long or short. There is no standard length of time, even with the same mother in her second, third, or tenth litter. An individual birth can take as little as ten or fifteen minutes; on the other hand, there can be up to several hours between deliveries. If the lapsed time between kittens does seem overly long to you and/or you sense that your cat is struggling, do call your vet or take her to a twenty-four-hour emergency clinic. Sometimes a kitten can get stuck and medical attention will be needed to prevent serious complications. Most cat births, however, proceed without problems.

Newborn kittens find their way to a nipple through scent and sensation.

The Newborn Kittens

At birth, kittens are deaf and their eyes are sealed shut. But through some ancient instincts of touch and smell, each one makes her way to the mother's teats and begins to suckle. Newborn kittens eat very little at a time (about a teaspoon), but they nurse frequently. To stimulate waste elimination, the mother cat licks the anal area of each kitten frequently.

Newborn kittens instinctively huddle together and near to the mother for warmth. They do nothing but eat and sleep. Unlike newborn horses, they do not have enough strength in the muscles of their legs to stand. So they drag themselves in a swimlike motion. It is exhausting for a kitten to drag herself (using forelegs only) to the teat. Once there, a kitten may nurse on and off for up to eight hours a day.

With all of that sucking and sleeping, kittens gain weight very quickly. Most weigh about 3.5 to 4 ounces at birth. That weight can double in the first week.

During the first few days of life, most kittens choose a nipple and pretty much stay with it. Some scientists think this is a precursor to the

Myth, Magic and Medicine

For centuries, and sometimes still today, unwanted newborn kittens were routinely drowned. There is even a Polish legend about what happened when a litter was thrown into a river. It is said that nearby willows saw the mother cat crying for her little ones from the sloped bank. Sensing her pain, the willows dragged their branches into the water for the kittens to grab. With the kittens holding on tightly, the branches stood upright again. In memory, every spring the pussy willow tree bursts with little "kittens" of fur.

Myth, Magic and Medicine

All kittens are born with blue eyes. When they're about six weeks old, the eyes begin to change color. The color of the eyes that each cat will have as an adult is not established until the cat is about three months old.

In ancient Egypt, it was believed that the life-giving rays of the sun were kept safely in cats' eyes during the night.

In Peru, Quechua natives fear a mythical cat with glowing eyes called the Ccoa. It is said to have the power to bring down hail or lightning from the sky.

territorial instinct that cats display later in life. The most preferable place is near the mom's armpit; the weakest kitten often gets the farthest back teat.

Kittens begin to acquire the ability to hear at about the fourth day of life when the auditory

Fame and Fortune

One of the most famous cat illustrators in history was the Swiss-born artist, Théophile-Alexandre Steinlen (1859–1923). He moved permanently to Paris at the age of twenty-three and became a French citizen. Today he is referred to as just Steinlen, and the name is virtually synonymous with studies of cats in motion. Kittens were his favorite subject.

By the time a kitten is five weeks old, the mother often stands away (both physically and psychologically) and encourages the kitten to stop nursing.

canals begin to open. By two weeks, the ear canals are fully open, but the kitten still doesn't have the full range of hearing. That comes at about three months old.

The eyes of most cats begin to open between day five and day ten of life, and they usually take about three more days to open fully. But the kitten still doesn't have very good vision. Only after about four weeks can a kitten begin to judge distance and depth accurately. Vision is fully developed at about four months of age.

By the time they're three weeks old, most kittens are able to stand and start to walk, even if they're a bit shaky. Their ears are also beginning to stand up firmly. By four weeks, kittens often hold their tails upright and their heads high.

The Caring Cat Mother

In the beginning, the mother cat must do everything for her litter of kittens. She keeps them warm and safe, she provides their food, she removes their waste material, and she keeps the nest clean. A mother cat spends three-quarters of her time in the nest with her kittens for the first four to five weeks of their lives.

For added safety, however, a queen usually moves her kittens to a new nest area soon after their birth, or at least before their fourth week of life begins. She picks each kitten up by the scruff of the neck and carries her to the new nest site. The kitten instinctively relaxes during this process: her forelegs go limp and her tail and hind legs curl inward. The relaxed body of the kitten and the mother's accurate grip assure safe transport. Then the mother goes back to the original nest for the next kitten, until all are resettled.

Over time, as the demand for her milk increases and the supply diminishes, the mother begins the process of weaning. The first movements toward separation usually occur near the end of the third week. Slowly the mother cat becomes less available and somewhat less tolerant of the kittens' demands. As the kittens grow older, the mother cat is sometimes caring and affectionate, and sometimes impatient. Eventually, she pushes the kittens away, especially as owners begin to provide food for the kittens and they discover that it tastes good!

CHAPTER 14

 **Kittens!**

In This Chapter

➤ Abandoned kitten or kittens

➤ How to tell the boys from the girls

➤ Kittens at five to six weeks old

➤ What to expect at seven to ten weeks old

This chapter almost calls out for a consultation with Dr. Benjamin Spock, who wrote *The Common Sense Book of Baby and Child Care*. No, I'm not saying that raising kittens is as complicated as raising children. But, well, in some ways, almost. There are two major differences: (1) You have a live-in nanny and teacher in the mother cat and (2) it doesn't take nearly as long. A cat who is a little past the age of one year is the human equivalent of an eighteen-year-old. Ready to vote, guard the territory, have babies, and make a commitment to lifelong companionship.

The experience of raising a kitten is full of awe and wonder. The best I can do in this short space is to give you a few hints about what to expect. As you read, just remember that dealing with each and every kitten is a unique blend of joy, laughter, frustration, sometimes anger, and always love—warm, tender, satisfying love.

Someone Said

"A kitten is in the animal world what a rosebud is in a garden."

—Robert Southey (1774–1843) English romantic poet

The Foundling

If kittens are born in your home, there is little to do for the first month of their lives except watch. Mom does all the work. Once the kittens' eyes are open, you can begin to put your fingers next to their faces and to handle them (with the queen's permission) so that they will become accustomed to human contact and human scent. But don't hold a kitten too long, and be sure to put him back in exactly the place you took him from.

But what if you find an orphaned kitten or two (or more) huddled in the weeds under a lamppost in an urban parking lot? Or what if someone has cruelly dumped a kitten or even an entire litter into the foundation plantings near your front doorstep? Be aware that very young kittens in those situations may or may not survive, no matter how much you try to help. Call in your brain to overrule your heart and put aside even the possibility of feeling guilty if a kitten does die. Then get to work.

Myth, Magic and Medicine

Even among indoor home births, the mortality rate for kittens is high. If you include stillborns, some estimates from cat authorities are as high as 20 percent. Among feral cats, the kitten mortality rate is dependent upon climate and location, and it's not specifically known. But it is certainly much higher. Sometimes only one or two kittens survive to become independent.

First try the local shelters. Not all will accept newborns, but try anyway; they may be able to help. If you decide to proceed independently, have the foundling checked by a vet to be certain he doesn't harbor contagious diseases or parasites. Meanwhile, keep the kitten(s) warm.

At about one week old, a kitten's body temperature is usually around 100 degrees Fahrenheit. He needs to maintain that body temperature despite his inability to do so naturally. In normal situations, kittens get their warmth from their mothers. Without the mother cat around, you'll have to keep a kitten box (or even a room) at about 80 degrees minimum for about twenty days. You can also wrap old-fashioned hot water bottles in towels to add warmth in a kitten box. Some people use circulating hot water pads or grain bags heated in the microwave and wrapped in towels.

Feeding the foundling kitten is a round-the-clock job. Most important: do not use cow's milk; it does not adequately substitute for mother's milk, and some kittens cannot tolerate it. Your best option is to purchase orphaned kitten formula at your pet supply store. Ask your veterinarian for recommendations on both formula and feeding tools.

If you cannot get the formula and you live in a rural area, sheep's milk can stand in for cat's milk.

Very small kittens need to be fed at a minimum of every four hours —every three hours is better. This can be increased to six-hour intervals as the kittens grow. Kittens over 5 ounces can usually do well at six- to eight-hour intervals.

If you know of a queen in your area who has recently given birth to a relatively small litter, you can attempt to facilitate a cat adoption. Many nursing cats will accept a new kitten or two of approximately the same age and size as their own. Hold the new kitten together with the mother's own babies so that some scent can be transferred. If the mother is accepting, let her lick the new kitten. In this way she is transferring her scent to the newcomer. Watch as the new kitten begins to nurse to be sure that the mother and the other kittens continue to be accepting. Cat adoption of this kind usually works best with very young kittens.

Some nursing queens will accept a newcomer as their own.

CATch Words

Our word *kitten* comes to us from the Middle English *kitoun*, or going back even farther, from the Old French *chitoun*.

The first actual appearance of the word *kitten* in English occurred in 1377. Some experts associate it with the Turkish word for cat, which is *keti*.

In British and American slang, to be having kittens is to be very nervous or upset.

How to Tell the Boys from the Girls

It's not easy to tell a boy kitten from a girl kitten, and the difficulty has resulted in many misnamed pets. Among my own cats, the beautiful silver-gray we named Schumann, had to be renamed Clara after a night of caterwauling outside our bedroom window. Yes, there were kittens.

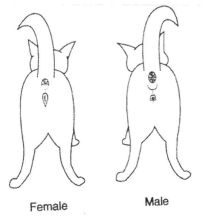

Female   Male

Distance is the key to differentiating sexes in young kittens; the two openings in the anal area are farther apart in a young male. Of course, your vet can tell boys from girls with certainty. So why do *we* have so much trouble?

Unlike dogs and most mammals, the cat penis does not hang down parallel to the abdomen. It is relatively small, and when the cat is standing it points in a direction opposite the nose.

In general physical appearance, most male kittens cannot be differentiated from females until they reach puberty at about five months old, and even then people can't always tell. The male cat is usually (but not always) larger than the female. After the age of five months, the boys begin to develop thicker skin on their necks, presumably to protect them in fights with other male cats. Their cheek ruffs grow to make their heads look larger.

CATch Words

Cheek ruff is extra hair on the outer part, or cheeks, of a male cat's face that grows once the cat has reached maturity.

Weaning

By six weeks of age, most kittens are fully trained to the litter box (get one with 2- to 3-inch-high sides), and they will be exploring your house. If you don't want open season on draperies and furniture, not to mention electrical cords, it is probably a good idea to confine them to one room.

Kittens should be almost completely weaned by this time. Most will, however, try to get whatever they can from a tolerant mother (like teenagers, right?). Many begin to eat strained baby food meats as young as four weeks. Now is the time to buy specialty kitten chow.

Cute and cuddly, fierce and fiery, kittens are comic miniatures. Do play with them! They will chase string and shadows and pounce on each other's tails. There will even be some roughhouse biting and scratching among littermates. Play activity starts out tentatively at about four weeks and increases until it peaks at about eleven weeks. By then, most responsible breeders are finding homes for the kittens.

Handle the kittens, cuddle them, challenge them. Just about all cat experts agree that kittens who are lovingly handled during their early life make better companion cats for the remainder of their lives. They also handle stress of all kinds better.

Seven to Ten Weeks

Kittens should be seen by a veterinarian when they are between six and eight weeks old. Feline distemper shots are usually given at that time. Feline leukemia virus vaccinations are usually started at about nine weeks. Rabies inoculations and other vaccines can be given at other intervals as required by state law or as thought necessary by your vet.

Because state laws, manufacturer's recommendations for certain vaccines, differ widely, it's impossible to give you a hard-and-fast schedule for vaccinating your litter in these pages. Note,, that rabies vaccine cannot be given before the kitten is 12 weeks of age. At that time the veterinarian can give the kitten a 1 year protection against rabies.

By the time they are eight weeks old, kittens are beginning to think and act like cats. By ten weeks, they may be slimmer and smaller than adult cats, but their proportions and postures are essentially the same. The kitten's motor coordination is well developed at this time, and if it weren't for their inexperience and overexuberance, they could hunt and act as cats.

Someone Said

"A kitten is the most irresistible comedian in the world. Its wide-open eyes gleam with wonder and mirth. It darts madly at nothing at all, and then, as though suddenly checked in the pursuit, prances sideways on its hind legs with ridiculous agility and zeal."

—Agnes Repplier (1855–1950) American writer

Fame and Fortune

A stray kitten spent more time at 10 Downing Street than any of Britain's Prime Ministers. His name was Wilberforce, and he lived (and moused) there from 1973 to 1987, serving under four British heads of state: Edward Heath, Harold Wilson, Jim Callaghan, and, of course, Margaret Thatcher, who once bought a tin of sardines for him in a Moscow marketplace. Wilberforce was known as the best mouser in Britain. He died in retirement in 1988.

Someone Said

"My love she is a kitten,

And my heart's a ball of string."

—Henry S. Leigh (1837–1883) British poet

Although they are beginning to look and act a lot like adult cats, most careful breeders will not release kittens until they are almost twelve weeks old. It is during the time from six to twelve weeks that the mother teaches her kittens all the necessary survival skills that she knows. She also teaches them how to interact with humans.

Myth, Magic and Medicine

A kitten starts kneading, or paw paddling, at the mother cat's mammary glands at about three weeks of age. The instinctive purpose is to stimulate the flow of milk. The action of the forefeet, however, is exactly the same as what we see in the contented adult cat before she settles down on a comfortable couch or on her owner's lap.

Finding Homes

Some owners fall in love with and keep some or all of the kittens. This weakness (or perhaps reward) can lead to a houseful in no time at all. In fact, if a female cat is allowed outdoors, she may be pregnant again even before her kittens are ready to leave home. Unlike most mammals, cats can resume the estrus cycle while they are still nursing kittens. Think seriously about spaying after the first litter.

Begin your quest for homes as soon as the litter is born by telling friends, family, and neighbors that you now have kittens. (Tell it with glee!) But don't invite anyone in to see the babies until they are at least three weeks old. Before that, they are blind and deaf and cannot walk (not a good time to choose a kitten to take home).

CATch Words

Cat and Kittens is a popular public house sign in the United Kingdom. It refers to the large and small pewter pots in which beer was once served. Stealing these pots (which occurred with regular frequency) was called cat and kitten stealing.

Cat and the Fiddle is another name for many British public houses. The phrase probably comes from the nursery rhyme *Hey Diddle Diddle, the Cat and the Fiddle*. There is also a possible connection, however, to the once-popular game of Tipcat.

According to most surveys, your best hope for placing a kitten is with friends, relatives, and neighbors. After exhausting the list of everyone they know, some enterprising home breeders take all of the kittens in a box (after they are at least six but preferably twelve weeks old) door-to-door in and around their neighborhood. Others take them to an office, a Girl Scout or Cub Scout meeting, even to a Little League game. Responsible breeders guarantee to take the kitten back if it doesn't work out.

It may be the happiest time of the year, but Christmas is a problem for many cat breeders. People fantasize about how cute a kitten will look in the stocking hanging from the mantel. After the holiday madness is over, however, many kittens lose their homes. Some breeders will not allow a kitten to be picked up until just before the New Year, although they will supply photos or DVDs to Christmas buyers.

If you have a purebred, you will of course advertise your kittens. Today, advertising isn't just putting an ad in your local newspaper. Don't forget that cat fancy groups have very effective newsletters and websites. Posting on social-networking sites can also gather a lot of attention. In fact, those social networks also work for letting the world know you have the cutest moggy kittens in the world looking for good homes.

Kitten-Proofing

Kitten-proofing a house is a little like toddler-proofing. Your kitten will stick his little nose into everything that looks interesting (to a kitten, that's just about everything) and will try to manipulate, grab, or tear it with his tiny claws. Before you allow your kitten the run of the house, try to put valuables and breakables away or out of reach. Be especially careful about exposed electrical wiring, aluminum Christmas ornaments, jewelry, balls of yarn, children's toys, and nylon stockings—not to mention fish tanks and caged birds, of course.

Someone Said

Here's a poem that says it all:

The Christmas Kitten

I once was a cuddly kitten,
But now I am a stray,
'Cause when I was no longer fluffy,
They sent me on my way.
They've kept their big watchdog,
As he can bark and growl,
But I could fly at strangers,
If I caught them on the prowl.
I slink around their garbage can;
I mew outside their door.
But it's clear from their behavior,
They don't want me anymore.
Now I'm cold and hungry,
And getting very thin,
What have I done to hurt them
Why don't they let me in?
I crouch in sheds and boxes,
In my bedraggled fur,
So shivery and dejected,
I cannot even purr.
They have another kitten,
Their children's whole delight;
But probably next Christmas,
It will share my wretched plight.

—Author unknown

C Steinlen's "Awful End of a Goldfish"

Houseplants and Outdoor Plants

Kittens like to chew, especially on greenery. Some common indoor houseplants like philodendron and English ivy can be toxic. Among the other indoor and outdoor plants poisonous to kittens are azalea, chrysanthemum, daffodil, jack-in-the-pulpit, larkspur, marijuana, nutmeg, poinsettia, rhubarb, and skunk cabbage.

Among the nontoxic plants are jade, prayer plant, begonia, and coleus. But if you leave even these plants on a windowsill or within jumping reach on a table, you might come home from work and find them quite shredded. In fact, you may have to keep plants out of your kitten's living space for a year or so.

Pills, Garbage, Candy, and Toys

Prescription and nonprescription medications come in interesting shapes and colors, if you can look at the world from a kitten's point of view, that is. *They're really fun to bat around; they roll so nicely! And, hmmmm, maybe they taste good too.*

Be sure to keep all your medications capped and out of reach. Cats have unusual reactions to many substances. Tylenol and aspirin can kill kittens. And many things in the trash or left out on a table can cause serious illness. Other dangers are potato skins and their eyes, wrapped and unwrapped chocolate kisses, small safety pins, coins, buttons, and anything else that you would keep out of a toddler's grasp.

And don't forget that kittens lick their feet. Anything that they scratch at or walk through can leave residue on their toes, pads, and nails. When grooming themselves, kittens can ingest harmful substances even though we humans see no trace of anything unusual.

The Importance of Play

Like children, kittens learn through play. Their very first toy, at about six or seven weeks of age, is usually the tail of a littermate. They bat at their littermates' flicking tails but if the other owner of the tail moves away, the batting kitten may or may not follow (chase).

Some experts believe that tail chasing is an instinct that precedes hunting behavior. Strangely enough, however, some kittens seem to be tail chasers from a very young age without instruction, while other do not develop the chasing and swatting instinct until later—perhaps learning from their mother or from watching their littermates.

Someone Said

"The playful kitten, with its pretty little tigerish gambols, is infinitely more amusing than half the people one is obliged to live with in the world."

—Lady Sydney Morgan (1778–1859) Irish novelist

What to Do with Prey

How kittens learn to handle prey is another area where questions about learned behavior versus instinct come up. When a mother cat is allowed outdoors, she may bring back a dead mouse and introduce her kittens to a new animal in their world. Usually she will not allow them to eat it but will let them watch as she eats it. Before her dinner, they are allowed to sniff at it and get the idea that it is different from them.

When the kittens are nine weeks or older, the outdoor mother may bring live prey back to the nest and literally teach her offspring how to kill it. Here's where the controversial discussions come in. Kittens who are reared by indoor mothers also learn to kill prey. So is the behavior learned or instinct or both?

Did You Notice the Cat?

Every owner of an indoor-outdoor cat finds a gift of dead prey in the house from time to time. Sometimes, however, the "gift" is still alive. People chase about trying to capture it; would young kittens do the same? It depends.

At the time that our friends Debbie and Ernest had two three-month-old kittens (Maverick and Matilda) living with them (shelter cats but not related to each other), a field mouse got into the kitchen through a garage door left ajar. Debbie quickly closed all the kitchen doors so the visitor could go no further. But then what?

Ernest began chasing from corner to corner with a bath towel in hand, hoping to throw it on top of the mouse, catch it, and let it go. Matilda was delighted. She ran wildly after the mouse, coming ever so close to a catch time and time again. Kitchen chairs fell over, a coffee cup was broken, there were a few screams, and finally Debbie thought maybe she should open the garage door. When she did, it was only a few minutes before the desperate mouse departed.

And what was Maverick doing all this time. He sat in the middle of the kitchen floor and watched. No interest whatsoever.

Learning about Human Nature

Kittens learn about people by interacting with us. The interaction begins with human handling while the kitten is still thinking only about eating and sleeping. But as the kitten gets older, the best human interaction is play. By chasing, pouncing, and batting with a person, the kitten accepts the human as a part of the litter—someone to share with, have fun with, and keep warm with. Kittens who know human contact from their earliest weeks are usually more socially adaptable and make better pets.

Music and Cats

Kittens and cats seem to enjoy music. In fact, some ailurophiles suggest leaving the radio playing on an all-music station while the human inhabitants are away at work. Those cat fanciers swear that the sound is company for both kittens and cats. They say it keeps them happier and out of trouble.

And what do the kittens and cats hear when the radio is playing? We know they hear more than we do. But what is it about the rhythm, tempo, and tonality in music that felines find so intriguing. I'm sure they'd tell us, if only they could speak our language.

Did You Notice the Cat?

Italian composer Domenico Scarlatti (1685–1757) loved his cat, Pulcinella. The beautiful cat was particularly fond of walking around on the keyboard of Scarlatti's harpsichord. One day her prancing caught the composer's attention. He wrote down what he heard and the cat created music. Today, Scarlatti's Fugue in G minor (L499) is known in the musical world as the Cat's Fugue.

Other notable composers have also found inspiration in the cat. Tchaikovsky wrote "Puss-in-Boots and the White Cat." When Chopin's cat spent some time on the piano keyboard, the Polish pianist wrote the "Cat Waltz." Stravinsky wrote "Cat Lullabies." In collaboration with the French writer (and cat lover) Colette, Maurice Ravel wrote the opera *The Child and the Enchantments*. (The opera has a brilliant cat duet sung by Tom Cat and She Cat.)

Fame and Fortune

Of course we all know Andrew Lloyd Webber's music for the Broadway hit *Cats*. But other contemporary composers have paid tribute to their cats too:

➤ Ian Anderson, a member of Jethro Tull, writes about his cats on the official Jethro Tull website. The group has also recently joined Facebook. His cat Rupi was the subject of the title song in his 2004 solo album *Rupi's Dance*.

➤ Cats were the favorite pet of Beatles star John Lennon. As a boy he rode his bicycle to the local fishmonger's store to buy hake for his cat. (Hake is a fish related to the cod family.)

➤ British musician Freddie Mercury performed with and wrote songs for the rock group Queen. A true ailurophile, he had many cats, and he wrote songs about them. A favorite was a female tabby named Delilah, and *Delilah* is a song title released on the Queen album called *Innuendo*. Freddie Mercury dedicated his first solo album to his cats: Tom, Jerry, Oscar, Tiffany, Delilah, Goliath, Miko, Romeo, and Lily.

➤ Whitney Houston, award-winning singer, named her cat Marilyn Miste.

➤ Yoko Ono, a Japanese musician, author, peace activist, and wife of John Lennon had two favorite cats named Misha and Sascha.

➤ Joel Thomas Zimmerman is better known as deadmau5 (pronounced "dead mouse"). His cat is called Professor Meowingtons PhD.

CHAPTER 15

Good to Eat (Maybe)

In This Chapter

➤ What cats need to eat every day

➤ Table scraps and other treats

➤ Special needs diets

➤ Outdoor food

If cats were to go on vacation, they'd certainly would have liked to have spent some time in the Fulton Street Fish Market in New York City, alas, now moved to The Bronx and lacking the charm. Less metropolitan cats have already staked out territories around deep-sea fishing resorts and lakeside fishing camps around the country. Cats like the taste of fish.

One of my favorite childhood memories was going for lobster dinners at a shack-type restaurant at the mouth of the Niantic River on Long Island Sound. The outdoor picnic tables were covered with oiled paper. The lobsters were brought out on oversized paper platters. And cats were everywhere. They curled around your legs as you ate, waiting for accidental droppings of lungs or cartilage. The bravest ones jumped on the seats and sat beside you all during dinner. They had all learned not to walk on the tables.

The Need for Protein

Cats come from a long line of carnivores. Their digestive system has evolved to top-notch efficiency at processing animal protein. Unlike us, they cannot survive as vegetarians; although, living with us, they have adopted some very human omnivore tastes, like Brie, for instance.

True omnivores such as rats need only about 4 percent of their diet to be composed of protein. Cats need almost 20 percent in order to remain healthy. Some commercial cat foods, however, claim to be vegetarian. The company adds plant protein and synthetic matter in just the right portions.

Of course, fish aren't the cat's only preference nor are they available everywhere in our country for the taking. Suburban and country feral cats get their protein from the small prey that they capture. Their most common foods are birds and rodents of all kinds. City feral cats not only feed on small prey but also on human garbage.

Someone Said

"Cats know how to obtain food without labour, shelter without confinement, and love without penalties."

—W. L. (Walter Lionel) George (1882–1926) English writer

Your Cat's Nutrition

Now let's stop fantasizing about the wild life and turn to the cats who "belong" to us. Many cats eat when hungry at various times throughout the day. This particular preference works well for owners who put out dry food and allow their pets to self-feed. Moist food, however, should not be left out for a cat to eat at will because it can easily spoil, especially in warm weather. The bacteria in spoiled food affect cats in just the same way as they affect us. Everybody gets sick.

Despite their preferences for many small meals, cats do adapt well to being fed on a schedule. If you have an indoor cat, you get to decide what, when, and where she will eat. Your decisions will make a difference in her life.

With supermarkets, Walmarts, and pet supply stores everywhere, you have several choices for feeding your cat: moist commercial canned or packaged food; semimoist soft tidbits; hard commercial dry food; fresh home-cooked food, including human snacks; and commercial cat treats.

CATch Words

Neophobia is a term for a cat's tendency to reject unfamiliar flavors. Felines also quickly learn to turn their noses up at any food that they have tasted once and found unpleasant.

Pica is the term for the tendency of some cats to enjoy chewing on indigestible materials, for example wool, nylon, plastic (especially those bottle rings that hold six soda cans together), paper, string, and even coal. This chewing preference can endanger their health and even cause death if enough of a substance is ingested.

Moist Commercial Cat Food

The small containers of commercial cat food come in a vast variety of flavors like salmon, chicken, and shrimp. Most also contain other nutrients and a good deal of gelatin.

Hold on! Don't shake your head as though you're being cheated by the gelatin; most cats will tell you they like the jelly part. It's probably more the texture that holds the appeal, not the taste. In any case, moist cat foods may be as much as 75 percent water. Given the cat's low fluid requirements, the moist food might just keep them from drinking from the nearest dripping faucet.

Many manufacturers now have gourmet or premium cat food lines. Each container is carefully filled with exactly the same ingredients, in the same proportions. But that doesn't necessarily make them better. Many cats fed on select diets put on excess weight.

On the other hand, premium foods are at least consistent. Less expensive brands may vary the proportion of ingredients based on cost. Premium foods also claim that they are more efficiently digested and produce less waste.

Be cautious in making changes in your food selection and routine. It may not always be a good idea to buy whatever is on sale, offered as a buy one get one free deal, or has a coupon available. Remember cats don't like change, and sudden changes in food can cause an upset digestive system and sometimes diarrhea.

Fame and Fortune

Among the heaviest cats on record are:

➤ Himmy, a neutered male tabby lived in Queensland, Australia. He made the *Guinness World Records 2008* at 46 pounds 15.25 ounces. He was ten years old when he died of respiratory failure.

➤ Tiger, a long-haired Persian mixed breed, once held the record at 43 pounds.

(Please note: Guinness is no longer accepting candidates for this record because they do not want to encourage overfeeding.)

Whether you choose gourmet or the less expensive, everyday moist food varieties, do stop to read those labels, at least occasionally. One college professor friend of mine who reads everything noticed blueberries and grape seeds in one ingredients list. Should cats eat blueberries or grape seeds even if they do have millions of antioxidants?

Myth, Magic and Medicine

Taurine is a colorless amino acid that is essential in a cat's diet. In 1978, scientists discovered that insufficient taurine leads to macular degeneration and eventually blindness in cats. In 1986, a link was found between insufficient taurine and cat heart disease.

Commercial cat food manufacturers now routinely add this amino acid to their cat food formulas. It is not included in dog food, however, because most dogs have no need for it. This is just another reason why cats should not be fed on dog food!

Semimoist Food

Semimoist food comes in a variety of flavors—even mixed flavors. It is 25 to 40 percent water. It doesn't spoil when left out for several hours like moist cat food, but it does become brittle and certainly less appealing over time. If you choose this feeding method, be sure to read the label. The mix should not contain propylene glycol, which is known to cause blood problems in some cats. Most manufacturers have eliminated this ingredient.

Dry Food

Dry food comes in boxes, large bags, and even plastic bins for economy purchases (or multi-cat households). Many widely available brands are carefully formulated to meet feline nutrition needs. But not all brands! Check the ingredients list and if you have questions, ask you veterinarian for an opinion. Dry cat food also stores well, and it doesn't spoil when left out for the cat. Not spoiling even in the heat of summer is very handy if you happen to be going away for a few days. It might be a good idea, therefore, to accustom your cat to eating dry cat food at least some of the time. Usually dry cat food contains less than 10 percent water.

There is, however, a drawback to leaving dry cat food in your garage for your indoor-outdoor cat. Other animals can follow her lead and you may very well be feeding the neighborhood feral cats and some uninvited guests such as a raccoons, a possums, or even a stray dog or coyote.

Your Home Cooking

Yes, some people cook for their cats. And some people feed their cats entirely on table scraps. Both options can work, but it's a good idea to check with your veterinarian to be sure the cat's protein and other nutrient needs are being met. The vet may suggest vitamin tablets or supplements just to be on the safe side.

Myth, Magic and Medicine

In Great Britain, there is a superstition that it is bad luck to allow a cat on the dining table.

The French don't seem to agree:

➤ National leader Charles de Gaulle had a favorite pet, Gris-Gris. (*Gris* means gray.) Was the cat allowed on the table? Well, he was allowed everywhere else!

➤ Writer George Sand (real name Amandine Dudevant) who was both mistress and loving caretaker of Frederic Chopin, ate breakfast from the same bowl as her cat, Minou.

➤ 1921 Nobel Prize for Literature winner Anatole France was loving and permissive with his cat, Hamilcar.

➤ The prolific poet, dramatist, novelist, journalist, art critic, and literary critic, Pierre Jules Théophile Gautier allowed his cat, Madame Theophile, to "steal" food from his fork.

➤ Alexandre Dumas, the author of *The Three Musketeers* and numerous other works of historical fiction, called his cat Le Docteur.

➤ King Louis XV allowed his white cat to play on the table during Counsels of State and sometimes durng dinner.

➤ King Louis XVI and his wife Marie Antoinette allowed their Angora cats to walk about on the tables during court parties.

➤ Cardinal Richelieu (King Louis XIII's chief minister) lived with and loved dozens of cats, and they went everywhere they wanted to go.

Treats

Treats might be the chicken skin you remove before you eat the meat or perhaps the shrimp and spinach dip left in the dish after the Super Bowl party. Some cats like ice cream. There are lots of ways to spoil your cat—just remember to avoid chocolate!

Cat food manufacturers have not ignored the human temptation to express their love for their cats with treats. Virtually everywhere that groceries are sold, you can buy bags of cat food treats. They come in both hard and semimoist varieties. The hard versions are even advertised as helping to keep your cat's teeth both cleaner and tartar-free and her breath smelling sweeter (to humans).

Someone Said

"Cats eat what hussies spare." (*Hussies* is a very old word for housewives.)

—British proverb

Reading the Label

Reading cat food labels is not fun. It sometimes feels as though you should have studied for the test on label reading and received a graduation certificate confirming your competence. But you don't have to understand everything.

First of all, understand that all of the ingredients in any type of cat food are listed by weight in descending order. Meat, fish, or poultry should appear first in the best of foods. Cereal grains and soybeans are also acceptable near the top of the list.

You should also realize that the guaranteed analysis printed on most labels is not much of a guide to the quality of the product. The analysis is not required to separate the digestible protein, fat, and fiber in the food from the indigestible (filler). The numbers that you see are for the crude protein, fat, and fiber. *Crude* means digestible and indigestible are mixed together in determining the analysis.

The oversight group for cat food is the Association of American Feed Control Officials (AAFCO). It sets standards for what is considered nutritionally complete. Your choice for a daily feed for your cat should meet those standards. Some treat foods do not meet the standards and should be labeled "not to be fed as a sole diet" or "for intermittent feeding only."

Someone Said

"A cat isn't fussy—just so long as you remember he likes his milk in the shallow, rose-patterned saucer and his fish on the blue plate. From which he will take it, and eat it off the floor."

—Arthur Bridges (1984–) American actor

Milk

A saucer of milk has been associated with cats and kittens for centuries. You may be surprised to learn, however, that cow's milk is not needed in a cat's diet, even though most cats do like it. Many kittens become lactose intolerant as they approach adulthood and are often quite allergic to cow's milk, which contains considerable lactose. They will still drink it, however, so check out the milk allocation if your cat is having stomach problems.

Milk should never be used as a substitute for fresh water. A cat's water bowl should be refilled regularly. Milk also should not be left out for long periods unattended because it does spoil. Light cream or half-and-half, although richer and tastier, is just as bad, maybe worse, for your cat's digestive system. Some companies are now producing formulated milk especially for cats, but it has not become widely popular to date.

Special Diets

Pet food and pet-related merchandise are becoming such a major item on most shoppers' weekly grocery lists that some supermarkets actually have entire separate aisles for dogs and cats. It's easy to find kitten diets, weight-conscious diets, and diets for older cats. More expensive, but generally available, are the so-called natural diets which are supposed to contain best-quality ingredients and be manufactured under more stringent guidelines.

For even more special diet products, you may have to make a trip to a pet supply store or your veterinarian. It's always a good idea to have a veterinarian advise you before switching your cat's food to one of these products. Be certain you have your goals firmly in mind. There are low-calorie diets for slimming down. There are low-phosphorus, low-protein foods for cats who have problems with their kidneys. Some special diet formulas ensure acidic urine production; some promise to help with the smooth functioning of the entire digestive tract.

Cat Salads

Dog owners who walk their pets on a leash become quite accustomed to watching Fido stop every few feet to sniff the grass. The dog is sniffing for the scents left by previous passersby, both other dogs and cats. It's part of the territory thing. But many owners are surprised when they see their dogs stop to eat some grass. Cats eat grass too.

Cats may be carnivores, but they also know that grass and other greenery can help the digestive process. Sometimes they eat grass to help induce the vomiting of a hair ball. Many experts suggest that owners of indoor cats keep a small planter of grass growing indoors for the occasional cat salad. Of course you may think this is silly and choose not to do it, but be warned that if there's no grass, Kitty might choose from among your more expensive and more precious houseplants; some of which may cause digestive problems, some of which are poisonous.

Vitamins and Supplements

Lots of humans are hooked on filling their cupboards with pill bottles. They think the vitamins, minerals, and other supplements inside the various containers can solve virtually any human health problem. Meanwhile, many of these same vitamin and supplement advocates eat greasy fast food and wash it all down with sugar-laden "soft drinks" (which are really hard, hard, hard on the systems of the body). Fortunately, cats don't follow this lead.

Thanks to the science behind commercially produced cat food, most domestic cats do not need supplemental vitamins. Everything they need for good health is in the food formula.

Many veterinarians say that they see more health problems with pets suffering from vitamin excesses or toxicities than those related to vitamin deficiencies. And guess who gives the cats the extra vitamins.

Keep in mind that if your cat food contains at least the minimum required amount of the most important vitamins (and some foods contain many times the minimum), giving your cat still more could do harm rather than good. And never give a cat vitamins meant for humans (not even a children's dose) or dogs. To repeat: the cat digestive system is different from ours and our dogs'.

Myth, Magic and Medicine

Until the early twentieth century, virtually everyone (educated or uneducated, rich or poor) had little or no knowledge of the importance of cat nourishment or how cats might influence human health. In fact, cats were blamed for many diseases and also given responsibility for many impossible curative powers.

➤ In 1344, there was an outbreak of St. Vitus Dance (a nervous-system disease) in the French town of Metz. Someone in authority decided that cats were the cause and the town's cats were rounded up and publicly burned.

➤ One of the worst Black Death (bubonic plague) epidemics of the Middle Ages (1347–1348) was blamed on cats. Today we know the disease is spread by rat fleas. But back then, the Lord Mayor of London and many other officials all over Europe ordered that all cats be destroyed. Besides killing many innocent cats, the order actually allowed the rat population to increase, thus prolonging the spread of the disease.

➤ Written advice from 1602 told how to beat out and retaliate against a witch who might be casting spells, especially on a child. First, you must find a black cat who is seven years old and the seventh cat to be born in a litter. To improve health, kill the cat, roast her heart, and give some of it to the child to eat at bedtime for seven consecutive nights. For retaliation, take the blood from that heart and paint it on the witch's doorpost or throw it on her doorstep during the night. The proximity of the cat's blood will cause a sore and great pain in the witch's belly. (Of course, these procedures couldn't happen too often because of the caveats: the cat had to be black, seven years old, and the seventh born.)

Outdoor Food Sources

Catching and eating prey is a basic cat instinct. Indoor cats work around this basic drive by using toys and other play objects to pounce upon and catch. Often the owners really do have to spend a considerable amount of time playing with their indoor cats to keep them happy.

Catching outdoor prey may fill a good part of a day with adventure and challenges for outdoor cats, but how good is the end product in terms of nutrition? Actually, quite good. With small rodents, the cat usually devours the entire animal. There's plenty of protein and even calcium and other minerals. With birds, the cat doesn't much like feathers, but otherwise the captured and killed prize satisfies her taste preferences, provides all the necessary nutrition for maintaining good health, and fulfills instinctual cat drives.

There is, however, a problem: parasites. When your cat is eating prey, you and your cat don't know what microscopic cells or worms or other parasites for that matter are in that prey. You don't know where the prey has been or what it has eaten. In some cases, poisons or chemicals on the skin of prey can seriously harm a cat.

The other outdoor food source is human garbage. Some cats hang around the back doors of restaurants; some form colonies near condominium or apartment building dumpsters because stuff does accidentally fall out more than just occasionally. And besides, some "kindly" people actually throw food on the ground for the cats, especially at tourist sites like the steps near the fountains of Rome.

The discussion could go on, but let's just say that prey and garbage are definitely a contributing factors to the much shorter life expectancy of a feral or indoor-outdoor cat. Food as a killer beats out weather and cat fights and comes in right after car accidents.

Fame and Fortune

You'll only see this piece of art on the Internet or perhaps reprinted in books because the nineteenth-century Japanese watercolor titled *Sleeping Cat* is held in a private collection. We don't know the name of the artist, but how beautiful is this fat cat!

About Weight

The Duchess of Windsor (Wallis Simpson, the American divorcée who persuaded King Edward VIII to abdicate the throne to the United Kingdom) once said, "A woman can't be too rich or too thin." The words have echoed in American society ever since, driving some young girls to anorexia and making both men and women unhappy every time they get on the scale.

The influence has even trickled down to cats. How many owners have put Kitty on a strict weight-reduction diet because some friend said she seemed to be getting fat. Well, what is considered fat for a cat?

Like human weight, a cat's weight is determined by many factors. How much she is being fed is only one of them. DNA actually determines normal (not being starved or stuffed) weight just as much as it determines height. (Have you ever seen a skinny English bulldog or a fat Italian greyhound?) The brain and its chemicals also act upon body weight, often working to get the body back to the size and fat content it was before a weight-loss diet. And hormones and emotions have myriad effects on both weight loss and weight gain.

Did You Notice the Cat?

Being overweight has been a human concern for centuries, but it hasn't always had a negative connotation. In Albrecht Dürer's 1504 engraving, neither Adam nor Eve look particularly svelte, and the cat at their feet would be called overweight today.

OK, so we need something besides pounds to gauge healthy weight. Most cat authorities will tell you that if you cannot easily feel your cat's ribs, she is too fat. On the other hand, if you can see your cat's ribs through the fur, she is too skinny. That advice leaves a lot to personal judgment, however. Other measuring sticks to determining the ideal weight of your cat is to ask yourself if she is happy, if she moves about easily, if she can she jump up onto her favorite chair, if life still holds a lot of pleasurable moments for her. Consider all this while she sits purring in your lap and again before you cut her food ration in half.

Despite that good advice, I do believe that weight is a serious concern. Like humans in the United States, more and more cats are becoming obese. A recent survey estimated that 25 percent of indoor cats are now overweight. So keep both your brain and your heart in control. Don't just shrug off those growing stats. An overweight cat should be evaluated carefully, with all factors taken into consideration.

As in the human population, being overweight contributes to the onset of diabetes, arthritis, lethargy, some skin problems, and some cancers. At highest risk for putting on weight are placid, neutered indoor cats who don't get enough exercise and eat too much specialty food and table scraps. You can help your cat stay healthy by being aware of what she is being given to eat. You might also have your veterinarian check for thyroid problems if your cat is overweight.

CHAPTER 16

Cat Health Challenges and Handicaps

> ## In This Chapter
>
> ➤ Signs that your cat might be sick
> ➤ The flea and other skin dwellers
> ➤ Parasites inside your cat
> ➤ Ringworm, the fearsome fungus
> ➤ Handicaps

A healthy cat is one of the most beautiful animals on Earth. All his complex systems function together like a perfect piece of art or music to create a look of intense alertness, pride, and competence. (Not to mention love and joie de vivre

But as with humans, there's a lot of stuff in the world that can cause disease and discomfort. Some of it we can prevent; some of it we can treat and sometimes eliminate.

Someone Said

An excerpt from *Verses on a Cat*

You would not easily guess,
All the modes of distress
Which torture the tenants of earth;
And the various evils,
Which, like so many devils,
Attend the poor souls from their birth.

—Percy Bysshe Shelly (1792–1822) English lyric poet

The Flea

Who doesn't know at least something (the annoyance factor, for example) about fleas! There are many different kinds of fleas, each of which prefers a different host animal. In fact, the species continues to thrive on our planet. Back in the Middle

Ages, rat fleas spread the devastating Black Plague epidemics through Europe. And rat fleas are still around. Even today, there are some outbreaks of plague reported from time to time, especially in the western United States. Fortunately, we now have antibiotics epidemics of plague are no longer sustained and passed on from fleas. However even today, fleas carry blood parasites and tapeworms! They are never welcome in any home.

The most common negative reaction many cats have to fleas is flea bite allergy or hypersensitivity. In cats who have this sensitivity, even a few bites can cause skin reactions like itching, redness, bumps, and even hair loss. Some humans are allergic in the same way.

Sometimes cats are given anti-inflammatory medications to calm the reactions, but those prescriptionare not really a designed or indicated for long-term use. The very best thing you can do is keep a cat from getting fleas.

Ask your vet about flea collars and (more important) preventive medications applied to the skin or taken by mouth. Indoor cats in households without a dog can usually be kept from encountering fleas. Most dog fleas don't particularly like to live on cats, but they will jump up on Pussy if there's no other choice. They'll jump on humans too.

If a mother cat is allowed to go outdoors, she is likely to return to nursing her kittens with at least a few fleas hidden in her coat. The problem is that fleas reproduce with the speed of summer lightning!

Myth, Magic and Medicine

This image is a greatly magnified, fully matured flea. Fleas have strong survival behaviors and pass through several stages from egg to adult flea. A female flea will lay approximately twenty eggs at a time. They might hatch in a few days or in as long as two weeks. The larvae go through several molting sessions and then spin themselves into a cocoon in which they can continue to exist (being well protected), until they reach adulthood. That time lapse could be several months in your basement concrete floor or deep in your carpet fiber.

Usually when the weather is warmer and more humid or the temperature in the house is kept high, fleas are soon ready to emerge from the cocoon. Once out, they immediately look for a cat to jump on. These fleas live on blood sucked from a cat's body.

Dr. Shannon does not recommend that you get rid of fleas by using over-the-counter (purchased in all kinds of stores) flea-killer products for your cat. Some of them are toxic to the cat; some of them just don't work.

If you must use these products, be absolutely certain that the container is labeled specifically for cats. Many dog flea repellents are simply not safe for cats. Also never use more than one product at a time because you do not want to intermingle chemicals, especially if this is your cat's first exposure to flea medication.

Ticks

Ticks are found in wooded areas. You are unlikely to encounter one in your home if you keep indoor cats. Outdoor cats and dogs, however, are prey for the tick. These insects can transmit Rocky Mountain spotted fever and Lyme disease (which can cause severe arthritis and recurring fever and infection) to cats, dogs, and humans. Vaccines are available that prevent or at least reduce the aftereffects of infection.

Sometimes ticks climb directly on a human walking in the woods, with or without a cat or dog nearby. Sometimes after gorging themselves your blood or your pet's blood, they'll drop off and you'll find a gray oversized insect on the floor. I pick them up with a paper towel and flush the invader down the toilet. Some folks pop ticks and throw them in the garbage. I find the blood explosion repulsive. The best way to kill these bloated ticks is to drop them into a jar of alcohol

Ticks that have not eaten recently look like tiny mites. They are more agile in this form and can easily get onto the hair of an animal. Then they bury their heads in the skin and suck blood. When they are full to capacity, they look like gray or brown lima beans stuck to the skin.

The United States Center for Disease Control (CDC) has the following recommendations for removal of ticks embedded in the skin:

> ➤ Use fine-tipped tweezers to grasp the tick as close to the skin's surface as possible.

> ➤ Pull upward with steady, even pressure. Don't twist or jerk the tick; this can cause the mouth-parts to break off and remain in the skin. If this happens, remove the mouth-parts with tweezers. If you are unable to remove the mouth easily with clean tweezers, leave it alone and let the skin heal.

> ➤ After removing the tick, thoroughly clean the bite area and your hands with rubbing alcohol, an iodine scrub, or soap and water.

Definitely avoid folklore remedies such as "painting" the tick with nail polish or petroleum jelly, or using heat to make the tick detach from the skin. These folk- procedures are seriously risk laden. Ask your vet for information on the new tick-removal tools on the market.

If you see a tick on your cat or dog, don't try to pull it off by hand. Usually the body will break off and the head will remain embedded in the skin, possibly causing infection. Instead, follow the CDC recommendations. You can also try soaking a paper towel or cotton ball with alcohol and applying it to the head of the tick. Then wait two minutes or so, and remove the head and body with tweezers.If the area becomes red, swollen, or painful, see your veterinarian or (if the tick was on your body) your doctor.

Lice and Mites

Lice are another blood-feeding insect. They can bury themselves into the hair or fur of any warm-blooded animal, including humans , but different kinds of lice are species specific. Some lice prefer the head, some the body, and some the pubic area. And lice each prefer a specific animal.

Lice infestations of humans have increased worldwide since the mid-1960s. Scientists haven't kept careful track of cat infestations. Currently there is no product or treatment that can guarantee lice eradication with one application. Most experts suggest shampooing, combing, shaving, hot air, and silicone-based lotions available for cats at a vet's office. For human lice infestation, you should consult your doctor promptly. While human lice stay on humans and cat lice stay on cats, other paracites such as mites, ticks and fleas are not always so species specific. If you suspect infestation, don't wait too long before you seek professional help.

Smaller even than lice, there are several kinds of mites that infest cats, and they can cause several different diseases. They are truly minute in size (almost invisible), and they are more difficult to eradicate than fleas or lice. In most cases, you'll need veterinary help.

Parasites on the Inside

As a child, I thought worms were something squirmy that you threaded on a fishing hook. Little did I know that they are one of the most common health problems that cats and dogs face today. A majority of cats have worms at some point in their lives. Common symptoms requiring immediate attention are:

➤ a distended abdomen (sometimes called a pot belly);

➤ loss of appetite and weight loss;

➤ restless and uncomfortable behavior; and

➤ rubbing the anal area on carpets and floors or outdoors on grass.

The most common worms in a cat's world are roundworms, tapeworms, hookworms, coccidia, and trichinae. Common or not, however, you should never treat worms with your own remedies. It is essential that your veterinarian determine what kind of parasite infestation your cat is fighting before stepping in with the proper treatment. You'll need to gather stool samples, sometimes more than once.

Myth, Magic and Medicine

Many cat owners believe that regularly adding fresh shredded carrots or small amounts of diced garlic to a cat's food will keep him from getting worms. Don't count on it!

Infectious Diseases

Just as humans can get many viral and bacterial diseases, so can cats. For both species, some viruses are particularly dangerous and deadly. Others are like the common cold— they go away.

Feline Leukemia Virus (FeLV)

Feline leukemia virus was once the leading killer of cats but medicine seems to be gaining ground on this disease both in prevention and treatment. The virus thrives in bodily fluids,

CATch Words

Roundworms are the most common cat worm problem. Most cats are infected at least once during their lives, usually as kittens. The roundworm resides in the small intestine and resembles a 3- or 4-inch piece of spaghetti. They are sometimes visible in a cat's stool. Veterinarians routinely treat round worm infestation with prescription tablets.

Hookworms can enter a host in several ways: through contaminated feces, the milk of an infected mother, or by penetrating the skin. The most common symptom is diarrhea, but that's not the major worry. Hookworms can cause anemia. (Adult worms survive by sucking blood from the host.) Hookworms today are elimated with one or two doses of prescription medication or by injected medication.

Tapeworms are segmented worms. Owners sometimes see the grain-sized segments crawling near the cat's anus. Cats get tapeworms by eating fleas or mice that contain an immature stage of the parasite. Veterinary treatment is either by injection or by medication by mouth.

Coccidia are single-cell parasites. Cats and kittens get them by sniffing infected feces. Although adult cats, when medicated for elimination of coccidian, usually do well, kittens and older cats can become very ill and sometimes even die. Veterinary treatment is with oral medication.

including cat saliva tand it can spread through mutual grooming eating and drinking from the same dishes, and through bite wounds. Mothers can also pass it on to their kittens during nursing.

Outside the cat body, however, the virus does not live long. Dryness kills it quickly, which is why it is passed through fluids.

FeLV can cause cancer and anemia, and it renders the immune system virtually helpless. Without a good working immune system, the cat is susceptible to a large number of secondary infections.

There is now a vaccine available and it is effective in 80 to 90% of its usage. Blood tests can accurately determine if a cat is infected with the virus, even though the cat may appear to be healthy when in the early stages of the disease. Therefore, if you love cats, have every new or perspective cat tested, preferably before bringing him home. FeLV can spread to other cats, but it does not spread to humans.

Feline Immunodeficiency Virus (FIV)

This disease is similar to human immunodeficiency virus (HIV) and causes similar symptoms, but it is not the same disease. It is transmitted from one cat to another through bite wounds. Like HIV it suppresses the cat's immune system, but it may take years for symptoms to show up. It can be diagnosed through a blood test. It can eventually be deadly. FIV is not contagious to humans.

The only test for FIV available today is an antibody test. This limitation has caused some problems in health evaluation because sometimes a cat that has been vaccinated will show up positive. Also cats who have been exposed to the disease but do not have it could show up with positive antibodies. Therefore when a cat tests "positive" for FIV it does not necessarily have FIV. Most cats and shelters, however, assume that they do have the disease. Many cats test positive but live normal lives. If you get a positive test, talk with your veterinarian or a cat specialist.

Feline Infectious Peritonitis (FIP)

This is a disease that affects many different organs at the same time and is routinely fatal. Fortunately, it is relatively rare and affects only about 1 percent of the cat population.

Feline Calicivirus Virus and Herpesvirus

These viruses have symptoms like the human cold and are responsible for 80 to 90 percent of upper respiratory diseases in cats. Almost every cat gets one or the other at some time. Some cats never stop shedding the viruses, and while they appear healthy, they can infect other cats.

These diseases are serious when contracted by kittens and aging cats. The symptoms are similar to a cold: runny nose, sneezing, runny eyes, fever. Antibiotics may help to prevent complications from secondary infections but they do not cure the virus..

Feline Distemper

Fame and Fortune

Cats rarely make national news. But the story of one sweet, strong, and healthy orange tabby was included in the June 25, 2010, issue of *The Week*, a recent rival of *Time* and *Newsweek*.

The cat's name is Lima. She was outdoors with her owner Cherry Woods one June day in Pearland, Texas. Two large pit bulls approaching 50 pounds each aggressively came at Cherry Woods. Even though Lima is a small cat, she would not tolerate the insult or the attack. She jumped on the dogs, clawing, hissing, and biting. Cherry's husband Harold came running from the house and dragged his wife from the fray. She suffered only minor injuries, and Lima was just fine. Being pit bulls, the dogs just went on their way (unsupervised).

Harold commented about Lima: "She's the most reclusive, timid animal I've ever seen." But the quiet cat was willing to risk her life for the mistress she loved.

Feline distemper is a highly contagious and deadly disease. Its symptoms are diarrhea, vomiting, and severe dehydration. It is spread by saliva and direct contact. The death rate among kittens is quite high and virtually all cat care organizations recommend immunization.

Rabies

Up until the mid-twentieth century, the call "Mad dog!" would send people scurrying into their homes or to whatever shelter they could find. The words meant a dog with rabies had been spotted in the street. Everyone feared being bitten and infected with this disease that affects the nervous system and almost invariably results in death.

Cats can get rabies too. In fact, today in the United States rabies is reported in cats more than in any other domestic animal. (In the wild, it is common among raccoons, coyotes, and foxes.) Most states require that all domestic pets receive the rabies vaccine. Boosters are needed every two or three years.

Myth, Magic and Medicine

From medieval times through the early twentieth century, cats in Europe were often associated with superstitious cures and sometimes diseases.

In 1721, a Scottish proverb advised that to cure a man with a raging fever, "cast the cat o'er him." Most people believed the cat would take on the fever.

As late as 1888, an English midwife advised, "If the baby is ill and not thriving, take a cat by the four feet, swing it round and round the infant several times, then throw it out of the hole in the roof for letting out the smoke (sky vent) or an upper story window." People believed that if the cat died, the child would live because the witches or brownies have left the child and gone into the cat. If the cat lived, they believed, the child would die.

But despite the threat to human health, research by the American Society for the Prevention of Cruelty to Animals (ASPCA) estimates that less than 4 percent of pet cats are vaccinated. The probable reasons for this lapse are that few municipalities require licenses for cats, and most owners of indoor cats feel that their pets are not threatened. Animal protection organizations recommend vaccination.

Ringworm

Ringworm is a disease caused by a fungus. It looks like an expanding circle of red, flaky, bald skin. It can spread from one cat to another in a multi-cat household, and it is contagious to humans. It is particularly difficult to get rid of in children.

Elimination of the fungus in a household is time-consuming and expensive. You will have to call upon your veterinarian for antifungal dips or baths and antifungal salve to be applied to skin lesions. There are also prescription oral medications available. This treatment may go on for several months. And what's worse, the fungus tends to come back even after you think treatment has been successful.

When cleaning your home, you should use bleach or other strong disinfectants frequently to keep areas free from the fungus. This is especially important in areas that are generally wet, like the shower.

Faults in the Skeleton

We think of cats as incredibly graceful and able to go just about anywhere at will. But as with dogs and humans, cats can sometimes have problems with bones and joints. The most common problem points are hips and knees, but spinal arthritis also occurs..

Hip Dysplasia

We usually hear of hip dysplasia as a common problem in the larger dog breeds. But it does show up in cats, although less frequently. Hip dysplasia begins as an abnormal looseness of the hip joint. It can develop into severe arthritis.

Most cats don't complain or show symptoms of dysplasia until it becomes so severe that they cannot jump anymore. It is more

Someone Said

"Balanchine trained his cat to perform brilliant jetés and tours en l'air. He says that at last he has a body worth choreographing for."

—Bernard Taper (1918) American journalist, author of *Balanchine:*

A Biography, University of California Press, 1996

common in very old cats and in very heavy cats. There are, however, medications to reduce the inflammation. If the prescriptions don't work and a cat seems to be in excruciating pain, there are surgical procedures for relief. Be aware that this is major surgery.

Patellar Luxation

In nonmedical language, *patellar luxation* means dislocation of the kneecap. It is sometimes associated with arthritis and hip dysplasia. Patellar luxation is rare in American mixed breeds, or moggies, which means that the patellar luxation gene is probably recessive. It does occur with more frequency in purebreds, especially the Abyssinian, the Devon rex, and the Chartreux.

Surgery is usually necessary to fix the problem. Successful surgery may also help prevent the later development of arthritis.

Do Cats Get Cancer?

The big C. The word still strikes fear in the hearts of most people. Cats get it too. There are many, many kinds of cancer, which is one of the reasons science has not yet found a cure that works for all of them. Essentially, cancer is the uncontrolled growth of unwanted and unnecessary cells. The cause is generally unknown. Cancer strikes cats in most of the same places and systems as it does humans.

Lymphosarcoma

You guessed right, that means a cancer characterized by enlargement of the lymph glands. It is a common cancer in cats it is thought to be caused by the feline leukemia virus in some cases. (FeLV, see above). I apologize for the repetition but this is so important: Have a new cat tested for FeLV before you bring him home to mix with your other cats.

Lymphosarcoma can be treated with chemotherapy, but it cannot be completely cured. Its symptoms are lethargy, loss of appetite, and anemia.

Squamous Cell Carcinoma

You'd think with all that fur, cats wouldn't get skin cancer. They do. In fact, squamous cell carcinoma is the most common cancer in cats. In cats, it is caused by repeated sunburn to facial areas, particularly areas that are not protected by dark pigment or hair. White cats and cats with white ears are especially susceptible.

If your cat goes outdoors and has white ears, you can try applying sunblock products, but it's really hard to control a cat's comings and goings and the amount of time the cat spends in the sun. Indoor cats are protected from this disease.

The disease starts with red edges on the ears. It progresses slowly, but once the tumors develop the cat's ears become ulcerated and often bloody. The only remedy is surgical removal of the ear flaps. The disease, however, need not be fatal if it remains confined to the skin.

Mammary Cancer

In people language, that's breast cancer. If you notice a lump in the area of your cat's nipples, have a biopsy done by your veterinarian. Diagnosed early, the cancer can be cured. You

Did You Notice the Cat?

It wasn't until they had almost finished their bagels that Diana and Joe wondered where Sabrina was. She always came for breakfast. They called. She didn't come. So they started the search. She was found in a corner behind the living room couch, a place they had never seen her in before.

Sabrina looked as though she was asleep, but both Diana and Joe knew it wasn't sleep. Sabrina was dead, and her loving owners didn't know why. They asked their vet to do an autopsy. He found uterine cancer. The cat was only seven years old.

I'll never forget hearing Diana's voice on the phone. "She never made a fuss when she was in season, so we never had her spayed." Their vet had advised that they do the spaying at about six months, but "She never made a fuss. She never made a fuss." Diana eventually got another cat, but she never forgot Sabrina.

If you don't plan to raise kittens, the best way to prevent uterine cancer is to have a female cat spayed.

can also dramatically increase your cat's chances of never getting this disease by having her spayed before her first estrus season.

Uterine and Ovarian Cancer

Your cat cannot get these diseases if she is spayed. They often go undiagnosed (symptoms are few and often unnoticeable), and these cancers are deadly once they are advanced.

Signs That Your Cat Might Be Sick

Because your cat can't tell you (in words) that he's sick, and will in fact try to hide it from you, you should be aware of the behavior clues that signal the need for a vet visit. The following is an alphabetical list of some symptoms and behaviors, along with some of the illnesses they might indicate:

➤ Breathing difficulties: Asthma,heart isease, foreign bodies, head cold, leukemia, upper respiratory system disorder

➤ Changes in the skin: Allergies, external parasites, fungus infection, improper diet

➤ Constipation: Blockage of the intestine, dehydration, foreign bodies, infectious peritonitis, head cold, kidney stones, renal disease,spinal arthritis,uterine infection, worms

➤ Coughing and sneezing: Cat flu, head cold, heart disease, upper respiratory system disorder

➤ Diarrhea: Hair balls, improper diet, infectious peritonitis, kidney problems, leukemia, poisoning, worms

➤ Fever: Bacterial infection, flea infestation, hair balls, kidney problems, upper respiratory system disorder, viral infection

➤ Increased thirst: Diabetes, flea infestation, kidney problems, liver disease, leukemia, poisoning, uterine infection

➤ Running eyes and nose: Cat flu, feline pneumonitis, injury, upper respiratory disorder

➤ Scratching ears and shaking head: Ear infection, ear mites, fleas

➤ Swollen body: Distemper, fleas, foreign bodies, infectious peritonitis, leukemia, worms

➤ Vomiting: Foreign bodies, hair balls, hyper thryoidism,improper diet, infectious peritonitis, pancreatitis , poisoning, worms

Handicapped Cats

With a little human (or humane) help, a handicapped cat can enjoy life just as can a handicapped person. Many cats and dogs do just fine running about with three legs. Some can even navigate with partial paralysis. Blind and deaf cats need a little more attention, but if they could talk, they'd tell you that their quality of life is pretty good. Cats with these handicaps or with chronic illnesses can be high-spirited, curious, loyal, affectionate, and every other adjective you can attach to a much-loved pet.

Trouble Walking

There are devices now available to help cats who have missing limbs or have partial paralysis. There are also support groups for owners of handicapped pets. Many veterinarians and cat shelters have information on local clubs, and the Internet is a great resource; search the key words "handicapped cat."

Walking around with wheels as your back legs is not as much fun as jumping from the couch to the rocking chair, but handicapped cats do still purr, and quite often too. You may have to change or move a few things, but these are small matters for both you and Wonder Cat.

Blindness

Blindness might be caused by a birth defect, but much more often it is the result of illness or injury. A blind cat will have to be an indoor cat, but he really won't mind. With your help and on his own, the cat will learn the placement of doorways and furniture and the location of food and water bowls, and, of course, the litter box.

You may be surprised by how well a blind cat navigates. Remember, cats have an acute sense of smell and extraordinary hearing that also helps with balance. Their whiskers also help them make judgments about where they can or cannot go.

Talk often to your blind cat. Your voice will reassure him about who is out there in a dark world. Also talk to your blind cat before you touch him so that an unexpected touch will not cause a startle reaction.

Deafness

As with humans, genetic deafness occurs occasionally in kittens. It is quite common in white cats with blue eyes. Again, most deaf cats survive only as indoor cats. Many owners, however, say that the deaf cat is easier to care for than the blind cat. In their silent world, cats without the ability to hear use their other senses to get around, and they can love you just as much as any other cat.

If you choose to keep a deaf cat, you might talk with your veterinarian about suggestions for making his life (and yours) a little easier. For example, it is often suggested that you walk heavily when approaching the cat from behind, because the cat can actually feel the vibrations of your tread. As far as dinner is concerned, you can usually work out a dinner-signal system other than the shake and rattle of the dry cat food, but most cats just appear in the kitchen at feeding time.

Chronic Illness

Cats with chronic illnesses such as diabetes need more attention than the average cat. They may need special food and a stricter feeding schedule. They may need to have medication or shots administered at given times. And they may need to see the vet more often than do ordinary cats. But they will still love you. And you can care enough to provide the very best.

If You Can't

If you have a handicapped pet and you come to feel that you can no longer care for him, don't beat yourself up with guilt. You can list the cat with local shelters and advertise him on the Internet. You can also seek out a no-kill shelter organization and make reservations to have your pet placed there. (You'll have to make reservations because most such shelters have waiting lists.) And, of course, you can talk with relatives and friends about taking over your cat's care.

Someone Said

"I believe cats to be spirits come to earth. A cat, I am sure, could walk on a cloud without coming through."

—Jules Verne (1828–1905) French science fiction author

If your ill or handicapped cat is in untreatable pain or you are too ill to continue his necessary care, you can also consider euthanasia. If you've ever seen the plight of many persons confined to nursing homes, you'll know why sometimes being "put to sleep" is the kindest option.

CHAPTER 17

Old? Who's Old?

Just like kittens, older cats are sometimes a problem and often a joy. They are usually more affectionate and attentive than their prime-of-life cousins. They sleep a lot. They like their comfort. They don't ask that you play with them quite so often. And they love good food. How very human of them!

Myth, Magic and Medicine

How old is a cat in people years? It's hard to tell exactly because each cat, just as each person, ages in an individual way. But here are some generally accepted aging comparisons:

Cat years:	1	2	7	10	15	20
Human years:	15	25	50	60	75	95

This is all well and good for an estimate of behavior trends, but there are many cats who live quite actively far into their twenties, and there are quite a number of reports of queens having healthy litters at age twenty-five. For example, Kitty, from Croxton, Staffordshire, England, gave birth to her last kitten (her 218th) in 1987 when she was thirty years old.

Cats will always be cats, but things do change a bit when they pass the human equivalent of about seventy to seventy-five (that's fifteen in cat years). In this chapter, we'll look at some of the challenges and some of the special joys to expect from our geriatric cats.

Working Cats

Like some humans, especially writers and artists, some cats work all their lives. Believe it or not, they take on and maintain new responsibilities, and catching mice is not their only job. Older cats feel particularly strong bonds to people and places, and they will routinely check on their favorite humans and check out all the places they consider theirs. Why? Just to make sure everything is purring along as it should be.

For most cats, work is never considered *work*; it's just an important part of their lives, their whole lives. Everyone who really knows about cats knows that one of their most important jobs is comforter. And it is truly a lifelong job. For example, you've read in chapter 2 about Oscar the nursing home cat who routinely kept dying residents company during their last hours. And you probably know of many cats who cuddle every day with their elderly owners, giving love, warmth, and the very satisfying and bonding purr.

Stories of famous people and their comforter cats are everywhere. World-class French artist Henri Matisse (who died in 1954) was often forced to remain in bed due to poor health. His favorite black cat was always there beside him. Much farther back in time, Saint Gregory the Great (circa 540–604) gave up all his worldly possessions except his cat "with which he played oft and held it in his lap deliciously." In the mid-twentieth century, American poet Joyce Horner read about the saint during her last year in a nursing home suffering from crippling arthritis. The story, she says in her memoir, *That Time of the Year*, "made me wish for a cat then and there." She never got to have one.

Someone Said

On a Cat, Aging

He blinks upon the hearth-rug,
And yawns in deep content,
Accepting all the comforts
That Providence has sent.
Louder he purrs, and louder,
In one glad hymn of praise
For all the night's adventures
For quiet restful days.
Life will go on forever,
With all that cat can wish,
Warmth and the glad procession
Of fish and milk and fish.
Only—the thought disturbs him—
He's noticed once or twice,
The times are somehow breeding
A nimbler race of mice.

—Alexander Gray (1882–1968) Scottish economist, writer, and poet

Cats Under Stress

Many of life's stressful situations for humans are also stressors for cats, and both older humans and older cats seem to feel the anxiety of stress more intensely. Like humans, cats usually respond to excessive stress with changes in their behavior patterns. Some cats overeat, consuming everything they can find whenever they find it. Some cats refuse to eat. Restlessness, not using the litter box, and over-grooming to the point of licking a spot to baldness are other common responses.

Someone Said

"Sleep sweetly in the fields of asphodel, and waken, as of old, to stretch thy languid length, and purr thy soft contentment to the skies."

—Agnes Repplier (1855–1950) American essayist

Among the most common stressors for an older cat are

➤ extended absence of a loved family member;

➤ introduction of a new human into the household (this includes both spouses and babies);

➤ introduction of a new cat into the household;

➤ long hours, or even days, of being left home alone;

➤ stresses in a human's daily life that changes the behavior of that loved person;

➤ tensions and arguments between married owners, divorce, and separation from one owner (who gets the cat is often a point of negotiation);

➤ moving to a new home; and

➤ loss of a companion cat in the household.

Most cats eventually work out their anxiety and grief, but if serious behavioral problems persist, you may want to get some professional help.

Did You Notice the Cat?

Always fond of animals, Albert Einstein had a tomcat whom he called Tiger. Tiger tended to get depressed whenever it rained for a length of time. Einstein empathized. He was overheard saying to Tiger, "I know what's wrong, dear fellow, but I don't know how to turn it off."

Depression is Real for Cats Too

Some cats, like humans, suffer periods of depression, not just bad moods but something akin to clinical depression. But unlike humans, they can't see a shrink and get a prescription for Xanax or Prozac.

The almost eerie aspect of cat depression is that the same symptoms are discussed in psychiatric textbooks (yes, for people). Think about this list: a lack of interest in life, un-groomed and uncared-for appearance, listlessness, changes in eating habits (either refusing food or binge behavior), changes in sleep patterns, and personality changes (including unwarranted anger and aggression and withdrawal from all social encounters).

Many of the situations listed in the previous section in Cats Under Stress can contribute to a bout of depression. For veterinarians, cat therapists, and owners, the challenge in working with depression is finding ways to alleviate or change the cause of the stress. And, sadly, sometimes it simply can't be done. The answer then is to try to make some changes that will make life better in different ways. There are also some medications available for cats.

Fame and Fortune

The artist, illustrator, and writer Edward Lear was devoted to his tabby, Foss. (See drawings in chapter 1.) He didn't want Foss to feel the stress of an impending move to France, so Lear had his architect design a replica of his old house in England. A new residence was built to exact specifications in France, and Foss hardly noticed the change. (Well, he surely noticed that it smelled different, but he didn't object much. The rooms, the furniture, and the people were the same.)

Foss is famous as the cat in Lear's *The Owl and the Pussycat*. When Foss died, Lear had him buried in the garden close to home.

Older Cats and their Weight

What is it that the majority of people hate most about going to the doctor? It's not the examination, it's not the questions, it's not filling out the insurance claim forms. It's getting on that damn scale. I've known women who search their closets for the lightest clothes they own in hopes of reducing their weight by a few ounces.

Fortunately, cats don't care about numbers or weight charts. That's the vet's business. In older cats, however, weight often causes concern for their owners. Studies supported by pet-food manufacturers show that close to 80% percent of older domestic cats in the United States are overweight. Being overweight is defined as being 14 percent above the ideal weight.

Of course, determining the "ideal weight" for each different breed and body type, in fact each individual cat, is a problem that cat care providers still haven't completely solved. At what point does body fat become a risk factor for death and serious disease? Today we have a BMI (body mass index)calculator for cats (provided by Hills Corporation). This calculator measures te cat's neck, length,leg diameter, etc. in order to get the cat's BMI as against a theoretical ideal.

Myth, Magic and Medicine

A recent news release from Hill's Science Diet provided the following information:

➤ "If you feed a 10 lb cat one cup of milk, it's the equivalent of a 5'4" woman eating four and a half hamburgers or five chocolate bars."

➤ "Five extra pounds on a medium size cat like an American Shorthair [*sic*] is the equivalent of nearly 37 pounds extra weight on an average woman."

You can go to www.petfit.com to learn more about a program Hill's Science Diet is conducting to help owners help their pets to lose weight.

Being a little overweight is one thing, obesity is quite another. There may not be an exact number where obesity starts, but you'll be able to sense when your cat has a serious problem with weight. The question is what you do about it.

Helping your cat lose weight may well be one of the hardest things you've ever done. It's not like human weight-loss programs where cheating happens to almost everyone once in a while. If you put your indoor cat on a strict diet, where else can she get food? Despite the ads about balanced nutrition and frequent small feedings, a cat on a diet feels hungry. Will you be able to ignore your cat as she sits next to the table looking at you with those imploring eyes?

If, on the other hand, you have an indoor-outdoor cat, the problem becomes even more complex. If you cut down on the amount of food being fed to your cat at home, she is likely to go out in the world and find whatever she can to eat, which may include not only mice and birds, but also the neighbors' garbage cans and even the debris outside the local fast-food chain.

Someone Said

When rats infest the Palace a lame cat is better than the swiftest horse.

—Chinese proverb

The best advice I can offer is to talk with your vet and do some research on low-calorie foods and snacks that cats might like even though they contain little or no fat and fewer calories. There are even a number of products available that are made specifically for senior cats on a weight loss program. Changing or restricting a cat's diet may be hard, but most authorities say that an older cat is better off on a restricted

CATch Words

Diabetes mellitus (often mistakenly called sugar diabetes) is a disease that often affects overweight middle-aged and older cats. It is caused by inadequate insulin production or the body's inability to use the insulin that is available. Blood sugar rises, but the body cannot allow the glucose to enter the cells and thus nourish them. The cat feels hungry all the time, but eating doesn't give her back her energy. There are medications available for treatment of this disease, and diabetic cats can live long and happy lives. But you will need the help of your veterinarian.

diet and will probably live longer. . Just don't be so strict that the quality of life becomes painful

It is well known that obesity in cats and people causes problems and costs a lot in health care dollars. Diabetes, respiratory problems, and joint disorders are the most common illnesses associated with obesity and old age. There is some research that also suggests an association with some forms of cancer. Do talk with your veterinarian about your decisions and how to carry them out.

How is the Older Cat Different?

Like humans, some cats feel old and act old sooner than others. Of course, their fur-covered faces don't show the wrinkles and sagging skin, but there are other clues to aging, some of them very apparent to an attentive person. Many aging cats don't hear as well or see as well as they once did. They tend to jump less (even without diagnosed arthritis) and they tend to get up more slowly. Their appetites may fall off as their ability to taste and smell diminishes. And like humans, many cats become less adaptable and less resilient to changes, especially changes in diet, routine, and environment.

Some owners say, however, that their cat's older years are the best years. As they age, cats lose some of their wariness, their fierce independence, and their tendency to aggressiveness. The thing they want most is to be with the ones they love.

Many ailurophiles are certain that cats, particularly older cats, have a sixth sense about human character. Senior cats are very selective about the persons they will associate with.

Someone Said

"It's funny how dogs and cats know the inside of folks better than other folks do, isn't it?"

—Eleanor H. Porter (1868–1920) American novelist and children's writer

Some Things Won't Get Better

For centuries, explorers (both on land and sea, and in theoretical and practical science) have been looking for the fountain of youth. No success yet so we're all still getting old. One of the most difficult aspects of aging is the realization that many things that are beginning to bother us just won't get any better, ever. That's pretty tough to swallow. But looking from the outside, it's almost as hard to watch age slowly undermine your cat's perfect body and joy in life.

The fact is that although humans and cats suffer many of the same health problems as they age, cats rarely complain. In fact, one of the problems of living with an aging cat is detecting when he or she needs help or medical attention. Let's go over some of the most common incurable conditions usually associated with aging.

Arthritis

When aging cats develop arthritis, they usually feel it in several joints at the same time. The pain, stiffness, and lameness resulting from the deteriorating joints are usually at their worst as the cat gets up from sleeping. With movement, the arthritic feeling usually diminishes, although it doesn't go away completely.

The fact is that although humans and cats suffer many of the same health problems as they age, cats rarely complain. In fact, one of the problems of living with an aging cat is detecting when he or she needs help or medical attention. Let's go over some of the most common incurable conditions usually associated with aging.

Kidney Disease

Many cats have decreased kidney function in their old age; they drink more and need to urinate more often. They must therefore have a litter box readily available in the area where they usually stay since they may not be able to retain a large volume of urine for a long period of time. The best plan is to place several litter boxes in inconspicuous but easily accessible places. If you live on two or more stories, be sure each has its own litter box.

If you suspect that your cat has kidney disease, tell your vet and ask him or her to check for high blood pressure, which can either cause kidney problems or be the result of them.

Hyperthyroidism

Hyperthyroidism is caused by an overproduction of the thyroid hormone. The symptoms are a significant increase in appetite with insidious weight loss, a marked increase in activity,

Did You Notice the Cat?

Many cats continue to act like their ordinary selves even when they are hurting deeply. Able Seacat Simon was one of those stalwart souls. He was the rat catcher on the HMS *Amethyst* during the Yangtze River incident in 1949. After being stitched back together after injuries from cannon bombardment, he continued right on with his duties catching rats. And most important of all, he visited wounded sailors, raising morale throughout the ship.

He was given the honorary title of Able Seacat and awarded the Animal Victoria Cross, the Dickin Medal, and the Blue Cross medal in August of 1949. Thousands of letters were written to him, so many that a naval officer, Lt. Stuart Hett, was appointed "cat officer" to deal with Simon's correspondence.

Unfortunately, Simon died on November 28, 1949, from a virus complicated by his war wounds. He had a ceremonial funeral and was buried at the PDSA Ilford Animal Cemetery in East London. In 1950, the American writer Paul Gallico dedicated his novel *Jennie* to this extraordinary cat.

increased thirst and urination, and a greasy-looking coat. Sometimes there is vomiting and diarrhea. It causes high blood pressure and can lead to heart and kidney disease. It can be treated with antithyroid drugs, surgical removal of the thyroid gland, or treatment with radioactive iodine-131. Some cats recover thyroid function after treatment; others must remain on thyroid medication for the rest of their lives.

Diabetes Mellitus

Diabetes can start (and often go on unnoticed) in the early teens, but it is more commonly an older and overweight cat disease.

Despite their increased thirst and increased appetites, diabetic cats often lose weight at the onset of the disease because their bodies cannot make use of the nutrients overloading their blood. Medication to control the symptoms of diabetes can be given orally, or insulin can be given by injection. Most cats will gain back all the weight they lost once the medication dose is established. Some will gain more. In either case, both their calorie and their carbohydrate and fat intake must be carefully monitored.

Heart Disease

Cardiovascular problems can develop at any age, but they are far more common in elderly cats. The first sign of trouble is usually decreased activity. If your cat seems suddenly tired more often, has trouble climbing stairs quickly, or simply stops playing with you, you should see your veterinarian.

As with humans with cardiovascular problems, medications and special diets are readily available for cats. Have your vet instruct you on symptoms that might be signs for emergency treatment.

Tumors

Both benign and malignant tumors occur in cats, and their likelihood increases with age. Breast cancer can develop in both males and females. However, it is seven times more common in unspayed females than in spayed females. Treatment and prognosis depend upon the type of cancer, its location, and its size.

Someone Said

"Old cats mean young mice."

— Italian proverb

Fame and Fortune

During the eighteenth dynasty of Egypt, Crown Prince Djhtmose (more frequently referred to as Thutmose) had a cat called Ta-Miu (She-Cat) whom he loved very much. When the cat died, the prince had her mummified and entombed in a beautiful sarcophagus.

Carved into the stone were all the royal titles of Thutmose: Crown Prince, Overseer of the Priests of Upper and Lower Egypt, High Priest of Ptah in Memphis, and Sm-priest of Ptah. The limestone coffin for this royal cat is so much a work of art that it is the single largest item for which Thutmose is remembered. Ta-Miu's sarcophagus can be seen today in the Cairo Museum.

Someone Said

"Cats are connoisseurs of comfort."

—James Herriot (1916–1995) English veterinary surgeon and writer; author of *All Creatures Great and Small* (1972)

Dental Disease

Dental disease is both the most common and the most ignored disease among cats in America today. Ironically it can be controlled or sometimes even completely cured. Dental diseases lead to, or even cause, other diseases, infection, pain, and emotional problems. Be sure that your veterinarian checks your cat's teeth at every visit.

Last Days

Despite the medical miracles of the twenty-first century, some older cats suffer from their illnesses and linger on even when nothing more can be done to improve conditions or make them more comfortable. Fortunately for these cats, euthanasia is an option.

Some owners hesitate to take this step because they cannot bear to part with their much-loved companion. But when there is great pain and discomfort and no hope of recovery, it may be the kindest gift you can give to your pet.

The decision to end your cat's life is always a difficult one, and you should discuss it with the family and with your veterinarian. Do not hold back, however, because you fear that the process will be painful to the cat. Modern techniques are truly painless.

CHAPTER 18

 **Professional Help**

In This Chapter

➤ The veterinarian as health care mentor

➤ Pet insurance and how it works

➤ Behavior problems and help from therapy

➤ The death of your cat

At least the first half of the twenty-first century will probably be called The Age of Instant Everything. You name it—instant answers, instant communication, instant food, maybe even instant gratification.

With everything changing faster than we can keep up, most of us ailurophiles feel ongoing comfort that our cats are still exactly like the cats who sat with royalty in ancient Egypt, who curled under the robes of popes, who were the companions of countless writers, artists, musicians, and scientists, and who still persistently choose to sleep between the pillows of our beds.

For us, cats are an integral part of home. Getting to our homes and our cats is both calming and satisfying. But the truth is, we can't keep our cats and keep them healthy without some professional help. As Hillary Clinton wrote about raising a child, "It

Someone Said

"With their qualities of cleanliness, discretion, affection, patience, dignity and courage, how many of us, I ask you, would be capable of being cats?"

—Fernand Mery (1897–1983) French veterinarian and author

"There are no ordinary cats."

—Colette (1873–1954) French novelist, author of *Gigi*

takes a village." Loving and living with a cat may not require a whole village, but owners do need to call upon outside professionals from time to time.

Your Veterinarian

Your cat's veterinarian is his health mentor. Unfortunately, cats can neither read nor talk, so you, the owner, must choose the person to do the mentoring. Your choice can make a big difference in the life and life expectancy of your pet, and in your life too.

Finding a Good Vet

Finding a good vet is just like finding a good doctor. A cat can't discuss his symptoms so vets, like pediatricians, must be both perceptive and intuitive. A cat also can't verbalize his evaluation of the medical experience, so vets must also be trustworthy.

If you buy a purebred cat, the breeder can usually recommend a vet who not only knows the breed but also the lineage of your cat. But if you are like most of us and welcome an "ordinary" cat into your life, you will have to do a little research to find a health care provider who meets your standards.

Cat-owning friends are a good source for recommendations, as are shelter personnel who work with a number of vets. If you are moving to a new area, you can also contact the American Association of Feline Practitioners (AAFP) at www.catvets.com and ask for a referral in your area. While there are a great many general practice vets who run finely tuned clinics but do not belong to AAFP, a referral from this group assures you that you are choosing a veterinary hospital that is genuinely interested in cats.

What to Look for in a Veterinary Clinic

Needless to say, a veterinary clinic should be neat, clean, and free from unpleasant odors. There should be up-to-date equipment for examining, weighing, treating, and doing the necessary tests. Privacy is also a factor; there should be enough examining rooms so that you don't feel crowded or pushed along.

Probably most important is attitude and communication. First and foremost, your vet and the staff should listen, and listen carefully! Remember, a cat cannot talk, so the diagnosis must come from what you can tell the vet and what the medical people can observe and test for. Secondly, the vet and staff should encourage you to ask questions. If a test is suggested, don't hesitate to ask why, what it's for, and what it will show. Ask for a treatment plan and a prognosis.

Check out the clinic's emergency policies. When an emergency happens, every second can count. You don't want to be checking out the phone book or your smart phone for a vet hospital that is open. Are late night calls accepted and answered? Will someone open up the office just for you at 2 a.m.? Do they share after-hours duty with other vet hospitals? If so, get a list.

Finally, be certain that your veterinary clinic keeps accurate records. Of course, all vaccinations and boosters should be recorded. But it's also very important to keep records of weight and of the general appearance of skin and coat, head, face, eyes, ears, mouth, and of general temperament and agility. Records should also be kept of treatment for diseases and parasites. This information becomes especially important as your cat gets older because the records establish baselines from which to judge change

Myth, Magic and Medicine

Beware the practitioner who promises miracles. When people are desperate for hope, they grasp at promises, potions, and procedures that would be totally disregarded under normal circumstances. If your cat is seriously ill, beware the quack and his "miracle cures."

Money-hungry practitioners go back centuries, if not millennia. In late eighteenth-century London, for example, two matching black cats and a "dramatic" doctor became quite famous. The cats were called the doctor's devils. In fact, they were demonstrators for Gustavus Katterfelto (circa 1743–1790), a Prussian conjurer and quack who performed in England from 1780–1784 during the height of a national flu epidemic. He entranced his audience by using static buildup in his cats' fur to set sparks between them. He claimed to be the greatest natural philosopher since Isaac Newton.

The Cat Specialist

Veterinarian Donna Shannon remembers a saying from vet school: "Cats are not small dogs." That sounds simple enough but the complexities in a medical practice are immense. Donna says:

The more I learn about cats the more this saying proves to be so true. The cats-only vet has the opportunity to learn the nuances of cat metabolism, behavior, handling, and medication (both selection and dosage. This is important because many medications that humans and dogs can tolerate very well simply cannot be given to cats. Why? Because cats lack the enzymes to break down the chemicals in the prescription medication and they therefore develop toxic reactions.

If your town does not have a cat specialist veterinarian, be sure that the general practice vet you choose runs a practice with a large percentage of feline patients! A good general practitioner is aware of the smaller doses required by cats among the medications that are tolerated by several species. Their technicians are trained in the special handling techniques that underlie a successful and thorough examination.

What the Vet Can Teach You

I started out attempting to do a section here that would explain how to give a cat a pill, how to give a cat a shot, and generally how to care for a sick cat. But I got bogged down with the inadequacy of words and pictures. There are simply some things that are taught better in person. A good veterinarian can and will teach you the how-to practices that you will need with your sick or older cat.

While you are learning, be sure to ask questions if you don't understand. Have the vet stand by your side while you do exactly what was instructed. After you get home, don't be afraid to call the office if you run into trouble or just have a plain old anxiety attack.

Myth, Magic and Medicine

Cats, like people, can be affected by passive smoking. Research in the United States has determined that cats who live in homes with persons who smoke regularly are more than twice as likely to develop feline lymphoma cancer than cats who do not inhale second-hand smoke.

How long will it be before pet insurance companies increase the premiums for cats with smoking owners?

The Cost of Services

A lot of people don't like to discuss money, especially when a needed service is being suggested by a professional. But talk about money is what you must do. Today, most vets will give an estimate of costs for each procedure before you decide to go ahead with it. At that point you should decide how and when you will pay for medical care. If the cost is more than you can afford to pay, ask if there are alternative choices. Or ask if a payment plan over time can be arranged. Most veterinary clinics also take credit cards.

CATch Words

Quack is today's word for the 1638 term *quacksalver.* It means a charlatan; one who pretends to have medical skill.

Pet Insurance

Pet health insurance is a fairly recent development, but with pets living longer and vet fees going up (like everything else), it is a growing industry. Unfortunately, it is almost as complex as the human health care industry.

The cost can approach $500 a year, usually paid monthly. And there are all kinds of policies, some for accidents only, some for diseases only, some with higher premiums for older pets or certain breeds, some that exclude certain preexisting conditions—the list seems nearly endless! Many do not cover yearly checkups or preventive medicine.

Someone Said

"The cat is a wild animal that inhabits the homes of humans."

—Konrad Lorenz (1903–1989) Austrian zoologist, winner of the Nobel

Prize in physiology (1973)

"As the cherub is to the angel, so the cat is to the tiger. . ."

—Elizabeth Marshall Thomas (1931–) American anthropologist and author of *The Tribe of Tiger: Cats and Their Culture*

Like human health insurance, some policies require you to use only vets who are approved members of the health care insurance group. Other plans allow you to choose your veterinarian, but they are usually reimbursement plans. In these agreements, you pay the bill and then submit it to the insurance company. The company may promise to pay 90 percent of the bill, but don't be surprised if there are limits on maximum payments.

If you have a good relationship with your veterinarian, ask him or her to recommend a health insurance company. Also coming into being in some major cities are veterinary HMOs, which can significantly cut the cost of both preventive and emergency care.

In the mid-1990s, there was only one company offering pet health insurance, Veterinary Pet Insurance (VPI). Underwritten by National Casualty Company, it was available in only thirty-eight states. Today, there are many corporations competing for your pet health insurance dollars. They are underwritten by such giants as Purina or Nationwide Insurance. Just search for pet health insurance on the Internet and you'll get answers to all of your questions, including what's covered and how much it costs. Each company offers many different plans at different costs.

Pet Therapists

Pet therapy can do a lot of good for both people and animals. Vets and shelters report that the most common reasons for giving up a pet are motivated by behavior problems.

CATch Words

Cat's-paw is an American and British idiom for someone who is tricked into doing something foolish or even dangerous for someone else. The term comes from a fable by Jean De La Fontaine called "The Monkey and the Cat" (published 1679). The monkey used the cat's paw to scrape chestnuts out of the fire. And the cat, of course, got burned. In human culture, the person who is persuaded to grab the hot potatoes out of the burning charcoal pit is the cat's-paw.

"There is more than one way to skin a cat" is an American adage that has nothing to do with the actual act of skinning a cat. In the 1800s, there were many variations on advice for ways to get rid of a cat including "there are more ways of killing a cat than choking her with cream." Most sayings are long forgotten, but during the twentieth century, "there is more than one way to skin a cat" came to mean having a variety of available solutions to a problem. We still use the colloquialism today.

Within the American Veterinary Medical Association, animal behavior therapy is slowly becoming an accepted specialty. Some courses are even being introduced at veterinary colleges. And some veterinary colleges and clinics maintain referral lists of competent pet therapists for owners in need. There are fees, however. So discuss time, service, and cost before you begin. And interview the recommended therapist, casually, over a cup of coffee if possible. Perhaps the most important factor in success in this field is a sense of simpatico between owner and therapist. Today Veterinary Behavior Specialists are licensed in most states

Among the most common problems among cats are aggression (often fearful aggression that the cat might call self-defense), jailed frustration (the indoor cat watches the outdoor world with teeth chattering and sometimes exhibiting unpleasant behavior), excessive marking and spraying, chewing sweaters and tearing draperies, refusal to accept other pets in the home and the resulting fights, and psychosomatic illnesses.

As I mentioned in the last chapter, pet therapists do not need a license to practice. They survive and prosper on referrals, so they must continually prove themselves. But don't expect them to possess magical fairy dust that will transform Jezebel into Pollyanna in just a few visits. Be aware also that pet therapists don't focus solely on the pet's behavior problems. A big part of a pet therapist's job is to evaluate the home situation and educate pet owners.

On the other hand, remember that you are still the master of the house. Keep your brain in control over your heart. If something that you are asked to do seems preposterous, it may be just that. Remember: not all problems are solvable and not all behavior must be accepted.

Cat Retirement Communities

What exactly is a cat retirement community? In the human world, there is a euphemism for housing developments built for people who no longer participate in the working world; we call them active adult communities. And until the recent real estate bust, retirement housing was the fastest growing segment of the new construction housing market. But what do cats retire from and to?

If you search for cat retirement on the Internet, you'll get lots of answers. Long-term care for cats is a growing industry in the United States. Essentially (if you can afford it), it's where you send your cat when you can no longer take care of him but still want him to have all the comforts of home.

Someone Said

"There are so few who can grow old with good grace."

—Sir Richard Steele (1672–1729) Irish writer and politician, cofounder of the magazine *The Spectator*

Some of the common reasons for the placement are:

➤ an owner who can no longer take care of an animal because of ill health;

➤ an owner who is moving into an assisted living complex or a retirement community that does not allow animals;

➤ military deployment or long-term assignment to a foreign country;

➤ a cat who must be retired because of behavior issues or social issues with other pets in the household;

➤ a cat who requires hospice care; and

➤ an owner who dies and leaves provision in the will for the care of his or her pets in a specified retirement community.

Fame and Fortune

Many accurate records have been kept about cats who were able to reach phenomenal ages; but then again, many bogus claims have also been posted. Here are a few statistics that have been validated:

➤ According to the Guinness World Records, the oldest living cat as of 2014 is a female called Pinky. She was born on 31 October 1989 and lives in Hoyt, Kansas. At age 13, Pinky was diagnosed with cancer and as a result her left hind leg was amputated. She has been an indoor cat most of her life.

➤ Creme Puff of Austin Texas was born on August 3, 1967, and celebrated her thirty-eighth birthday on August 6, 2005. She died three days later.

➤ Even more astounding: Puss was born at the very beginning of the twentieth century in 1903. He passed away on November, 29, 1939, one day after his thirty-sixth birthday.

In the majority of communities, the facilities are luxurious. There are no cages and cats live in houses; many even have their own room. And the food is good, so say the cats. But the cost is high. Minimum fees for a cat of seven years or older can run from $5,000 to $25,000 for lifetime care. The fee can be paid in cash in advance, through life insurance with the cat retirement community named as beneficiary, through a charitable remainder trust with the organization paid annually and the balance taken as a tax-deductible contribution, or as a clause in the will. A suggested wording is, "I give $_____ to the [name of cat retirement organization] to provide life care for my cat(s) [names], if they are alive when I die."

It's a good idea to check out the financial solvency of the retirement community before you commit, however. There have been notable bankruptcies and closures, causing problems on many levels.

The No-Kill Shelter

The no-frills economy version of the cat retirement community is the no-kill shelter. When they accept cats, they promise not to euphonize them. (In ordinary shelters, cats over seven years old are usually put down because the chances of adoption are very slim and space is

Fame and Fortune

Many famous entertainment personalities have contributed generously to animal rights and animal welfare. Next to Cleveland Amory, Doris Day is among the most noted and hardest working.

An American singer and actress born on April 3, 1924, she has spent most of her retirement years working to help animals. In 1971, she cofounded Actors and Others for Animals and appeared in a series of newspaper advertisements denouncing the wearing of fur alongside Mary Tyler Moore, Angie Dickinson, and Jayne Meadows. Day's friend, Cleveland Amory, wrote about these events in *Man Kind? Our Incredible War on Wildlife* (1974).

Throughout the 1980s and 1990s, Doris Day promoted the annual Spay Day USA, and on a number of occasions, actively lobbied the United States Congress in support of legislation designed to safeguard animal rights. She also founded the Doris Day Animal League (www.ddal.org). The group was merged into The Humane Society of the United States in 2006.

limited.) As opposed to cat retirement communities where the cats are committed to remain for the remainder of their lives, cats in no-kill shelters are available for adoption.

Did You Notice the Cat?

Most owners hold their cats very dear, very much like members of their family, in life and in death. This love seems not to have diminished in all the time that cats have been the companions of humans.

Myobu No Omoto was the favored cat of Japanese emperor Ichijo (980–1011). When a dog had the audacity to chase the beautiful feline, the emperor had the dog's owner imprisoned.

Many no-kill facilities are bare-bones, however, and cats spend their time in cages. Because space is limited, there is usually a fairly long waiting list. For more information and a list of shelters across the United States, go to www.nokillnetwork.org. For a worldwide list, including profiles of sanctuaries in every U.S. state, some of which are well funded and include free-range care, go to Wikipedia and key in "list of animal sanctuaries."

Euthanasia

Euthanasia is a tough subject that no one wants to talk about. Sometimes, however, it is a merciful gift. Most important, it is not painful to the cat.

Euthanasia is usually done in the veterinary clinic. In most cases, however, loved ones are allowed to remain with the cat during the process, if they choose to do so. Some vets will come to your home for the procedure. It is a quick, easy, and painless procedure.

Sometimes the cat is tranquillized prior to the start of the euthanasia process. The veterinarian then prepares a concentrated solution of anesthetic to be injected into a vein. The amount injected brings about unconsciousness in about fifteen to twenty seconds. Soon the heart stops beating and the cat never wakes up.

If you are present at the procedure, you may notice mild tremors that shake the body and there may be a release of urine or feces. Rarely, some cats gasp or even cry out. Be assured these actions are not signs of pain. They are the result of the muscle spasms and then limpness that accompany death.

Someone Said

"I have never known a cat that couldn't quiet me down just by walking slowly past my chair."

—Rod McKuen (1933–) American poet, composer, and singer

Unexpected Loss

Sometimes young cats are killed in accidents, especially roadway accidents. These deaths are sudden and of course unexpected. The effect on the cat's family can be devastating.

Well-meaning friends often suggest that you get a new cat or kitten. Some even bring a newcomer to your home as a condolence gift. Most experts suggest, however, that you do not try to replace a cat who has died unexpectedly with another cat. Although the new kitten or cat can be a distraction, he is never just like the pet you have lost.

Masking grief with distraction or by keeping busy rarely resolves the pain. It is far better to acknowledge your loss, work through your grief, and then, when the time is finally right for you, welcome a newcomer into your home. Welcome him for the individual he is, not as a replacement cat.

Do Cats Grieve?

Recent research has verified what every multiple cat household already knows. Cats do grieve at the loss of one of their household companions. Even kittens are sensitive to someone missing.

Symptoms of grief are loss of appetite, excessive meowing, pacing or sniffing around the house looking for the lost friend, lassitude, and unusual spraying among male cats. As with grieving humans, your cat may need extra attention for a time. Again do not be too quick to replace the lost cat with another.

The Lost Cat

Loss is the biggest risk in having an indoor-outdoor cat. The experience of searching for a cat who wanders off one day and is not seen again is harrowing. In many ways, it is more difficult than coping with unexpected or accidental death or euthanasia. Day after day drags on colored by a conflicting mixture of hope and fear. You worry about what could be happening, what could have happened. Usually, there is no answer, no closure.

Grieving

Grieving for a lost love is genuine and meaningful, whether the love is a person, an animal, a home, or even a precious heirloom. The validity and appropriateness of grief is not related to the value of the lost love on some socioeconomic scale. For the person grieving, the intensity and duration of grief can only be determined by the intensity of the love he or she felt for the departed. Grieving the death of your cat can be as emotionally deep and just as necessary as grieving the death of a beloved friend or relative.

It is important to let yourself cry. It is also important to talk about your pet—what you loved, what was funny, what were the unique routines, what were particular preferences. Some people gather photos together, others write poems. Still others find comfort in just sitting in the place that was often shared with the cat.

About the worst thing you can do when our cat dies is to feel pain on the inside and deny it to the world. Grief can affect the heart, quite literally. In the mid-90s, Harvard researchers added the death of a loved one to their list of triggers for a heart attack. They found that the risk of heart attack was fourteen times higher than normal the day after the death of a loved one, five times higher two days afterward, and elevated thereafter for about a month.

Doctors still don't know exactly why. Until more is known about the biological connection between psychological stress and physical illness, however, the best advice psychologists have to offer has been around for a long time: Recognize your grief, acknowledge it, and feel it. Time is necessary for recovery, but time does heal.

In Memoriam

Yes, it's true: some cats have funerals. But then, what is a funeral? It's a gathering of friends to say good-bye.

If a cat funeral would be helpful to you, your children, and other friends and family members, do it. The ceremony is an acknowledgment of separation from a loved pet. Don't let anyone tell you that you are being silly and simply don't listen to the supercilious comment that you're making too much of this.

Many owners choose to bury their cat in their own backyard, with or without a marker. Sometimes a small pile of stones will do, sometimes an outdoor chair placed close to the burial site, sometimes a favorite tree or bush newly planted to honor their dear pet. The estates of many of the rich and famous that I have visited have pet cemeteries with a small headstone for each grave.

Someone Said

"A cat improves the garden wall in sunshine, and the hearth in foul weather."

—Judith Merkle Riley (1942–2010)
American writer

Some owners wish to have their pets cremated. Many veterinary hospitals have the facilities to do this for their clients. If you wish to have your pet's ashes separate from others, however, you will have to make that request. (There is usually an extra charge.) The cremation can also be done at an animal crematorium.

Urns for keeping ashes are available at vet clinics, pet specialty stores, through dealers that advertise in cat magazines, and on the Internet. If you prefer not to use an urn, you can bury your cat's ashes in any place of your choosing with or without a marker. Or you can scatter them at a meaningful site— perhaps in a corner of the woods near your house where your cat chased mice or at the edge of a garden wall on which he enjoyed sleeping.

Pet Cemeteries

There are pet cemeteries in every state. Some are very beautiful and maintained much like human cemeteries; others are more casual. For a listing of pet cemeteries in every state go to www.nepanetwork.com/keepsakes/petcem1.htm.

The cost of a cemetery burial varies greatly. Inquire about charges for plot, the casket, and even the digging of the grave. There may even be a maintenance fee involved. Some cemeteries allow monuments; others do not.

America's largest and oldest pet cemetery is in Hartsdale, New York. It dates from 1896 when a vet working out of Manhattan offered to let a grieving pet owner bury her dog in his hillside apple orchard. Today it is the final resting place for more than 70,000 animals.

Normally pet cemeteries are completely separate from human cemeteries, by law. However, recent newspaper articles have publicized a movement among pet owners to allow their pets to be buried with them. For example, Senator Ken Jacobsen of Seattle, Washington, filed a bill in 2009 in the state legislature that would allow joint burial of people and their pets. In the state of Wisconsin, there are already two sites that allow pets and humans to be together.

The movement to allow pets to share our burial sites is also afoot in Europe. In January 2010, West Lindsey District Council in England gave permission for a site in the village of Stainton by Langworth, where animal remains can be interred alongside human remains as part of a green burial site.

Some Final Words

Have we spent too much time on burials and memorials? I don't think so. Love is the most precious emotion of life. It is never wrong to stand tall and acknowledge the love you feel and the love you have felt.

I would like to end this book with some words (an abridgement of Ecclesiastes, Chapter 3, I admit) that have been posted on my refrigerator in a plastic case with a magnetic backing. They have sustained me through many different seasons:

To every thing there is a season,
and a time to every purpose under the heavens.

A time to be born,
    And a time to die;
A time to plant,
And a time to uproot;A time to weep,
    And a time to laugh;
A time to be silent,
    And a time to speak;
A time to mourn,
    And a time to dance;
There is nothing better than to be glad and to do well during life.

All the cats I have known seem to know these words without ever having read them!

Cat-Myths Understood

In This Chapter

➤ Divine Cats

➤ Demonic Cats

➤ Powerful Cats

➤ The Astrological Cat

Cats have been lingering around human habitation since cave dwelling families tossed their left-over bones and berries out the back entrance. The felines came for food of course, but also perhaps, they came out of curiosity about this strange two-legged animal.

On the other hand, mankind has long admired the cat's beauty, agility, crafty intelligence, durability under stress, daring curiosity, and playfulness. And it follows, almost as the night the day, that human admiration turned into awe, and then fantasy. How could so much beauty and intelligence be combined in a beast?

With the human development of language came the grasping of and for concepts and it wasn't very long in evolutionary time before some persons (and groups of persons) began to think of cats as having divine powers. Other groups, however, were quite positive that the characteristics possessed by cats were demonic in origin. Throughout human history, there is perhaps no other animal that has inspired more myth and legend than the cat.

Did You Notice the Cat?

Man's earliest paintings found on the walls of caves are not limited in subject matter to bison, bears, deer, mastodons, horses, and stick-figure humans. Cats appear both as hunter/enemies and as moving bodies to be admired or perhaps used in ritual ceremonies.

These lions are part of a hunt mural in the Chauvet Cave in France. Authorities date the painting in the Paleolithic Era.

A Cat to Be Worshipped in Ancient Egypt

Who knows exactly when those luminescent eyes seen staring in the dark first inspired fear and awe. Surely it was long before humans learned to write. But centuries of research have gathered well-documented evidence that in the culture of the ancient Egyptians, cats were considered divine.

Museums around the world house hundreds of images and sculptures of Bastet, the Egyptian cat goddess. The earliest surviving works show her with the head of a lioness and the body of a woman. As such, she was a warrior deity and a protector of the land. She fought an evil snake named Apep.

Later representations, however, show Bastet (sometimes called Bast) simply in the form of a cat or as a composite figure with a catlike head and a female human body. Bastet protected her worshippers from diseases and from evil spirits. Said to be the daughter of Ra, the sun god, she was first associated with warmth and light, but later she became a moon and fertility goddess. Bastet was also the goddess of pleasure, music, dancing, and joy. She was regarded as the protector of the home, of women, and of children.

The temple of Bastet was located in the city of Bubastis (named in honor of the goddess and now called Tell Basta). The goddess was celebrated on a feast day each year. That day's activities attracted thousands of visitors from northern Africa and prompted music, singing, dancing, and almost universal drunkenness.

Myth, Magic and Medicine

Historic Egyptian sources advised that the ferocity of lion-like goddesses must be appeased by "feasts of drunkenness." Accordingly, Bastet's feast day was one big party. Her temple, however, was surrounded on three sides by water and this "sacred" lake kept most celebrators at a respectful distance. In their revelry, they told each other the story of the fiery and wrathful lioness (Africa's strongest and most resourceful hunter) who fell into the water of the lake and was transformed into a docile pet cat.

The Masculine Cat God

His name was Maahes, also spelled Mihow, Miysis, Mios, and Mahes, all of which come out sounding a bit like Meow. He was generally depicted with the head of a lion and the body of a man.

Fame and Fortune

The Lion/Cat gods of Egypt have come down to us as symbols of protection. Today, in the 21st century, they still stand guard at the entrances of many important buildings around the world. This watercolor painting by Lou Bonamarte features one of the lions who guard the entrance to the New York Public Library.

Mihow was considered the son of Bastet and he had many of her attributes. He was known as the protector of the innocent and the devourer of the guilty. As a member of the deity, he was a war god and weather god. Some sources say he was the same deity as the lion-god Apedemak, worshipped in Nubia and Egypt's western desert area.

The Highly Honored House Cat

Because they were associated with Bastet, cats were the most revered animals in ancient Egypt. In fact, so revered that they were protected by many very explicit statutes in Egyptian law. If a person killed a cat, the penalty was death. (No appeals.) There doesn't seem to be a mandatory sentence for smuggling cats, but their exportation from Egypt was strictly forbidden by trade laws. However the growth of the cat populations in Greece, Turkey, and other Mediterranean countries during Egypt's long era of power is a good indication of the willful disregard for these statutes. Not to mention the profitability of the cat trade!

Throughout Egypt (both the northern and southern civilizations), cats were treated as family members and many even ate from their owner's plates. When a family's cat died, its owners shaved off their eyebrows as a symbol of their mourning. Statues of cats were often placed near entranceways to ward off evil spirits (and other animals).

Why so much fuss about an animal that had become a common house pet? It all started with health and wealth. In a country where the weather is warm, stored grain and food are attractive to foraging animals. Cats were kept to catch mice, rats, and snakes. The better the hunter, the more valuable the cat. Among royalty and the very rich, some cats were considered so valuable that they wore collars studded with jewels. Given the cat's religious significance and legal protections, no one dared to steal them.

The cat was the most favored animal of all social classes throughout all the dynasties of Egyptian history. Many Egyptian mummies have been discovered with their mummified cats cuddled close to their bodies. People of lesser means, paid to have their cats properly prepared for burial. Some were even mummified. The first cat cemeteries in the world were

Someone Said

"Death be not proud, though some have called thee

Mighty and dreadful, for thou art not so..."

...John Donne

(1571? – 1631) British poet

Many ancient Egyptians believed that cats journeyed with their masters into the afterlife. Virtually every citizen would have agreed with John Donne.

almost certainly created in Egypt. Massive numbers of cat remains have been discovered in Bubastis and Beni Hasan. In the 19th century (1888), a farmer who was working his land in Beni Hasan turned over ground that was covering hundreds of thousands of cat skeletons.

The Cat in Ancient Greece

Although Egyptian law attempted to keep all Egyptian cats in their own country, more than a few were slipped out. Cats appeared on the Greek islands as early as 1800 BC. They did not rank as deity on Crete in the Minoan civilization of the Bronze Age, but they were closely associated with the powers of the immortals. For example, a 13" sculpture of a snake goddess includes a cat sitting on top of the goddess's headpiece. The cat is believed to be a fertility symbol. The ceramic statue dates from about 1600 BC and can be viewed at the Heraklion Museum in Crete. Cats are also depicted as hunters of birds in some early Minoan pottery and on wall frescos.

The ancient historian Herodotus visited Bubastis in 450 BC. He saw Bastet as similar to the Greek goddess Artemis. Artemis, like the Egyptian cat goddess Bastet, was the daughter of the king of the gods (Zeus in Greece, Ra in Egypt). Artemis was the goddess of the hunt, wild animals, childbirth, virginity, and relieving disease in women. She was depicted

CATch Words

The Greek name for Bastet or Bast was actually Ailuros. The English language has adopted that Greek word and transformed it into two words: ailurophile which means one who fancies or loves cats and ailurophobe which means one who hates or fears cats.

in sculpture as a strong woman, often carrying a bow and quiver of arrows, but never as a cat.

Other Divine, Powerful, and Saintly Cats

In India

In Hindu mythology one of the most popular deities is Narasimha, usually depicted with a feline head and claws but a masculine human body. He is said to be the fourth incarnation of Lord Vishnu. Acting as the avatar Narasimha, Lord Vishnu hunted down the demon Hiranyakashipu who could not be killed by a human, a god, or an animal. Because Narasimha is not any one of the three but a combination of all three, he was able to kill the evil one.

Narasimha is considered the great protector. He guards his worshippers against demonic deception and attacks. He is extremely powerful and often depicted engaged in life or death battles.

CATch Words

An incarnation is the physical embodiment of a god, a spirit, or an essential quality. A reincarnation is one in a series of earthly lifetimes or forms.

An avatar is a god or goddess appearing in bodily form on earth.

In South America

Among the ancient Mayan peoples, Ixchel (or Ix Chel) was the old-woman jaguar goddess of giving birth, midwifery, and medicine. She is depicted as a jaguar, or as an aged woman with jaguar ears and body markings.

In Norse Mythology

Among ancient Scandinavian deity, Freyja was not a goddess of cat-like appearance but she was always closely associated with cats. She rode in a chariot pulled by two giant cats called Cribcats. The many depictions of these servants of Freyja indicate that they were probably the ancestors of the Norwegian Forest Cat that we currently know. Strangely, in this breed the hind legs are longer than the forelegs. The coat is another marker of the breed: thick, coarse, double-layered, and virtually waterproof. The tail is long and very bushy.

Feyja is the goddess of youth, beauty, sexual love, and fruitfulness. As she traveled through Nordic farmlands she caused seeds to swell, sprout, and grow, especially when farmers left pans of milk out in the fields for her divine cats. She was worshipped with prayers for a good harvest. Friday is her day and it was considered the best day to be married in the

Scandinavian countries. In ancient China, there was a similar cat deity called Li Shou who protected the crops of farmers.

Freyja blessed all lovers and the presence of divine cats at engagement and wedding ceremonies was thought to be a positive influence on the marriage. In fact cats are associated with matrimonial superstitions in many areas of Europe. For example, young girls were told to feed the cats well so that the sun would shine on their wedding day. Also, if a bride feeds the cat before she goes to church, she will have happiness in her married life. And if a bride sees a black cat on the way to church to be married, she will have good luck all through her life.

In Slavic Countries

In Poland, Russia, the Ukraine, and other eastern Slavic countries, the spirit-being of the threshing house was named Ovinnik. He was depicted with a cat-like face and form. And like the cat, he could be protective or a mischievous.

In these northern lands, the threshing house was a two-story building for storing grain. Because stored grain is highly inflammable, the threshing house was usually built a good distance from the farmer's home. It was almost always a constructed of wood and heated by a furnace

The risk of fire was the obvious threat, but the Ovinnik could prevent an outbreak, if he was kept in a good mood. Naturally, this cat never went hungry. Local peasants regularly left him treats (or were they appeasements?) such as roosters or home-made bliny (a thin, egg-rich pancake).

In the darkness of New Year's Eve, farmers and other peasants would traditionally go out to the threshing house and await the touch of the Ovinnik. A warm touch predicted good fortune in the year ahead. Hmmmm....

In China

In Chinese mythology, cats were looked upon as the assistants to the Kitchen God, who was protector of the home. Ceramic pillows molded in the form of a cat were slept upon by the Emperor and peasants alike. It was believed that sleeping on the form of a cat would ward off evil spirits in the night. The Ming dynasty (1368 – 1644) were the first Chinese ailurophiles. During their reign, dogs were banned from the Ancestral Temple and the palaces; cats roamed free within the walls.

Fame and Fortune

The Japanese avidly adopted the idea of a powerful cat talisman. From the time of the Samurai, the people created the legend of the beckoning cat. Even today creative statues can be seen everywhere in Japan. Beckoning cats appear in homes, shop windows, restaurants, and even temples. They are considered a symbol of welcome, good luck, and prosperity.

Through much of Chinese history, many shopkeepers kept a collared and chained cat in their stores to ensure prosperity. The older the cat, the greater luck it could bring the business owner. The cats were kept chained because the businessmen believed that if the cat escaped, all prosperity would go with it.

In the Nations of Islam

The prophet Mohammed loved cats. In the Koran the cat is described as a pure animal for its cleanliness. (Dogs are not regarded in the same way.) The followers of Mohammed respect cats and treat them kindly. There is no history in Islamic nations of using cats to personify evil.

There is even a legend about the prophet's favorite cat, Muezza. The cat once fell asleep in the sleeve of his master's robe. Rather than wake him when it was necessary to leave, Mohammed cut the sleeve off.

Myth, Magic and Medicine

Saint Gertrude of Nivelles (626 – 659) is considered the patroness of cats. On the death of her father, she and her mother built a double monastery at Nivelles, and Gertrude became the Abbess. She resigned, however, in 656 and spent the last three years of her life studying Scripture, praying, and contemplating the visions she received. Her keeping of cats occurred hundreds of years before the papal Bull that prohibited cats in sacred buildings and monasteries. She is also a patroness of travelers because of her hospitality to those on the road and of gardeners for her care of plants.

Demonic Cats

While the idea of divine cats goes back many millennia, the image of the demon cat is even older and perhaps more wide spread. There is something fearsome in the cat's perfect symmetry, balance, control, intensity, and independence. Many people found it easy to blame the cat for misfortune. From there it was but a small step to attributing demonic power to individual cats or to the cat as a species.

Notice the combination of human and cat features in this engraving of a demon cat by R P Athanase Kircher, 1667

Someone Said

"The conceit that a cat has nine lives has cost at least nine lives in ten of the whole race."

Alexander Pope (1688 – 1744)

British poet and satirist

"Ah! cats are a mysterious kind of folk. There is more passing in their minds than we are aware of. It comes no doubt from their being so familiar with warlocks and witches."

Sir Walter Scott (1771-1832)

British novelist

Did You Notice the Cat?

Hans Baldung Grien (1485 – 1545) a student of Albrecht Durer, created a pen-and-ink and gouache drawing of the witches' Sabbath which now can be seen in the Muse de L'Ouvre de Notre-Dame in Strasbourg, France. Notice the cat reading in the book of spells and recipes in the lower right hand corner.

In medieval Christianity, the cat was said to be the incarnation of Satan himself and the feline species was attributed many malignant characteristics. Cats were finally linked formally with sorcery in the thirteenth century by Pope Gregory IX, the pontiff who founded the Inquisition. Pope Innocent VIII (1484 – 1492) confirmed the powers of the Inquisition and issued the Bull Summis desiderantes affectibus which resulted in the slaughter of hundreds of thousands of cats across Christian Europe. As a result, all cats were also removed from monasteries and convents (which of course resulted in an exponential increase in rats and mice among the clerics).

Despite massive cat kills, both cats and rats continued to enter European ports on trading ships. Unknown to the citizens of the time, rat fleas carried the bubonic plague. As the rat population increased with the diminished control from feral and domestic cats, plague outbreaks increased in number and they spread geographically.

Unfortunately "evil" cats were also blamed for other disease outbreaks such as cholera. For example in London in 1665, two hundred thousand cats were destroyed by order of the Lord Mayor, theoretically to stop the spread of an epidemic. Cats were also often destroyed because they were thought to be the embodiments of evil spirits. For example, it was a tradition for adults and children to throw stones at tethered cats on Shrove Tuesday (the day before Ash Wednesday). This cruel murder was considered a last fling before the self-denial of the Lenten season began.

Fame and Fortune

The demon cat-form Kasha is associated with many Japanese cat legends. He is commonly known as the Corpse-eating Cat Demon. In a typical story, a funeral procession is interrupted by a mighty wind and thunder and the coffin is swept away. Kasha retrieves the corpse. Sometimes he is depicted as having a split tail or two tails.

On St John's Eve (June 24, the summer solstice and the birthday of St. John the Baptist) great bonfires were lit on the hillsides of northern Europe, Scandinavia, and the British Isles. This night of the "summer Christmas" was celebrated with drinking, eating, and sexual changing partners. But there was always a fear of witches, and to keep them away from the festivities, their "demon cat familiars" were regularly thrown into to fires.

Cats were thought to be the ever-present companions of witches (often called "familiars"). Sometimes the cats were thought to be actual witches who had changed bodily form, and sometimes they were thought to be the devil himself in disguise. Cats and witches were burned together at the stake. Sometimes witches were drowned by being stuffed into a bag along with a dozen or more cats and thrown into the river.

Cats were said to participate with their witch companions in celebrating the witches' Sabbath, casting spells, and inhabiting or infecting with disease the bodies of people living and dead. They could assume the appearance of men or women and they could lead people into sin.

In Japan

Demon cats are fearsome figures in Japanese mythology. The Kasha (the name means "burning chariot") are demons rooted in both Shintoism and Buddihism. These mythical beasts have a human-like body, the head of a cat or sometimes a tiger, and a burning tail. They are said to travel the world stealing the corpses of recently deceased humans and dragging them into the fires of hell.

Fame and Fortune

The demon cat-form Kasha is associated with many Japanese cat legends. He is commonly known as the Corpse-eating Cat Demon. In a typical story, a funeral procession is interrupted by a mighty wind and thunder and the coffin is swept away. Kasha retrieves the corpse. Sometimes he is depicted as having a split tail or two tails.

The bakeneko (translated as "monster cat") are a mythical group of Japanese cats that haunt and menace households. Strangely, an ordinary Japanese house cat can turn itself into a babeneko. To do so, it must meet at least one of three conditions:

➤ *living beyond 10 years of age;*

➤ *reaching over one kan (3.75 kg or 8.25 lbs) in weight;*

➤ *growing its tail so long that it can fork into two. (When a cat has a forked tail or two tails it is called a nekomata).*

Once transformed into a bakeneko, the body of a cat can grow up to five feet in length. Besides the sudden growth and splitting of the tail, another sign that a cat is turning into a babeneko is an attraction to lamp oil. Folklore believing owners got worried when they caught their cats lapping lamp oil (which in Japan was made from fish oil).

The paranormal powers used to haunt the household include menacing or even eating sleeping humans, walking on its hind legs, flying, talking, bouncing around in ghostly fireballs, and bringing back to life a recently deceased person by leaping over his/her body.

In Washington, DC

Yes, legend has it that there is a demon cat in the capitol city of the United States. He (or she) is said to be a ghost that haunts the government buildings. Described as a black cat that is pretty much average in size, except... Except when it is alerted or frightened. Then it is said to grow to the size of a giant tiger. It might explode, or pounce at the viewer, or simply vanish in a moment.

Legends circulate that this American demon cat is glimpsed before presidential elections, strategic meetings, and tragedies. It is said that the cat was spotted by White House security guards on the nights before the assassinations of Abraham Lincoln and John F. Kennedy.

The last "official" sightings of a black cat in government basements was in the 1940s. The United States Capitol Historical Society tells the story of a security guard who may have been, well, drunk. He was licked by a cat while lying on the floor. Thinking that he was standing rather than stretched out on the floor (or that's what he said), he imagined that the scratchy cat's tongue belonged to a monster.

The Cat In Christian Art

A number of paintings of religious subject matter (not only from the renaissance but also into the following centuries) include cats. Most art historians and authorities believe that these cats were meant to symbolize the devil. Sometimes the cats are sedate and seem docile or are actually playing, but more often they are lurking as images of the presence of evil and temptation in all our lives.

This painting of the Annunciation by Lorenzo Lotto (1480 – 1556) hangs in the Museo Civico in Recanati, Italy. The cat in the center of the composition is frightened by the appearance of God's angel and is running away with its back arched and its head turned to look behind. Could he symbolize the devil fleeing God's power?

Someone Said

A cat is an animal which has more human feelings than most any other."

...Emily Bronte (1815 – 1848)

British novelist

Peter Paul Rubens included a quiet cat in his 1628 painting of the annunciation. The cat does not seem disturbed by the turbulence of the angel's arrival. Perhaps here he represents *lurking and latent evil.*

A painting of the Last Supper by Cosimo Rosselli (1439 – 1507) that decorates a wall of the Sistine Chapel includes two cats in the foreground and another on the left side. Are they meant to symbolize the ignored presence of evil even in the holiest atmosphere?

Weather Cats

For many centuries cats have been associated with rain and violent weather. In some cultures (even today), they are predictors of coming changes; in other cultures they are thought to be the agents of lightning and thunder.

In 1773 a British book, The Poetical Description of Beasts, described the antics of the cat before story weather:

Against the times of snow or hail,

Or boist'rous windy storms;

She frisks about and wags her tail,

And many a trick performs.

Sailors through the ages and in many countries actually become fearful when shipboard cats become too active. They said that when a cat is too frisky, she has a gale of wind in her tail. In other words, the cat is a predictor of foul weather. Beware! Beware!

In the legends and mythology of northern European countries, the cat is the predictor of rain. As far back as 1656, a book called *Nature's Secrets* reported "Cats...licking their feet, and trimming the hair of their heads, and mustachios, presages rainy weather." By the end of the 19th century, people watched to see if a cat washing her face moved her paw over the back of her ears. And if she did, children said: We shall have rain; the cat goes over her ear. By 1922 the prediction was expanded to include the theory that the wind will blow from the direction the cat is facing.

In his classic book *The Tiger in the House*, Carl Van Vechten tells of many rituals regarding cats and rain. For example, on the island of Celebes in Indonesia, ancient inhabitants tried to bring on rain by tying a cat into a sedan chair and carrying it three times around the parched fields. In a village in Sumatra the rain ritual required women to wade into the river and splash one another. Then a black cat was thrown into their midst and made to swim while being pursued by the splashing women.

Van Vechten also tells of other cat legends in the United States and Canada. For example, cats of three colors are believed to bring good luck in Canada, Washington, and eastern Kansas. (And also among Japanese sailors!) And a 19th century tradition among slaves in the American south taught that in the tip of every cat's tail were three hairs of the devil. Those hairs prompted the cat to prowl but they could bring bad luck to anyone who plucked them out.

The Astrological Cat

Julie Leiter, a member of the National Council for Geocosmic Research and the Astrological Society of Princeton has compiled the following astrological sun signs of the cat.

Aries (March 21 – April 20)

A real swashbuckler of a cat with a lot of energy, drive, and daring. Aries cats love being where the action is and will not back away from a fight. With a strong sense of self and a me-first attitude, they hate standing on the sidelines and will try to dominate others around them. Spontaneous and impatient, they are first at the food dish, and the toms are first in line for the queens.

Taurus (April 21 – May 21)

A cat who loves the good things in life – a soft cushion, a special place of its own, and gourmet dinners. Laid-back, adagio, and very sensual, Taurus cats choose food, stroking, and massage. So much "good stuff," however, could lead to, well, pudge. Taurus cats are possessive of the things they love, and they can be stubborn. Once habits are acquired, they're hard to break, so train these cats early.

Gemini (May 22 – June 21)

A curious and playful cat who doesn't want to miss a trick. Gemini cats are alert, clever, quick-witted, and interested in everything. Variety is the spice of their lives; they choose a little of this and a little of that – but not too much o one thing. They are great communicators and usually enjoy "talking" (or talking back) to whoever is around. Concentration is not their strong point.

Cancer (June 22 – July 23)

The homebody of the feline world, cats born under the sign of Cancer love the security of a warm hearth (or a warm bed). They are sensitive and can be somewhat shy and moody, but they will purr with pleasure at a little TLC. Queens make good mothers. Toms like to be mothered. Both genders love the night hours, and, in their own quiet way, they are very tenacious about getting what they want.

Leo (July 24 – August 22)

Truly "the cat who would be king," the Leo cat is proud, regal, and dramatic. Leos like center stage and usually get it. They love flattery and having a fuss made over them. Their vanity, however, will not tolerate belittling, and if you ever make fun of them, they might just go off to seek an appreciative audience elsewhere. But given their royal "due," they will be the happiest and most loving of cats – and lord it over you with the greatest aplomb.]

Virgo (August 23 – September 23)

A very intelligent and discriminating aristocrat, Virgo cats demand only the best and look down upon anything or anyone who is less than perfect. No dirty litter boxes or day-old food for these connoisseurs – they keep themselves neat and clean and expect their environments to be kept the same way. Virgos have a sense of what seems "right" and can become nervous if things are not "just so." If you win the approval of this cat, you've been bestowed the greatest of compliments.

Libra (September 24 – October 23)

Unhappy alone and a good friend to all, cats born in Libra need interaction with others – felines, humans, or even Fido. Usually very beautiful, they have a refined nature and love of peace and harmony. Too much discord and loud noise can mean nervousness and misery for them. Libra cats often have trouble making up their minds, like whether or not to go out while you stand there with the door open. But they are so charming and attractive that most humans are happy to be a part of their lives.

Scorpio (October 24 – November 22)

The animal of sensuous magnetism, the Scorpio cat is intense, passionate, and mysterious. Scorpios have strong desires and expect to get what they want. They will size up a situation instantly, and they can seduce you into doing whatever they want and have you think it was your idea. In fact, they can push your buttons so expertly that you will enjoy being manipulated. But don't cross swords with them – you are sure to lose!

Sagittarius (November 23 – December 21)

A live wire with a yen for adventure, Sagittarius cats are always ready to explore what's just around the corner or go out to conquer a new world. Very athletic, they will delight you with acrobatic feats and yowl loudly if their needs for exercise and activity are not met. Yet as they get older, they will develop a philosophical bent and prefer to sit on the front porch and contemplate where they have been and what they have done.

Capricorn (December 22 – January 20)

The status seeker, the Capricorn cat wants to climb to the top – so watch out for your curtains and look for these cats on the top of furniture or shelving (as close to the ceiling as they can get). Capricorns are serious, cautious, deliberate, and determined, and they work hard at whatever they do. They even work hard at playing! Somewhat insecure, they thrive in a positive environment and appreciate warmth and attention, although they usually won't admit it.

Aquarius (January 21 – February 19)

The original "KrazyKat," Aquarius cats are unpredictable, and that's how they like it! Just when you think they're your best friends, they become remote and detached, looking down at you from a distant perspective. Independence and individuality are their watchwords. With a strange electricity in their nature, they may appear downright "flaky" at times, and they often can't resist rebelling against what is expected or upsetting the status quo – just because. Yet the Aquarius cat is friendly and generally tolerant of your foibles.

Pisces (February 20 – March 20)

A sweet and dreamy cat who finds it easy to "make-bleieve," the Pisces cat can spend a lot of time entertaining both itself and you with imaginary scenarios. Deeply sensitive both physically and emotionally, their hearts yearn for total oneness with you (on their own terms, of course). Their taste usually runs to seafood, and a little water is less likely to bother them than most other members of the feline species. Be aware of what you are feeling when you're with a Pisces cat because they are very impressionable and tend to absorb your moods!

The Eastern Zodiac

The cat is *not* one of the 12 animals that each represent a whole year in the Chinese Zodiac.

There are many stories that explain why the cat was excluded. One of the most common is this one that is circulated widely on the internet:

The Rat and the Cat

A long, long time ago, the Cat and the Rat were the best of friends. They accompanied each other everywhere they went and they shared their food. One day, the Cat learnt that the Jade Emperor was going to elect twelve animals to represent the twelve calendar years, and invited all animals to a party. The Cat suggested to the Rat that both of them should make a presence.

When the day finally arrived, the Cat told the Rat, 'I am going to take a nap so that I will be in my top form. Can you please wake me up when it's time to go to the party?' 'No problem.' the Rat replied, 'Just relax and rest. I will wake you up when the time comes.'

After the Cat fell asleep, the Rat thought to himself, 'I am among the smallest of all animals and I don't stand a chance in making one of the twelve if the Cat will go.' So when the time came, the Rat left on his own without waking up the Cat, and was elected as one of the twelve Zodiac Animals.

When the Cat found out what the Rat had done, he was furious. The two became worst enemies. This is the reason why cats are not one of the twelve animals and they love to chase after rats.

In the Vietnamese zodiac, the cat replaces the rabbit used in the Chinese system. It is a cat year once every 12 years. The last one was 2011, the next will be 2023.

Persons born in a year of the cat are in fact a lot like cats. They are kind, proud and aloof, lovers of habit and tradition, caring mothers, clever, loving, and loyal. They can also be devious, crafty, aggressive, protective, and extraordinarily sensitive.

Celebrating Cats

In This Appendix

➤ Forming a cat-centered group

➤ Cat books

➤ Cat movies

➤ Cat activities

Sharing joy, concerns, cares, sorrows, challenges, and moments of laughter, awe, and insight, that's what happens when men and women (and children too) get together with a common interest, one that seems to unfold endlessly. Thinking and laughing together, perhaps an arm over a shoulder, helping hands offered sincerely, sometimes even a tear wiped away, all of this gives us a sense of belonging. To belong is one of our essential human needs, and we must communicate to belong. In other words, communication is essential for community.

Some people say that the Internet is a great communicator, and sometimes it is. But the Internet is also a separator. The printed word cannot compare with a hug. When people are gathered on front porches, in firehouses, in church basements, and around kitchen tables, they touch one another literally and emotionally. No matter how many friends you have on Facebook, no matter how well you can use Google, the computer cannot replace a gathering of living, talking, laughing friends. Human nature mandates that we make contact with one another.

Cats 4 Love (cats, characters, caretakers, and community)

What has all this got to do with cats? First of all, cats are social animals too. And second, well, why not share our love for cats? Why not let mutual interests in this fascinating animal strengthen our ties with each other and become the building blocks of mini-communities bound together with caring hearts. Why not start a Cats 4 Love (cats, characters, caretakers, and community) group of your own?

Maybe you're a little tired of reading novels and history books in your reading group. Maybe you're just a little jealous of those hundreds of dog breed groups that run shows and get-togethers. Yes, there are purebred cat groups, but there are also millions (literally) more pet cats who are just plain cats, each a unique individual. And wouldn't it be fun to share both the joys and cares of living with no ordinary cat?

There are countless ways to organize your meetings, to share insights, to contribute to your community or your family and the schooling of your children. The following is a list of just a few suggested topics and projects. You will come up with many more as your group is formed. You can organize it any way you like. You can connect with other Cats 4 Love groups, or not. You can hook up with cat shelter groups, or not. You can choose any name you like for your group too!

In this stereotyped, patterned, programmed world, here's a chance to make something just the way you want it to be.

Reading Group Suggestions

My vote for the best book about cats ever written so far is Carl Van Vechten's *The Tiger in the House*. Originally published by Knopf in 1920, the book is still in print. Van Vechten is one of the greatest researchers and writers in the modern world, and this one book could provide the material for a whole year's worth of fascinating meetings.

The chapter titles include:

➤ By Way of Correcting a Popular Prejudice [cats vs. dogs]

➤ Treating of Traits [this is a "why do they do that?" chapter]

➤ Ailurophobes and Other Cat Haters [Did you know that Napoleon hated cats? Hitler too, although he's not in Van Vechten's book. Ambrose Bierce defined a cat as "A soft indestructible automaton provided by nature to be kicked when things go wrong in the domestic circle." And Noah Webster wrote, "The domestic cat is a deceitful animal and when enraged extremely spiteful."]

➤ The Cat and the Occult [myth and magic, sometimes scary]

➤ The Cat in Folklore [Van Vechten means folklore all across the globe]

➤ The Cat and the Law [Did you know that "the English 'Rule of Nuns' issued in the early thirteenth century, forbade the holy women to keep any beast but a cat"?

There's a lot more to talk about in this chapter!]

➤ The Cat in the Theatre [One quoted line will give you a taste: "Naturally the presence of cats in theatres is frequently responsible for accidents." Van Vechten takes you around the world and through the ages.]

➤ The Cat in Music [Lots of surprises in this chapter.]

➤ The Cat in Art [Have you seen Picasso's cat portrait? It doesn't exactly entice a petting or suggest a purr. But there's a wonderful book recently published in Italy by Stefano Zuffi (available in the United States from Abrams), titled *The Cat in Art*. It has great reproductions and fine discussions from ancient Egypt to the present. Van Vechten also discusses cats throughout the history of painting. His words and the black-and-white reproductions will send you to Google images for more, more, more!]

➤ The Cat in Fiction [Of course, Edgar Allen Poe's *Black Cat* is mentioned among the many entries.]

➤ The Cat and the Poet [Van Vechten is just the beginning if you enjoy poetry. There are many cat poetry sites on the Web. Or better yet, try writing about your own cats. You could even form a cat literary group.]

➤ Literary Men Who Have Loved Cats [Who says cats are a woman's pets? How about Mark Twain, Victor Hugo, Anatole France? And of course, it would have been an oxymoron to say "literary women" in 1920. Where's Colette?]

Van Vechten ends his book with an expression of awesome love for his own cats.

Today, it seems there's always a cat book on the fiction or nonfiction best-seller list. I've mentioned several in these pages already. If the focus of your Cats 4 Love group will be a reading group, I suggest you go to the Internet and search for cat books. You will be absolutely amazed by how many responses you'll get. Here are a few of my other favorites:

➤ Cleveland Amory's books about Polar Bear: *The Cat Who Came for Christmas*; *The Cat and the Curmudgeon*; and *The Best Cat Ever*

➤ Dr. David Dosa's *Making Rounds with Oscar*

➤ New York City cat veterinarian Dr. Louis J. Camuti's *All My Patients Are under the Bed*

➤ Television personality Roger Tabor's *Cat Behavior* and his other books

➤ Vicki Myron and Brett Witter's *Dewey: The Small Town Library Cat Who Touched the World*

Of course, you can organize your group to meet in each other's houses. But if reading will be your primary activity, consider going to a local bookstore and asking for a time and space for your group to meet. The bookstore, of course, wants to sell books, but it also can host authors on tour. The existence of a Cats 4 Love group will entice authors of cat books to come to the store and share their stories with you.

Cats in the Movies

If you meet in private homes, you can watch DVDs together, along with snacking on coffee and doughnuts. The world has come a long way since *Breakfast at Tiffany's*. In that film, the role Cat was played by Orangey. As a young cat, Orangey also appeared in the movie *Rhubarb*.

Here are just a few suggestions for other cat films:

> *Caressing the Tiger*: A National Geographic special that you won't want to miss.

> *Cats and Dogs* and *The Revenge of Kitty Galore*: Two Warner Bros. animated films with a lot of stereotypes, but funny

> *The Adventures of Milo and Otis*: A beautiful film from Japan.

> The musical *Cats*: The play is based on T. S. Eliot's *Old Possum's Book of Practical Cats*

> *Homeward Bound: The Incredible Journey*: Sally Field voices the cat

> *Bell, Book, and Candle*: An early *Bewitched* movie starring Kim Novak as the witch Gillian and her "familiar" Pyewacket. Witches lose their power if they fall in love. Poor Pyewacket must make a decision: to stay or to leave.

> *That Darn Cat!*: It takes a Siamese cat secret agent to make this movie into a crime story!

> *Felix the Cat*

> *Black Cat*: An eerie thriller based on Edgar Allan Poe's story.

> *Ghost Cat*: An abandoned cat named Margaret and some very bizarre events

There are also a lot of documentaries available about cat care and cat behavior.

Rainy Day Activities Groups

There are a lot of activities groups that you can form for fun and creativity. Think about designing cat needlepoint. How about a quilt using a cat theme; it could be auctioned off or awarded as a raffle prize at a community gathering. The proceeds could go to local cat rescue groups. Or perhaps you might be interested in designing and making cat toys or scratching posts, which are great for selling at the Christmas bazaar.

Your group might also like to scrapbook together. And if some of you like to write or take photos, you might even think about self-publishing a book of local stories.

Community Contributions

Your Cats 4 Love group could also be an educational group. You could design programs on cat care for presentation at local schools or school fairs. For example, you might put together a short talk with photos of cats showing off different tail positions. Children could learn to approach a cat more safely by reading the cat's body language.

You might also escort school groups to a local cat shelter, where the staff will explain how and why cats are rescued, neutered, and placed in homes.

Keeping in Touch

But perhaps you'd prefer not to meet in person on a particular day of each month. Well, there is always the computer. You can form a group with cat lovers all over the world and share photos and stories.

Cats can be good friends in the privacy of your home, but they can also be a connection with the whole wide world. Have fun!

INDEX

ABOUT THE AUTHOR

All through her life, cats and dogs have been Carolyn Janik's faithful companions and precious friends. Among the cats she has lived with and loved were Brutus, Mozart, Brahms, Clara, and el Diablo. But her favorite of all was Emily Dickinson Kat (spelled with a K) who lived for 23 years. The newest member of her family is Miss Becky Sharp.

An inquisitive little helper who likes to sit by the computer and sometimes on the keyboard, Becky is a little over a year old (approximately). She was found in a cage next to a dumpster. A kindly veterinarian treated her, spayed her, and kept her for almost a year before Carolyn came upon her and fell instantaneously in love.

Carolyn Janik is the author of over 22 non-fiction books. Her real estate books have won national-level awards from Robert Bruss and Sylvia Porter. Her work has been featured in many magazines including Kiplingers, Redbook, Modern Bride, Parade, Money, and Family Circle.

Reviews of her books in Library Journal, Publishers Weekly, and syndicated newspaper columns have emphasized not only the clarity of her writing, but also the humor and pleasant readability.

Carolyn has appeared on Good Morning America and The Today Show along with countless other local and national radio and television programs. She has also done live presentations for City Bank and other real estate organizations, almost always ending with standing ovations.

The author's cat Becky   Photo: Dianne Blyler

Made in the USA
San Bernardino, CA
05 May 2014